The ABCs
of International
Finance

The ABCs of International Finance

Second Edition

BY

John Charles Pool
Stephen C. Stamos
Patrice Franko Jones

Lexington Books

D.C. Heath and Company/Lexington, Massachusetts/Toronto

Library of Congress Cataloging-in-Publication Data

Pool, John Charles.
The ABCs of international finance / by John Charles Pool, Stephen
C. Stamos, Patrice Franko Jones. — 2nd ed.
P.cm.
ISBN 0–669–27887–4 ISBN 0–669–24522–4 (pbk.) (alk. paper)
1. International finance. 2. Balance of payments. 3. Debts,
External—Developing countries. 4.International economic
relations. I. Stamos, Steve, 1947–   . II. Franko Jones, Patrice.
III. Title.
HG3851.P66   1991
332'.042—dc20   CIP 90–24529

Published simultaneously in Canada
Printed in the United States of America
Casebound International Standard Book Number: 0–669–27887–4
Paperbound International Standard Book Number: 0–669–24522–4
Library of Congress Catalog Card Number: 90–24529

The paper used in this publication meets
the minimum requirements of American National Standard
for Information Sciences—Permanence of Paper
for Printed Library Materials, ANSI Z39.48–1984.

Year and number of this printing:

91 92 93 94 8 7 6 5 4 3 2 1

Contents

Figures   ix

Tables   xiii

Preface   xv

Acknowledgments   xvii

1. The Trade and Debt Crisis   1

2. The Role of International Trade   11

   Theories of International Trade   13
   The Theory of Protectionism   23
   Problems of Developing Countries   31

3. The Mysterious World of International Finance   39

   The Balance of Payments Accounts   40
   The Theory of Balance of Payments Adjustment with
   Floating Exchange Rates   43
   Exchange Rate Systems   51
   Two Factors in Exchange Rate Determination and Balance
   of Payments Adjustment   56
   The Paradox of the Strong Dollar   57
   The Emerging Financial Crisis   60

4. The Historical Evolution of the International Monetary
   System   65

   The Discipline of International Finance   65
   The Special Case of the United States   67
   The Evolution of the Dollar Glut   69
   The Rise of the Eurodollar Market   72

The Demise of Gold   73
Petrodollar Recycling   75
The Oil Price Shock of 1973–1974   77
The Flight of Capital: 1975–1985   79
The International Monetary Fund   80
The Call for a New International Economic Order   84
The Plaza Agreement and Tokyo Summit   88

5. The U.S. Debt Problem   93

U.S. Industry: National and International Troubles   93
The U.S. Trade Deficit   100
Government Efforts   105
The Vulnerability of the U.S. Banking System   110
The Legacy of the Reagan Era   115

6. The Developing World Debt Crisis   125

Causes and Origins of the Debt Crisis   127
A Chronology of the Debt Crisis   129
Attempts at Managing the Debt   135
The Impact of the Debt Crisis   138
The Resource Transfer Flow   139

7. The Mexican Debt Crisis: A Case Study   149

Economic and Political Background: 1940–1968   152
Failed Ambitions for Reform: 1968–1976   152
José López Portillo and Petroleum: 1976–1982   153
Miguel de la Madrid's IMF Austerity Measures:
1983–1986   155
The 1986 Rescue Package   164
The Presidency of Carlos Salinas de Gortari
(1988–   )   171
The Brady Plan: Once Again, Halfway Is Not Far
Enough   171
A Mexican Family Copes with Hardship   176

8. The New Bretton Woods?   183

The Case Against   183
Agenda for a New Bretton Woods   185
Toward a Stable International Economy   204

Suggested Reading 207

Index 211

About the Authors 219

Figures

2–1. Volume of World Exports, 1960–1988 13

2–2. Production Possibilities Curve without International Trade 14

2–3. Gains from Trade with Absolute Advantage 15

2–4. Gains from Trade with Comparative Advantage 18

2–5. The Effect of a Tariff on a Domestic Economy 24

2–6. Percent of World Exports, Selected Countries 36

3–1. U.S.-Japanese Trade Flows, 1980–1989 47

3–2. Yen/Dollar Exchange Rates, 1973–1990 48

3–3. Currency and Goods in U.S.-Japanese Trade 50

3–4. Supply and Demand of Foreign Exchange 51

3–5. Trade-weighted Exchange Rates versus the U.S. Current Account 52

3–6. Managed Exchange Rates 55

3–7. U.S. Investment Income, 1970–1989 59

3–8. Government Bond Yields 60

3–9. International Investment Position of the United States, 1970–1989 62

3–10. Annual Net Flows of Foreign Investment, 1960–1989 63

3–11. Bilateral Investment Profile: United States and Japan, 1974–1989 64

4–1. U.S. Gold Reserve Assets and Dollar Liabilities, 1950–1975 74

4–2. Petrodollar Recycling   77

4–3. Crude Oil Prices, 1970–1990   78

4–4. How Capital Flight Adds to Latin America's Growing Debt, 1976–1985   81

4–5. The Debt Picture in Mexico, Venezuela, and Argentina If There Had Been No Capital Flight, 1985   81

4–6. Domestic Savings Deposits in the United States, Mexico, and Argentina, 1981–1985   82

5–1. Export Shares in Microelectronics and Telecommunications   99

5–2. Nondefense R&D Expenditures   100

5–3. U.S. Current Account Balance, 1960–1989   101

5–4. U.S. Merchandise Trade Deficit, 1980–1989   102

5–5. Major Powers' Share of World Exports, 1960–1989   103

5–6. U.S. Federal Deficit, 1960–1989   116

5–7. Gross Outstanding Federal Debt of the United States, 1960–1989   118

5–8. U.S. Gross Federal Debt As a Percentage of GNP   119

5–9. Investment As a Percent of GDP   120

5–10. Total Corporate Debt in the United States, 1980–1989   121

5–11. Total Household Borrowing in the United States   122

5–12. Consumption As a Percent of GDP   123

6–1. Total Debt of Developing Nations, 1974–1990   126

6–2. The Debt Trap   128

6–3. Resource Flow to and from Indebted Developing Countries, 1978–1991   141

6–4. Resource Flow As a Percent of Exports   142

6–5. Debt Flows Vocabulary Guide   143

6–6.   Net Flows and Net Transfers, All Developing
       Countries, 1980–1989   143

6–7.   Per Capita GNP in the Developing World,
       1967–1987   144

6–8.   Gross Domestic Investment Per Capita,
       1967–1987   145

6–9.   Value of Merchandise Imports, 1967–1987   146

7–1.   Mexico's Total External Debt, 1970–1989   150

7–2.   Mexican Capital Flight As a Percentage of Change
       in Debt   156

7–3.   Mexico's New Borrowing and Debt Service   158

7–4.   Mexico's Net Flow and Transfer of
       Resources   160

7–5.   Mexico's Trade Balance   162

7–6.   Mexican Inflation, 1981–1989   168

7–7.   Urban Real Wages in Mexico, 1980–1989   169

7–8.   Growth of Per Capita GDP at Constant
       Prices   170

7–9.   Mexico's Imports versus Exports, 1960–1989   172

7–10. Secondary Market Value of External Mexican
       Debt   174

8–1.   Index of the Dollar's Value against Fifteen
       Industrial Country Currencies   189

8–2.   Debt Relief Financing Options   203

Tables

2–1. Production Possibilities for the United States and Chile with and without Trade 16

2–2. Distribution of Costs and Benefits from Special Protection 26

2–3. U.S. Merchandise Exports by End-Use Category, 1965–1988 35

2–4. U.S. Merchandise Imports by End-Use Category, 1965–1988 35

3–1. Hypothetical Summary Balance of Payments for the United States 41

3–2. Positive and Negative Effects on Balance of Payments Accounts 41

3–3. Foreign Exchange Rates 44

3–4. U.S. International Transactions 54

4–1. U.S. Balance of Payments, 1946–1949 70

4–2. U.S. Balance of Payments, 1950–1957 70

4–3. U.S. Balance of Payments, 1958–1965 71

4–4. OPEC International Placements, 1976–1983 76

4–5. Estimated Net Capital Flight: Cumulative Flows, 1976–1985 80

4–6. Current and Capital Accounts of Developing Countries, 1978–1984 87

4–7. Percentage Change in Gross Domestic Product of Developing Countries and Industrial Countries, 1978–1985 87

5–1. U.S. Merchandise Exports by Product Group, 1965–1989   103

5–2. U.S. Merchandise Imports by Product Group, 1965–1989   104

5–3. U.S. Economic Data, 1977–1981   105

5–4. U.S. Dependence on Petroleum Imports, 1973–1989   106

5–5. Cost of U.S. Energy Imports, 1975–1988   107

5–6. The Reagan Economic Record, 1981–1989   109

5–7. Exposure of Major U.S. Banks to Six Troubled Developing Countries, March 1984   113

5–8. Exposure of U.S. Banks to Third World Debtors, June 1984   114

6–1. Debt Indicators for Developing Countries, 1974–1990   127

6–2. U.S. Economic Data, 1973–1990   132

6–3. Resource Flow to and from Debtor Countries, 1978–1991   140

7–1. Mexican Debt Profile   159

7–2. Mexico's Balance of Payments, 1960–1989   164

7–3. Exposure of Major U.S. Banks to Mexican Debt, 1982, 1985   166

7–4. Mexican Loan Package, 1986   166

8–1. Debt Relief and New Loans, 1980–1987   198

8–2. Big Lenders to Developing Countries   199

Preface

The international economic system is in flux. The key actors and the rules of the game have changed. As the Berlin wall tumbled, so did the distinctions between first, second, and third worlds. With the further consolidation of the European Community in 1992, the notion of the trading state has been called into question. Production and finance are not constrained by national boundaries; a product's parts may be produced in a dozen different countries and financed by a money center bank. We live in a truly global economic system.

But with this change comes confusion. How do we understand trade deficits that are in part comprised of U.S. multinational corporations importing component parts from its overseas subsidiaries? How do we explain movements of a dollar that is not only the unit of value and account in the United States but is used as a global currency? Given the signs of disequilibrium in the international economic system, such as mounting debt in both the industrialized and less developed world, what ought to be the policy recommendations for a stable international economic system?

This book attempts to provide the fundamentals for understanding our changing economic system. The principles of international trade and finance are highlighted by the historical context that shapes their development. The second edition of *The ABCs of International Finance* includes the following:

- An up-to-date statistical portrait of U.S. balance of payments, mounting domestic debt, and the continuing financial crisis of the less developed world. New figures characterize the fundamental disequilibrium in international markets

- Focus on the debt crisis in the less developed world as a long run, structural problem

- Expanded treatment of trade theory and exchange rate determination to explain the paradox of the U.S. trade deficit and a strong dollar

- Analysis of the Brady Plan to address less developed countries' debt, including a case study of Mexico

- Argument for a "New Bretton Woods" to restructure the international trade and financial systems

We believe that this book is suitable for students in a variety of courses. While international economics is the most obvious, we also envision its use in intermediate macro theory, economic development, and even introductory economics courses. The book is written in simple, nontechnical language, but it neither trivializes the international sector, as introductory textbooks usually do, nor does it mathematize the subject, which is the approach of most advanced texts. Therefore, the book is appropriate for students at many levels. We hope it helps them understand how, in the real world of the 1990s, there is no such thing as a national economy anymore— virtually everything depends on the smooth functioning of the international economy.

Acknowledgments

As with the first edition, this book is a result of the efforts of a number of people, many more than could reasonably be listed here. Among these are Jorge Castenada, John C. Chitwood, Norris Clement, Samuel Schmidt, James Crotty, Ross M. LaRoe, John Hodges, Harry Magdoff, Robert Rafferty, Tom Riddell, and Frank E. Wagner.

We are also grateful for the efficiency and attention to detail of Grace Von Tobel, the manuscript typist, and to Alice Van Buskirk and Linda Vollmer, whose editorial diligence throughout the many drafts of the first edition made the job of revision much simpler than it might have been. Many thanks also to Margaret H. Pierce, the efficient research assistance who cheerfully tracked down statistical sources for the second edition.

And, of course, love and appreciation to our families: Betty, Mike, and Laura Linda; Lucie, Barry, and Lisanna; and David, for understanding.

1

The Trade and
Debt Crisis

O ne of the most complicated areas in all of economics is international trade theory and its facilitating mechanism, international finance. Trade is easier to conceptualize: we make things and trade them to other countries; they do the same, and everybody gains. But the manner in which this process is financed is something understood by only a few people in the world, and even most of them can't (or won't) explain it.

Until recently most businesspeople felt they could afford to deal with the intricacies of international finance as an abstraction—something best handled by the gnomes of Zurich. But as the world has become increasingly internationalized and interdependent no one nowadays can escape the vicissitudes of international finance. We're all in this together.

Consider, for example:

By August 1986 the unemployment rate in the United States was 6.8 percent; but in Aliquippa, Pennsylvania, over 13 percent were unemployed. Aliquippa is in Beaver County, just north of Pittsburgh. The economic recovery that spread across the nation between 1983 and 1986 missed Aliquippa completely. The local LTV steel plant, which employed more than 12,000 workers several years ago, now employs only 800. What has happened here has happened throughout Pennsylvania. In 1976 there were more than 200,000 jobs in the steel and primary metals industry in the state, but by 1986 fewer than 100,000 remained.

To protect himself against a sharply devalued currency, Venezuelan businessman José-Manuel Sanchez sold 20 million bolivars worth of his stock in Venezuelan companies, and with the proceeds he bought $1 million worth of certificates of deposit from Chemical Bank in New York, depositing the rest in a West German bank.

In 1990 a twenty-one-year-old worker in one of Brazil's automobile factories was on strike for wages to match inflation. His wages, along with his bank account, had been frozen under the new government's economic shock plan to attack the inflation that had reached more than 60 percent *monthly*. Since this worker entered the work force at age sixteen, the currency valuation has changed three times—one cruzeiro back then now is only worth about .000001. The worker's family saves dollars to hedge against such instability.

In 1981 petroleum was selling for $32.50 a barrel. U.S. oil fields were crowded with geologists and drilling rigs. But by August 1986, petroleum prices had collapsed to $12.50 a barrel, and the oil fields have become symbols of debt, bankruptcy, and unemployment. Texas alone faced a $3.2 billion state budget deficit and an unemployment rate of almost 12 percent.

In 1986 a U.S. steel worker on strike complained that although she had accepted a $3.00 per hour reduction in wages and benefits two years ago, the company was now demanding another cut of $5.50 per hour in wages and benefits. Without this concession from the union workers the company claims it cannot compete against foreign steel producers and will be forced to shut down.

A formerly unemployed machinist from Chicopee, Massachusetts, is now working in a new high-tech industry located off Route 128 outside Boston. While he is delighted to be working, he now makes $4.85 an hour, compared with the $9.75 an hour in his former job. To make ends meet, his wife is working at a fast-food restaurant for $3.35 an hour.

Just off Interstate 90 in the middle of Minnesota, in a small breakfast diner, there is a poster tacked to the wall above the cash register. It reads, "FUTURE FARMERS OF AMERICA: WHO NEEDS THEM?"

An Iowa farmer who has just lost his farm wearily contemplates the irony of his misfortune: his overproduction of corn contributed to declining grain prices and eventually to the foreclosure on his farm. As he reads the evening newspaper, he learns that so much grain has been produced this year that there is no place to store it. On another page is a story about famine and starvation in East Africa, and below that story he reads that the president has offered to sell wheat to the Soviet Union at a 30 percent discount. Even at that price the Soviets aren't buying; they can get it cheaper elsewhere. Unable to comprehend the interdependence of these seemingly unrelated stories, he reflects on his new job in a service station—owned by his wife's brother.

In Smyrna, Tennessee, former Ford manager Jerry Benefield is the president of a thriving Nissan plant. Such Japanese "trans-plants" expect to export as many cars as Detroit automakers next year.

Mexican peasant Maria Nunez, a mother of eleven children, discovered this morning at the tortilla factory that the price of tortillas had increased again. Tortillas, the main staple of her family's diet, have doubled in price during the past six months. She was informed that the government had further reduced its subsidy. It had something to do with deficits, debt, and a loan from the International Monetary Fund in Washington, D.C.—which is a long way from her small farm in Santa Cruz just outside Guadalajara.

In Rochester, New York, a Kodak production line worker with twenty-two years seniority is laid off. Competition from the Japanese, he is told, is the reason. What, he wonders, as he drives his Toyota to the unemployment office, has become of the American dream?

The reason international finance is affecting everyone's lives in such a dramatic way is that through a paradoxical set of circumstances the U.S. banking system—the strongest in the world—has become extremely vulnerable to disaster, if not to a total collapse.

Ironically, this all came about because of the strength of the U.S. economy after World War II and the subsequent adoption of the U.S. dollar as the world's key currency. Since then the dollar has replaced gold as the medium of exchange for international transactions and has become the reserve currency for most nations. Therefore anything that threatens the health of the U.S. dollar also threatens the health, if not the very existence, of world trade and, as such, everyone's well-being.

The seeds of the present crisis were sown when the Organization of Petroleum Producing Countries (OPEC) was able to establish a near monopoly of the world's oil supply and increased oil prices by some 1,700 percent over the 1971–73 period. Industrialized countries dependent on petroleum had no option but to pay the price, leading to one of the largest transfers of wealth in history. Oil continued to flow to the West, and several hundred billion dollars (nicknamed *petrodollars*) flowed back to the Middle East in payment for it. The OPEC countries in turn were unable to absorb such a large infusion of funds without risking runaway inflation, so they simply deposited the money in the safest logical place: the banks of the industrialized world.

Now the banks had an unaccustomed but not unattractive problem: what to do with these unexpected new deposits? Banks survive and prosper by loaning out deposits at a rate higher than they pay for them. Given the recession of the mid-1970s (caused in part by the oil price shock), the only seemingly qualified borrowers were the countries of the Third World, which were in need of capital.

Therefore, on the now dubious but then seemingly logical assumption that governments don't go bankrupt and consequently are good credit risks, billions of dollars were transferred to the Third World. By 1990 this debt amounted to over $1 trillion. This seemed to make sense in the beginning because almost everyone believed that transferring capital to where it was needed was simply good economics. It seemed so logical that even the International Monetary Fund (IMF) made considerable efforts to facilitate the process. A new term even entered the economic vocabulary to describe it: *petrodollar recycling.*

But such an assumption is valid only if the borrowing countries are able to invest the funds in economic activities that produce a rate of return higher than the rate of interest on the loans. Unfortunately, this didn't happen.

Private banks, in their somewhat unaccustomed new role as international development bankers, didn't have the resources, the know-how, or the authority to monitor how their loans were used. As a result, much of the money simply disappeared, or was transferred into personal accounts (often right back to where it came from), or was invested in ill-conceived pork barrel development projects.

By the late 1970s the debtor countries began to realize that their export capacity was not sufficient to continue meeting their debt obligations (which were compounding at an increasing rate), and "rescheduling" became commonplace. Then, in August 1982, the Mexican government announced that it could no longer service its debt. For all practical purposes, Mexico was bankrupt. This sent a shock through the international financial system, especially since Mexico was a major oil producer and was therefore assumed to be one of the most creditworthy of the debtor nations. In a near panic atmosphere, the banking authorities quickly arranged a temporary bailout, rescheduling the Mexican debt. The crisis was averted, at least temporarily.

Since then the general situation has not improved: Argentina, Brazil, and most of the debtor countries have been forced to reschedule their mounting debts. The banks have had little option but to accommodate them and, thus, reluctantly pour good money after bad. To make matters worse, by 1985 the ten major U.S. banks were exposed to the Third World debtor countries by more than 200 percent of their net worth, making a default by *even one* of the major debtor countries enough almost certainly to trigger a banking panic, a run on the banks, and a potential collapse of the U.S. banking system.

In 1986 the breakup of OPEC, the concomitant declining oil prices, and an unexpected dramatic fall of interest rates seemed at first to signal the end of the crisis. Most of the debtor countries are also oil importers, so it now appeared that they would be able to service their debts more easily. Lower interest rates also relieved some pressure as the debts were rescheduled at lower rates. And some of the debtor countries, notably Argentina and Brazil, have seen their position improve somewhat.

However, some of the oil-exporting debtor countries, especially Mexico and Nigeria, now find themselves in a nearly impossible dilemma. Mexico, which is the more serious case, receives some 70 percent of its export earnings from oil exports. Mexico owes some $100 billion, $25 billion of that directly to U.S. private banks. Without oil revenues (as we shall show) there is no way Mexico can continue to service its debt over the long run. Therefore, while lower oil prices would in general appear to be good news for everyone, they may well push Mexico into bankruptcy. This alone could be enough to precipitate a crisis in the U.S. banking system. Furthermore, the United States' financial system is itself in crisis. Unsustainable macroeconomic policies led to an accumulation of government, business, and household debt.

Understanding this ironic turn of events requires an understanding of the role of the dollar in international finance, the theoretical subtleties and the realities of international trade, and the mechanics of international lending. These issues are the subject of this book. After examining them in some detail, we then take up the question of why previous policy prescriptions have failed and suggest some possible solutions to this increasingly pressing problem.

Chapter 2 analyzes international trade and demonstrates how and why everyone theoretically gains from specializing and trading. However, trade is directly related to the method of financing it. Because of the general acceptability of the U.S. dollar, the United States has for many years been able to run huge balance of trade deficits—that is, buying much more from abroad than it is selling. Since 1984 the U.S. trade deficit has exceeded $100 billion annually; this is historically unprecedented.

Any time a country has a trade deficit, financial transactions must take place to balance and accommodate the difference. As we see in chapter 3 when we examine the theoretical workings of exchange rate systems, financial flows should trigger changes in prices of traded goods, and the imbalance between exports and

A Quick Guide to Statistical Sources in International Finance

This book is rich in statistical information. But we encourage you to muck around in some of the original sources. For example, where we have presented balance of payments information on the United States, you might want to analyze the external position of Japan. Or while we have presented a case study of Mexico, you might be interested in the debt situation of low-income Africa. To play around with the data we suggest the following sources:

For information on the United States, consult:

The Economic Report of the President (annual, U.S. Government Printing Office, Washington, D.C.) The appendix section on "International Statistics" is the best source of annual data, some series dating back to 1946. *The Statistical Abstract of the United States* is also useful for time series data. For information on current years, consult the *Survey of Current Business* (Bureau of Economic Analysis, U.S. Department of Commerce). March issues are especially useful because they provide the summary of prior year's transactions.

For information on other countries, consult:

International Financial Statistics (International Monetary Fund). This appears monthly as well as in an annual supplement called the *Yearbook.* In the front are summary tables detailing, for example, world imports and exports. This is followed by country data on nearly all macroeconomic aggregates. To analyze the Third World debt situation, the *World Debt Tables* are an essential tool. This multivolume set published by the World Bank presents both aggregated as well as country-specific information. Another key source for information on the developing world is the *World Development Report,* also published by the World Bank.

imports should be self-correcting. But in reality there is an important difference between the theory of exchange rate adjustments, which are supposed to prevent such imbalances, and the present world economic situation in which little such adjustment has occurred.

A key point here is that in recognition of the fact that the huge U.S. trade deficits cannot continue forever without creating an even more serious crisis, the major Western industrialized nations (the Group of Five—the United States, France, Japan, Great Britain, and West Germany) have abandoned the free-flexible exchange rate system (which had been in place since 1973) in favor of a coordinated market intervention to control the value of the dollar in relation to other currencies, notably the Japanese yen.

As was planned, this intervention has caused the dollar to fall somewhat and has stimulated U.S. exports. But this in turn has merely exacerbated the problem of lack of confidence and contributed to the fragility of the system. There is a great deal of uncertainty over the ability of governments to intervene in foreign exchange markets over time and over the desirability of their doing so. Because the rules of the international financial game are in flux, future stability is in question.

In chapter 4 we examine and explain the all-important role of the U.S. dollar in the international financial system. If the dollar were not the world's key reserve currency (used for more than 50 percent of all international transactions), the debt crisis, which is really a dollar crisis, wouldn't have such serious implications for the U.S. economy. A country that allows its currency to be used as a key currency has many privileges, but in broader terms it also has responsibilities. The collapse of the dollar, like the meltdown of a nuclear power plant, would spread fallout all over the world and everyone would feel its effects. The United States, which has recently become a debtor nation itself, we shall argue has a responsibility to see that this does not happen.

Unfortunately, the U.S. economy is also beset with problems from other directions: strong competition from foreign manufacturers, the banking system's vulnerability to Third World nations' debt, and the savings and loan crisis at home. Chapter 5 looks at these woes, using the ailing farm and high-technology industries as examples. It then assesses the Carter, Reagan, and Bush administrations' efforts to get the economy moving again despite stagflation and trade deficits.

But the recovery of the industrial sector is limited by the debt explosion in the United States. Over the past two decades, the U.S. economy has been plagued by record federal deficits, which have resulted in an internal debt of over $3 trillion, an amount equal to over 50 percent of the U.S. Gross National Product.

The U.S. national debt more than doubled in the 1980s. In addition to government debt, business and personal debt now amount to more than $6 *trillion.* Total debt in the U.S. economy is more than $10 trillion. In 1985 the United States became a debtor nation internationally for the first time since 1914. This means that the United States now owes more to foreign interests than it is owed. This external debt will soon become a serious drain on U.S. internal resources. As the rest of the world has become more industrialized, efficient, and competitive, the United States has lost its once predominant position in the international economy. Therefore, we examine this situation in some detail, then put it into the context of the most serious problem of all: the vulnerability of the U.S. banking system to the internal and external debt buildup. We next examine the potential consequences of a collapse of the international financial system, which would most certainly follow a collapse of the U.S. economy.

Chapter 6 then focuses on the debt crisis of the Third World. The presumed purpose of international lending is to transfer capital from the wealthy industrialized nations to developing Third World nations that have little capital. However, what is occurring now is just the opposite: a net transfer of funds *from* the Third World *to* the industrialized world. This process has severely constrained the possibilities for long-run development in the Third World.

In chapter 7, we take up the case of Mexico. The inability of Mexico to meet its financial obligations triggered the Third World debt crisis. A systematic study of the various emergency packages and economic programs demonstrates the depth of the problem of development under the debt burden. The costs to the Mexican people have been enormous, and the future promises more of the same.

Then, in chapter 8, we examine the international economic policy options to address the triple debt crisis looming over the international financial system. The staggering developing world debt, coupled with rapidly growing U.S. internal debt *and* U.S. external debt, has created a fragile situation that is not sustainable over the long run. What should be done?

Economists have described and explained the problem. But solving it will take some enlightened politicians. At this juncture none appears in the horizon.

2
The Role of
International Trade

International trade has a long and illustrious history. As far back as classical antiquity, nations have traded. There are several reasons for trade. One is, of course, that everyone gains, or at least perceives that they gain, from the process. Otherwise, it wouldn't happen. Perhaps a more important reason is that all nations are interdependent. No nation can be self-sufficient—independent from international trade—without great sacrifices.

The United States, for example, is one of the more self-sufficient countries in the world, yet it depends on imports for most of its bauxite, diamonds, tin, coffee, nickel, manganese, rubber, tungsten, bananas, gold, platinum, and chromium. The latter two are crucial in the production of jet engines and in many other industrial processes, but they are nonexistent in the United States and come almost exclusively from South Africa.

So every nation needs imports, albeit some more than others. It follows then that if a nation needs imports, it also needs exports because there is no other way to pay for imports. All nations, therefore, need imports *and* exports. In other words, they need international trade. The gains from international trade are the same as the gains from any other kind of trade. When people specialize, productivity is increased. And when they trade, their incomes are higher, as is overall consumption.

In one sense, international trade is very simple: each nation specializes in whatever it can produce most efficiently and trades the resulting product to someone else for whatever it does best. Given that the distribution of skills and national resources is not the same throughout the world, everyone gains from the process. But in another sense the process is quite complicated. That's because everyone's self-interest is involved.

Chances are you don't make your own shoes or clothing. Instead, you specialize in doing whatever you can do best, and you sell your services (your labor) or your product in the marketplace. So either directly or indirectly, you trade with others, and both you and they are presumably better off for it. Almost no one—neither nation nor individual—is self-sufficient, and no nation these days tries to get along without international trade. You can understand this better if you try to build an automobile in your garage or to grow some bananas in your garden.

This process of specializing and trading was first elaborated in detail by Adam Smith in 1776 in the classic book popularly known as *The Wealth of Nations* (but, in fact, entitled *An Inquiry into the Nature and Causes of the Wealth of Nations*). Smith's work still provides the theoretical foundation and rationale for free-market capitalism.

In some 1,200 pages, Smith elaborated on the fact that people gain by pursuing their own self-interest. A private vice—selfishness—becomes a public virtue when people selfishly specialize in doing whatever they can do best, "truck" the result off somewhere, and "barter" it (exchange it for something else). The theory of capitalism says that free competition between buyers and sellers assures that the whole process works out to everyone's best interest, and that competition and trade are normal and important parts of the capitalist system.

What is often overlooked is that Smith wrote *The Wealth of Nations* not only as an explanation of how capitalism works, but also as a diatribe against the mercantilist trading policies of the eighteenth-century nation-states. The mercantilists felt that the primary objective of trading internationally was to export as much as possible and accumulate gold in return. This, they thought, was the "nature and cause" of the wealth of nations.

Not so, said Smith. Nations, as well as individuals, gain from specializing and trading. But Smith's ideal trade wasn't goods for gold, but goods for goods. This set the stage for a controversy that has persisted for more than two hundred years now. If Smith was right, as most economists nowadays believe he was, then there is no place in a rational world for protectionist, self-interested measures to restrict trade through artificial barriers such as tariffs and import

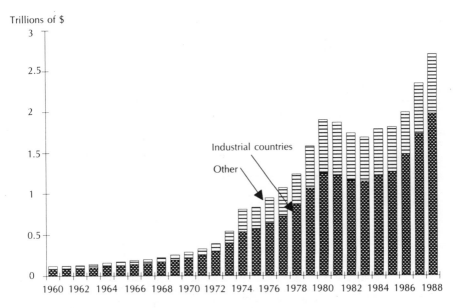

Trillions of $

Source: *International Financial Statistics Yearbook 1989.*

Figure 2–1. *Volume of World Exports, 1960–1988*

quotas. As figure 2–1 shows, in 1988 total world exports reached an astounding volume of $2.69 *trillion,* increasing more than twenty-two times since 1960. Clearly, international trade is no small issue.

Theories of International Trade

Various theories explain how international trade does—or should—function. The theories of *absolute advantage* and *comparative advantage* are not controversial. *Protectionism,* however, is hotly debated, for it affects special-interest groups much differently from the way it affects the general public.

The Theory of Absolute Advantage

Refined by Smith's follower David Ricardo and dressed up in modern terminology—the ABCs version—the theory of absolute advantage goes like this.

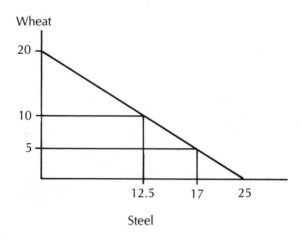

Assume 100 workers. It takes 4 worker hours to make steel and 5 worker hours for wheat. Your *production* possibilities are then 25 steel (100/4) or 20 wheat (100/5). You may choose to *consume* any combination of goods along the PPC— perhaps 10 wheat, 12.5 steel or 5 wheat, 17 steel.

Figure 2.2. *Production Possibilities Curve without International Trade*

With rare exceptions, almost any nation can produce any two given products, steel *and* wheat, bananas *and* refrigerators, guns *and* butter being but a few of the more obvious examples. The same nation can also choose to produce steel *or* wheat, bananas *or* refrigerators, guns *or* butter. The problem comes in deciding on what combination to produce, since the possibilities are infinite. Figure 2–2 depicts the various combinations possible in producing two goods in one country *without* international trade.

But countries are not always efficient at producing both steel *and* wheat, copper *and* corn. Obviously, if you are efficient at producing copper and need corn, then you should produce copper and trade it to someone who is efficient at producing corn. Or if you are efficient at producing bananas but need refrigerators, then you'll certainly want to leave the production of refrigerators to someone else and put your efforts into bananas. These are examples of what is called *absolute advantage.* With absolute advantage, because you

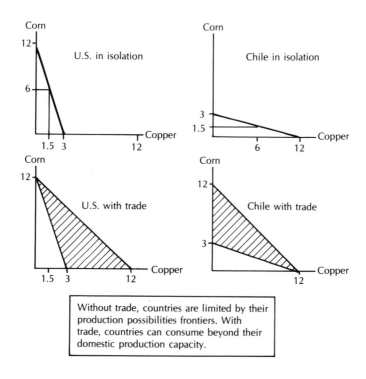

Figure 2–3. *Gains from Trade with Absolute Advantage*

use fewer resources in production you are clearly better than another country in the production of a good. The other country may be distinctly superior to you in the sale of another good. In such a case, it is easy to see that everyone gains from specializing and trading internationally. You can see absolute advantage demonstrated in figure 2–3, which is derived from the data in table 2–1.

To understand the theory of free trade, we need to employ some simplifying assumptions. Adam Smith and David Ricardo believed that the value of all goods could be represented by the number of labor hours used to produce them. While machines might be used, the contribution of a tractor, for example, can be broken down into the labor hours used to make the tractor. So, for example, we can say that in the United States it takes 5 labor hours to produce a bushel of corn and 20 labor hours to produce copper. Let's assume

Table 2–1
*Production Possibilities for the United States and Chile
with and without Trade*

Without trade:			
	Corn	or	Copper
United States	12		3
Chile	3		12
In isolation trying to produce both:			
	Corn	and	Copper
United States	6.0		1.5
Chile	1.5		6.0
Total production	7.5		7.5
Total possible production with trade:			
	Corn	and	Copper
United States	12		0
Chile	0		12
Total	12		12

that in Chile it is the reverse: 20 labor hours for corn and 5 for copper. Why might the required labor hours differ? It could be that the soil in the United States is fertile and doesn't need much work to grow corn, but the copper is much harder to extract in the United States than in Chile and takes many more labor hours. Based on these labor hours needed (also called input requirements) we see that the United States is absolutely more efficient in corn and that Chile is more efficient in copper.

For simplicity's sake let's assume that both the United States and Chile had the same number of labor hours: 60. With this endowment of labor, we can calculate that the United States could produce 12 bushels of corn (since it takes 5 labor hours to make 1 bushel, 60 laborers working an hour will produce 60/5, or 12). Alternatively, the United States could produce 3 units of copper (60/20). Chile, given the same number of worker hours, could produce 3 corn units (60/20) or 12 copper (60/5). We can easily see that the United States has a clear absolute advantage over Chile in corn production. If all U.S. resources went into corn production, then the nation could produce 12 units of corn, whereas Chile could only produce 3 units. On the other hand, Chile, with its abundant resources, could produce 12 units of copper. But even if it gave up completely on copper and put all its efforts into producing corn, it could only produce 3 units of corn.

Now, since both countries need corn *and* copper, if no trade exists and each is going it alone, both would have to divide their efforts between the two, let's say, for simplicity, into a 50–50 split. Under those conditions, the United States would be producing 6 units of corn and 1.5 units of copper. Chile would produce the opposite: 1.5 units of corn and 6 units of copper. Between the two, 7.5 units of corn and 7.5 units of copper would be produced.

It's obvious by now that each country can gain a lot by specializing in what it does best and trading to the other. If the United States puts all its effort into corn production, it can produce 12 units; while if Chile produces only copper, it can produce 12 units. Then they do a little trading. Now the countries can consume beyond what they produce. The shaded area in figure 2–3 shows these potential gains from trade. So clearly it would seem that everyone is better off when the two countries specialize and trade.

The point of all this is that countries can gain from specializing and trading. Productivity is increased, incomes are higher because more is sold, costs are lower, and consumption is higher. Everybody gains from international trade when absolute advantages exist—or at least that would certainly seem to be the case.

The Theory of Comparative Advantage

But there's more. What if the United States is more efficient at producing *both* corn *and* copper? Is there then any reason why the United States should trade with Chile? Common sense would tell us there's not. But, as David Ricardo demonstrated in the early 1800s, both countries can still gain from trade so long as even just a relative comparative advantage exists. To see why, take a look at figure 2–4. Then read on.

Let's think, for example, about trade between the United States and Argentina. Assume that both countries have 24 labor hours at their disposal. In the United States it takes 2 labor hours to produce a unit of beef and 8 for a unit of wheat. But for argument's sake,

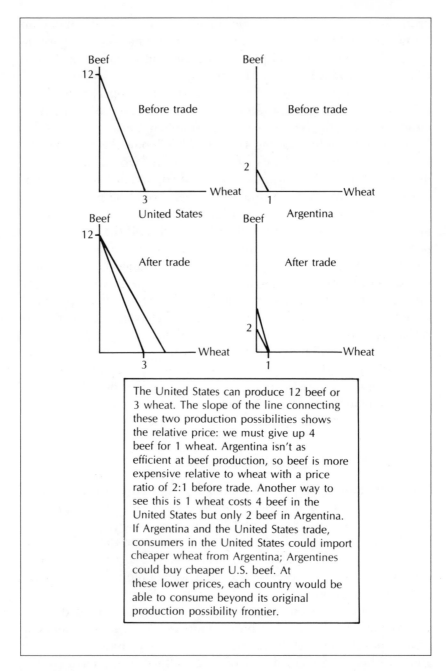

The United States can produce 12 beef or 3 wheat. The slope of the line connecting these two production possibilities shows the relative price: we must give up 4 beef for 1 wheat. Argentina isn't as efficient at beef production, so beef is more expensive relative to wheat with a price ratio of 2:1 before trade. Another way to see this is 1 wheat costs 4 beef in the United States but only 2 beef in Argentina. If Argentina and the United States trade, consumers in the United States could import cheaper wheat from Argentina; Argentines could buy cheaper U.S. beef. At these lower prices, each country would be able to consume beyond its original production possibility frontier.

Figure 2–4. *Gains from Trade with Comparative Advantage*

assume Argentina is less efficient, using 12 labor hours for each beef and 24 for each wheat. The United States is far more efficient in both. Given the 24 labor hours, the United States could produce 12 beef (24/2) or 3 wheat (24/8), while Argentina chooses between 2 beef (24/12) and 1 wheat (24/24) if the two countries do not trade. We can see these production possibilities in the top frame of figure 2–4.

Despite the United States' relative advantage in both wheat and beef, the country still gains from trade. Why? Because with specialization, there are still advantages in trading; otherwise, trade obviously wouldn't occur.

If the United States specializes in beef and sells it to Argentina and Argentina specializes in wheat and sells some to the United States, both countries still gain. Why? The gains come from differences in *relative prices*. Relative prices tell us how much of one good you must give up to get a unit of another good. Since the United States may produce 12 units of beef *or* 3 units of wheat, the relative price ratio is 4 beef to 1 wheat. Since you would have to give up 4 beef for 1 wheat (reducing 12/3), wheat is four times more expensive than beef. In Argentina the relative prices before trade are different. Argentina can produce 2 units of beef or 1 unit of wheat. Instead of giving up 4 beef, as in the United States, Argentines only have to exchange 2 beef for each unit of wheat. According to our model, wheat is cheaper in Argentina when expressed in terms of beef.

Based on these relative prices, we can see that wheat is *relatively* more expensive in the United States (you pay 4 beef for it) than it is in Argentina. The other way of expressing this is to say that because the United States is more efficient in beef production, beef is relatively cheaper there than in Argentina.

Because of these differences in relative prices, there are potential gains from trade. With beef cheaper in the United States than in Argentina, if the Argentines imported beef at this low price, consumers would have money left over to buy more beef or wheat. Likewise, if the United States imported Argentina's cheaper wheat and only had to pay 2 beef instead of 4, there would be greater potential to consume more of both goods. Despite the fact that Argentina is not absolutely better at producing beef or wheat, everyone is made better off because of trade in accord with relative comparative advantage—at least in theory.

Contemporary Theories of Trade

Later economists abandoned Smith's and Ricardo's assumption that all goods can be reduced to their labor requirements. Instead, their models included two factors of production: labor and capital (machines). But the argument for free trade is the same: there are gains from the good that you can produce most efficiently.

This theory was made famous by Eli Heckscher and his student Bertil Ohlin. It postulates that a country should export that good which uses relatively intensively the country's most abundant factor. Why? The answer is based in simple supply and demand concepts. If a country has a lot of capital, with an ample supply, the price is cheap. Likewise, an abundance of labor relative to capital makes for low wages. If capital is abundant (and relatively cheap), this country should be able to offer capital-intensive goods—machines, for example—to other countries at low prices. Countries overflowing with labor and cheap wages can sell labor-intensive goods at an advantage. Thus, if Indian labor is abundant relative to capital, India should export labor-intensive goods; while in Great Britain, if capital is more plentiful than labor, that nation should trade capital-intensive products. Therefore, the direction of trade (which country trades what) is determined by relative factor endowments—how much labor you have compared to how much capital.

Furthermore, an extension of this theory predicts that not only will trade increase the amount of goods available for the world to consume, but over time the benefits of trade will accrue to the least advantaged within nations. That is, if India is labor-abundant and exports labor-intensive goods, this will generate a new source of demand for labor. The price of the abundant factor—which had been very cheap because it was plentiful—would now rise, making those who were poor better off. Trade would also generate a tendency toward equality in factor prices between nations. As wages would be rising in India because of the international demand for labor-intensive products, they would be falling in the United States, which would be exporting capital-intensive products instead.

Trade then benefits everyone—theoretically. But when this theory that predicted that capital-intensive countries should be exporting capital-intensive goods was tested using historical data for the United States, the results were inconsistent. Nobel laureate Wassily

Leontief found that although the theory predicted that the United States would export capital-intensive goods, in practice just the opposite has occurred—the U.S. exports were more labor intensive.[1]

The Leontief Paradox, as this study came to be called, spurred much research into the determinants of trade. A critical factor that has emerged is the role technology plays in defining what good should be exported. Remember, the original Heckscher-Ohlin model focused on capital and labor. Just how these two factors are combined—the technology used—is a key to understanding competitive advantage. Later research by Raymond Vernon showed that the comparative advantage that the United States enjoyed over the rest of the world in the 1950s and 1960s was derived from its ability to develop and use technical know-how.[2] Thus new products are produced in countries with large research and development capabilities while older, more "mature" products can be replicated in the less industrialized nations. This tendency was accentuated by the growing importance of multinational corporations, which tended to keep research and development in the home country during the early stages of product development, and to transfer production to less developed countries as processes were standardized. Thus, developing countries might be exporting capital-intensive goods developed in industrial country research centers. With the rise of multinational corporations, the political boundaries of nation-states give way to economic considerations. Different stages of production are often completed in a number of countries, making the old theories of trading among nations difficult to apply.

The new wave of theories of international trade has challenged the static concept of a stock of labor and capital, analyzing instead the principal *actors* in creating dynamic technological systems. For example, MIT professor Paul Krugman argues for active intervention on the part of government to promote strategic high-technology sectors.[3] Harvard professor Michael Porter also supports the idea that national wealth does not come from endowments of capital or labor but depends on the ability of a nation's industries to innovate, creating new products and new processes.[4] But in contrast to Krugman, Porter advocates limiting government intervention and focusing instead on the availability of skilled labor, the nature of home market demand, the presence of related industries, and healthy domestic rivalry between firms.

Despite disagreements over what determines the products traded and how successful the results, economists of almost all pedigrees and all but the most myopic politicians seem to agree that international trade is beneficial to everyone. But it's not that simple. What complicates the issue is the apparently obvious fact that for a system of international trade to work, there has to be at least some degree of balance between what is imported and what is exported. Otherwise, someone gets more of the gains and someone else loses more than is fair.

Again, the analogy of individuals trading in the market is relevant. The idea of trading is to come out ahead. The winners in the exchange process are those who are good "horse traders" or good bargainers. Everyone tries to buy cheap and sell dear. If you win at this game, you can become wealthy; if you lose, you'll be poor. There are always winners and losers.

Now, if we extend this logic to the international arena, a similar process occurs. Everyone wants to be a winner, which in this case means every country wants to export more than it imports. In one sense, this is a curious kind of logic, because by exporting more than it is importing, a country is sending more of its goods out of the country than it is getting back, which seems a strange way to interpret the general welfare. This is, in fact, why Adam Smith railed against the mercantilists: all you accumulate when you have an export surplus is gold, or, more likely, another's currency, which is, in the final analysis, just paper.

But what's at issue here are problems of employment and domestic economic growth. These days some 30 percent of the U.S. economy is involved in and dependent on the international sector—exports constituted 14.2 percent of GNP in 1989, and imports were 15.5 percent. For most other regions, especially Japan and Western Europe, that figure is much higher. For example, more than 50 percent of the Japanese economy depends on exports. So, since every country wants to provide more jobs for its people, each tries to increase its exports as much as possible, while at the same time limiting imports, which of course costs jobs.

In the developing world, the acquisition of these jobs is critically important to increasing living standards. But even more valuable to developing world policymakers is gaining control over advanced technologies, which are closely held by industrial countries. Developing nations believe technology transfer is the key to sustained growth. In order to buy technology, however, the developing world needs to export to gain hard currency. But the problem is that since one country's exports are another's imports, it is clearly *not possible for everyone to have an export surplus;* nonetheless, everyone tries. This is why international trade is often called a "beggar-thy-neighbor" game, the object being to make yourself better off at your neighbor's expense.

The Theory of Protectionism

One result of this goal is "export fetish protectionism." It seems logical enough that if your objective is to maximize exports and minimize imports, then one simple way to do it is to put a tax on imports (a *tariff*) or to limit by law the quantity of imports (a *quota*). Tariffs and quotas have the effect of increasing prices in the domestic industries by protecting them from foreign competition. This *protectionism,* of course, saves jobs at home. However, it also raises a host of problems and is one of the most controversial issues in economics, as we shall see.

The theory of tariffs is fairly simple. Most economists agree that tariffs don't make economic sense, except in special cases such as a developing country trying to protect an *infant industry*—a new industry still struggling to establish itself. Other arguments for tariffs or quotas include the need for protection of industries critical to national defense; the temporary support of an industry subjected to an unexpected shock to give it time to adjust (like the gas-guzzling American autos during the oil crisis); or in retaliation for unfair trade practices by other nations. But protectionist measures have high economic costs. The reason is demonstrated in figure 2–5, which you should look at before you read on. At the top, a standard supply and demand graph shows the conditions that would prevail if a country were in isolation and not trading a product—for example, steel—internationally. The price would be P_1 and the quantity sold Q_1.

Now, if the country entered world trade, it would be facing a horizontal (perfectly *elastic*) demand curve, which means it could sell or buy all it wanted at the world price, P_2. Note, however, who gains and who loses.

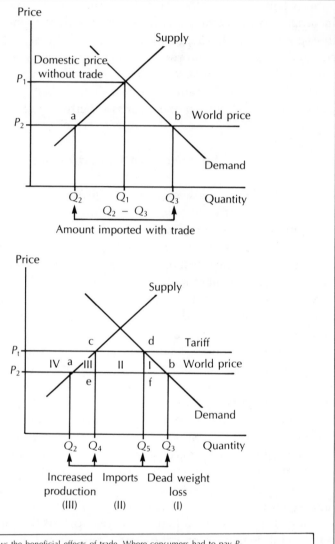

Panel (a) shows the beneficial effects of trade. Where consumers had to pay P_1, the domestic price without trade, the lower world price, P_2 allows them to consume more. Unfortunately domestic producers cannot match the world price and domestic supply falls to Q_2. $Q_1 - Q_2$ is imported. Panel (b) shows the effect of a tariff raising price to P_t. Consumers lose the areas I, II, III, IV (or P_t ab P_2) because the higher price cuts the surplus they enjoyed. Some of this loss is given to other parties. The government gains II (cdfe) in tariff revenues and producers gain IV (P_2 caP_2). But as a whole the nation loses because I + II + III + IV, the consumer loss, exceeds II + IV, the benefits to producers and the government.

Figure 2–5. *The Effect of a Tariff on a Domestic Economy*

Consumers gain since they now can buy steel products at the new lower world price, P_2. Also, since, the law of demand tells us that consumers will buy more at a lower price, we know they probably will; they'll now buy Q_3 at the lower price, P_2.

Obviously, in this scenario domestic producers lose. They were producing and selling quantity Q_1 at price P_1, but now it will only be profitable for them to produce up to quantity Q_2 (the point where the supply line intersects the world price line). The additional supply of steel (Q_2 to Q_3) will be imported, the net result being that a lot of jobs in the domestic steel industry will be lost to foreign competition.

So now protectionism enters the picture. The steel industry lobby puts pressure on the Congress to place a tariff on steel imports. The effects of this tariff are demonstrated in the lower graph in figure 2–5.

The tariff raises the domestic price of steel from P_2 to P_t. *Consumers lose because they (or we) have to pay a higher price and will accordingly buy less (as shown by the area from Q_5 to Q_3 less).* Producers, on the other hand, gain. At the higher price, P_t, they will find it profitable to produce up to quantity Q_4, or a gain of Q_2 to Q_4. The rectangle *cdef* represents the tariff—the tax collected by the government on steel imports.

The net effect of the protectionist tariff is to increase domestic production, to increase steel producers' profits, and to increase employment in the domestic steel industry. The government also gains tax revenues. The losers, of course, are consumers, who are subsidizing the steel industry by paying the higher prices and obtaining less steel. To put it another way, the effect of a tariff is to redistribute income from consumers to the steel producers and their employees, and, to a lesser extent, to the government.

Table 2–2 shows estimates of the distribution of the costs and benefits of protectionism for thirty-one industries in the United States. The data demonstrate that annual consumer losses exceed $100 million in all but six cases; in eighteen of the thirty-one cases it costs more than $100,000 a year to save a job. There are many different interpretations and estimates of the costs of protectionism. One study showed that tariffs and quotas raise the cost of imported goods by $50 million a year. Another study showed that because of trade restrictions, Americans pay twice as much for imported

Table 2–2
Distribution of Costs and Benefits from Special Protection

| Case | Consumer Losses (I & II & III & IV) | | Producer Gains (IV) Totals (million dollars) | Welfare Costs of Restraints | | |
	Totals (million dollars)	Per Job Saved[a] (dollars)		Gain to Foreigners (million dollars)	(II) Tariff Revenue (million dollars)	(III) Efficiency Loss (million dollars)
Manufacturing:						
Book manufacturing	500	100,000 over 1 million	305	neg.	0	29
Benzenoid chemicals	2,650	200,000	2,250	neg.	252 –	14
Glassware	200	200,000	130	neg.	54	13
Rubber footwear	230	30,000	90	neg.	139 –	33
Ceramic articles	95	47,500	25	neg.	69 –	6
Ceramic tiles	116	135,000	62	neg.	55 +	11
Orange juice	525	240,000	390	neg.	128 –	130
Canned tuna	91	76,000	74	7	10	4
Textiles & apparel: Phase I	9,400 –	22,000	8,700	neg.	1,158	1,100
Textiles & apparel: Phase II	20,000	37,000	18,000	350	2,143	3,100
Textiles & apparel: Phase III	27,000	42,000	22,000	1,800	2,535	4,850
Carbon steel: Phase I	1,970	240,000	1,330	330	290	50
Carbon steel: Phase II	4,350	620,000	2,770	930	556	120
Carbon steel: Phase III	6,800	750,000	3,800	2,000	560	330
Ball bearings	45	90,000	21	neg.	18	neg.
Specialty steel	520	1,000,000	420	50	32	30
Nonrubber footwear	700	55,000	250	220	262	16

Color televisions	420	420,000	190	140	77	7
CB radios	55	93,000	14	neg.	32	5
Bolts, nuts, large screws	110	550,000	60	neg.	16	1
Prepared mushrooms	35 –	117,000	13	neg.	25	0.8
Automobiles	5,800	105,000	2,600	2,200	790	200
Motorcycles	104	150,000	67	neg.	21	17
Services:						
Maritime industries	3,000	270,000	2,000	neg.	10[b]	1,000
Agriculture and fisheries:						
Sugar	930	60,000 690/acre	550	410	5	130
Dairy products	5,500	220,000 1,800/cow	5,000	250	34	1,370
Peanuts	170	1,000/acre	170	neg.	9	14
Meat	1,800	160,000	1,600	135	44	145
Fish	560	225/head 21,000	200	170	177	15
Mining:						
Petroleum	6,900	160,000	4,800	2,000[c]	70	3,000
Lead and zinc	67	30,000	46	4	11	5

Source: "Trade Protection in the United States," 31 Case Studies. Reprinted in Federal Reserve Bank of St. Louis, Jan./Feb. 1988.

Note: neg. = negligible.

[a] Unless otherwise specified, figures are per worker.

[b] Estimated duties collected on ship repairs performed abroad.

[c] In this case, because of the way the quotas were allocated, the gains to importers accrued to domestic refiners rather than foreign exporters.

Jeff Danziger, © 1986 *Christian Science Monitor.* Reprinted with permission of Los Angeles Times Syndicate.

clothing as they would without them, and they pay $2 billion more for goods made with steel, $500 million more for books, and $104 million more for motorcycles. Moreover, in 1985 Americans paid $2,500 extra for each imported car and $1,000 extra for each domestic automobile.[5] In 1986 one textile-quota bill passed by the Congress (but vetoed by the president) would alone have cost American consumers $14 billion, and it would have saved 100,000 jobs—at a cost of $140,000 per job.[6]

So the protectionist issue is primarily one of deciding what is the appropriate price for society to pay for protecting special interest groups. Clearly, it's a complicated long-run policy question (unless you are the one losing your job).

In addition to the difficult problem of job loss, another reason for protectionism, despite its costs to consumers, is retaliation against other countries not perceived to be playing by the free trade rules. Given that international trade is a beggar-thy-neighbor situation where everyone "does to others as they do to you," it is not surprising that the one thing almost everyone agrees upon is that protectionism begets protectionism—tariffs and quotas almost always cause retaliation.

There are thousands of examples. A recent one is especially instructive. The United States and Canada (the United States' largest trading partner) have agreed—in principle—that a common-market elimination of tariffs between the two countries would be mutually beneficial for both in the long run. Talks along these lines began in 1985.

But in 1986, under pressure from northern timber interests, President Reagan imposed a tariff on the import of Canadian shingles. The United States imported around $157 million worth of shingles from Canada in 1985, a small percentage of total imports from Canada of $69 billion. Almost immediately, Canada retaliated by imposing new restrictions on U.S.-made books, computers, and semiconductors.

Because of the unexpected rapid retaliation, some senators who had sponsored the bill were forced to rethink their position. One, Sen. Daniel Evans (R–Wash.) was quoted in the *Wall Street Journal* as saying, "[This is] a good case study of what can happen when nations unilaterally attempt to protect their own positions through trade restrictions. . . . It's a splendid example . . . if we're only wise enough to understand it."[7]

If trade restrictions simply result in retaliation by a nation's trading partners—as they almost always do—we are, at best, looking at a negative-sum game in which everybody loses. Total trade is reduced, prices are higher, less is produced and sold, and jobs are lost on both sides. If there is any clear-cut, logical argument against protectionism, it is the inevitable retaliation.

Because of the costs of protectionism, nations have since the end of World War II sought to provide an international framework for the reduction of barriers to trade. The General Agreement on Tariffs and Trade (the GATT), currently with a membership of ninety-six countries covering 80 percent of world trade, established a set of rules for international trade and provides a mechanism for multilateral negotiations to promote free trade. The fundamental principle of the GATT is the most-favored nation clause: do unto all nations as you would your best ally. That is, a member country must extend to all signatories the most favorable treatment it extends to one partner. Although there are exceptions to this rule, its purpose is to foster a fair trading system made efficient by open global competition.

The GATT has organized seven series of international negotiations since 1948 to reduce tariffs and nontariff barriers in the global trading system. It has successfully worked to reduce average industrial tariffs from 40 percent in 1947 to under 5 percent today. The most recent, called the Uruguay round (1986–90), has grappled with several pressing issues: the international protection of intellectual property, such as patents and copyrights; trade in services, particularly telecommunications; restrictions of foreign investment; restrictions and subsidies in agriculture and textiles, two sectors historically protected in industrial countries because of special interest group pressure; and the integration of developing countries, especially the newly industrializing countries, more fully into the GATT.[8] A critical challenge in the coming years will be the fuller participation of China, the Soviet Union, and Eastern Europe.

In addition to its multilateral efforts, the United States has engaged in bilateral pressure to promote free trade. The 1988 Omnibus Trade and Competitiveness Act mandated that the U.S. trade representative and the administration identify "priority practices, including major barriers and trade distorting practices, the elimination of which are likely to have the most significant potential to increase U.S. exports."[9] Under the "Super 301" provisions of this code, the United States targeted Japanese practices in the areas of supercomputers, satellites, and wood, as well as two cases in India and one in Brazil. However, despite the United States' rhetoric supporting free trade, the portion of U.S. goods covered by protectionist barriers doubled to 25 percent since 1980.[10] The motivation for increased protectionism came from systemic U.S. trade deficits caused, in large part, by the overvalued dollar—a topic to which we will return.

Problems of Developing Countries

As we have seen, while the theory of free trade according to comparative advantage should generate greatest gains for all, domestic interest groups within nations often demand protectionist barriers to promote jobs or spur new technological growth. There is also a demand for new rules in international trade because of inequalities between trading nations.

The theory of comparative advantage, as we have seen, says that if each nation puts its best foot forward and specializes in what it can do best, everyone will produce and consume more when they trade and everyone will have higher incomes as a result. But the pure theory breaks down in practice. Economist Carlos Diaz-Alejandro once asked, if you met a Martian who had studied trade theory in outer space, how would you explain the existing economic disparities on Earth? Why is it that some countries are so dismally poor while others keep getting richer?

The example David Ricardo used when he first proposed the theory of comparative advantage was the relationship between Great Britain and Portugal: Britain produced wool, Portugal produced wine, and they traded. Both, according to Ricardo, should gain. However, as one writer has pointed out, that didn't quite happen.

> Britain and Portugal began their partnership in 1373, when they formed an alliance against Castile, the Spanish empire. In 1580, Castile expanded into Portugal. Sixty years later, Britain began to offer Portugal military support against Spain in exchange for a series of economic concessions. A critical concession was made in the Treaty of Methuen, signed in 1703.
>
> According to this treaty, the Portuguese agreed to impose no tariffs on wool cloth and other woolen goods from Britain on the condition that the British lower their duties on wine imported from Portugal to two-thirds of those currently imposed on imported French wine. Since the British had already lowered the duties on Portuguese wine in 1690, they clearly stood to gain more from the treaty than the Portuguese.
>
> The impact of the Treaty of Methuen on the Portuguese economy was tremendous. British wool exports to Portugal jumped by 120 percent between 1700 and 1710. During the same period, the Portuguese sold 40 percent more wine to the British and wine production expanded fivefold. But the group of small-time Portuguese artisans who made woolen products could hardly compete with

the cheap imports of British wool, and were eventually forced to abandon their enterprise.

By the 1850s, Portuguese economic growth had stagnated, and Portugal had become economically dependent on Britain. While the development of the textile industry had laid the foundation for the British Empire, specialization in wine had succeeded in transforming Portugal into what looked like a small South American republic that just happened to be attached to Europe.[11]

Clearly it made a difference that Britain held military and political power over Portugal and that Britain expanded in an industry where the benefits of technology became evident. In today's trading arena it matters whether you are a large country such as the United States or a small island like Jamaica.

Most economics textbooks explain the theory of comparative advantage by using the now fabled example of the secretaries and the lawyers.[12] Imagine that lawyers can type faster than their secretaries, yet they do the legal work and leave the typing to the secretaries. Why? Because lawyers have a comparative advantage. They can earn more doing the legal work, so (theoretically) between the lawyers and secretaries, their total product is greater—as is their income—than it would be if the lawyers spent less time on legal work and more time typing.

But, of course, it is the lawyers' income that is higher, not the secretaries'. The arrangement is clearly to the lawyers' advantage. However, if the secretaries learned a new skill—such as legal work—they would increase their comparative advantage, and their income.

So when we compare two countries trading under conditions of comparative advantage, a similar process usually (but not always) occurs. Most of the time, industrial countries trade more sophisticated, expensive products. Essentially, there is a premium paid for the technology embodied in these goods. Smaller and/or underdeveloped countries may have only one or two comparative advantages: abundant cheap labor or abundant cheap raw materials (for example, tin in Bolivia, copper in Chile, and oil in Mexico).

If it is the abundant labor that is being traded, then specializing in labor-intensive products (those requiring more labor than capital to produce) merely ensures that labor will remain cheap and income low. Politically this creates an incentive to suppress rising wages. If incomes rise, the rationale for trade is gone since costs of producing the good will have to rise as well.

The case of raw materials is more complicated. Generally speaking, it seems to make sense for resource-rich underdeveloped countries to export raw materials and trade them for processed capital goods, such as tractors, to develop their agricultural sector, which should eventually make them more self-sufficient. But there is a catch here. For specialization to be mutually beneficial the products have to be traded at constant cost ratios. That is, the terms of trade, or how much copper you must give up to get a tractor, must remain relatively constant. If they don't, the smaller country—now totally dependent on income from the exportation of a primary product—must give up more and more copper to import a tractor. Some economists argue that the terms of trade have steadily declined for developing nations. They contend that poorer nations must export more and more agricultural and primary products just to maintain past import levels of capital goods. It becomes an uphill scramble to export more to continue to buy the capital goods critical for growth. It is hard to get wealthy that way.

In recent years the terms of trade between primary product exports from the underdeveloped countries to the more industrialized countries have deteriorated by some 30 percent. This loss of income is primarily responsible for the huge foreign debt buildup and for much of the international financial crisis. As we will see in chapter 7, one of the more dramatic examples is that of the Mexican economy, which was nearly devastated by the decline in prices of oil in the mid-1980s, oil being its primary export and comparative advantage.

Recently in the Philippines there was a rather dramatic example.

Sugarcane was first produced on the archipelago as a snack food. Not until the mid-1800s did the colony's Spanish rulers decide to explore the possibilities of large-scale sugar production for export.

The island of Negros, which had an ideal environment for sugar production, was converted into a monocrop zone. By the late 1800s, half of the nation's sugar was being harvested in Negros. In the years of U.S. colonial rule, the United States encouraged the sugar industry by enacting a series of tariffs and import quotas that gave Philippine sugar a competitive advantage over sugar from other countries. When the United States cut off trade with Cuba, the U.S. government increased the quotas for the Philippines. The new quotas increased the country's dependence on U.S. markets, and propelled further increases in sugar production at the expense of diversification. Land that had produced food was increasingly used to produce sugar.

The fate of Negros became tied to the ups and downs of world sugar prices. In the spring of 1985, a 40 percent drop in the expected sugar harvest, combined with historical lows in the world price of sugar, wreaked a famine of alarming proportions on the island of Negros. Yet, according to Roberto Ortaliz, the president of the National Federation of Sugar Workers, proper use of the arable land on Negros could feed up to fifty times the total Filipino population of 55 million.[13]

But difficulties with international trade are not limited to Third World nations. The United States was for many, many years the dominant industrial power in the world. Exports of U.S. industrial products (including automobiles, capital goods, and agricultural products) fueled the expansion of the world economy in the postwar period. But by the 1970s a series of unexpected shocks changed all that. High oil prices, rising wages, declining productivity, an overvalued dollar, and a host of other factors—to which we will return later—caused U.S. heavy industry to seek protection from increasingly efficient and aggressive foreign competition. Tables 2–3 and 2–4 show, for example, the decline in exports of agricultural and industrial goods as a result of the strong dollar in the mid-1980s, as well as the rise in imports of all categories, save petroleum.

With the help of U.S. postwar reconstruction aid, the Japanese and Western Europeans became formidable competitors in the world market. More recently, the so-called newly industrialized countries, or NICs (Brazil, South Korea, Taiwan, and others), learned that they too could produce and sell industrial products. As can be seen in figure 2–6, the result has been a dramatic shift in the distribution of world economic power. The U.S. share of world exports has fallen from 17.5 percent in 1968 to approximately 12 percent in the 1980s, while Japan has increased its share from less than 6 percent to nearly 10 percent, West Germany has maintained steady growth, and South Korea has experienced a rapid surge in exports.

In the 1990s global competition will be even more formidable. New challenges facing the United States in the international trading system will include the strengthening of the European Economic Community. By 1992 the twelve nations that compose the European

Table 2–3

U.S. Merchandise Exports by End-Use Category, 1965–1988

(billions of U.S. $)

Year	Total Products	Agricultural Products	Industrial Goods	Capital Exports	Automotive Exports	Other
1965	26.5	6.3	7.6	8.1	1.9	2.6
1970	42.5	7.4	12.3	14.7	3.9	4.3
1975	107.1	22.2	26.7	36.6	10.8	10.7
1980	224.3	42.2	64.9	74.2	17.5	25.4
1985	215.9	38.9	53.6	75.6	24.8	37.1
1986	223.4	29.6	54.0	76.5	24.7	31.1
1987	250.3	29.5	62.6	87.7	27.5	42.8
1988	319.3	38.1	81.5	112.4	32.5	54.7

Source: Department of Commerce, *Survey of Current Business,* "Merchandise Exports and Imports by Principal End-Use Category," various years.

Note: Military shipments are excluded.

Table 2–4

U.S. Merchandise Imports by End-Use Category, 1965–1988

(billions of U.S. $)

Year	Total Products	Petroleum Products	Industrial Goods	Capital Imports	Automotive Imports	Other
1965	21.5	2.0	9.1	1.5	0.9	8.0
1970	39.9	2.9	12.3	4.0	5.7	15.0
1975	98.2	27.0	23.6	10.2	12.1	25.3
1980	244.8	79.3	54.0	31.2	27.9	57.4
1985	328.7	48.8	62.7	61.4	62.2	93.4
1986	368.4	34.4	69.9	72.1	78.1	113.9
1987	409.8	42.9	70.8	85.1	85.2	125.7
1988	446.5	39.9	83.0	101.8	87.9	134.4

Source: Department of Commerce, *Survey of Current Business,* "Merchandise Exports and Imports by Principal End-Use Category," various years.

Economic Community hope to achieve free movement of goods, capital, and labor across national borders. With a single economic market, the potential gains from free trade within the Community are estimated at $240 million. Moreover, the combined gross domestic product of the twelve nations exceeds that of the United States. German unification presents the possibility of an even larger

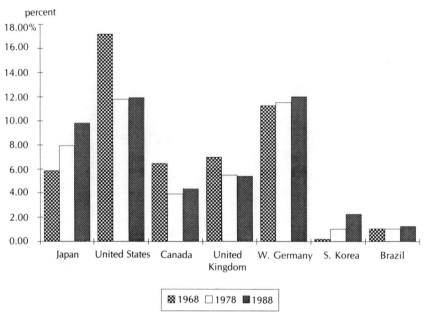

Source: *International Financial Statistics Yearbook 1989.*

Figure 2–6. *Percent of World Exports, Selected Countries*

economic base. The Europeans hope to take advantage of a huge internal consumer market and economies of scale in production to become a world-class economic power.

So, international trade has become a complicated and paradoxical issue. Despite these problems of trade between rich and poor nations, it would be misleading and irresponsible to say that nations shouldn't trade because the theory of comparative advantage doesn't always work out the way Mr. Ricardo envisioned it. Nations *do* gain from trade. It's just that often some gain more than others. This is a problem with serious implications. As the rest of the world has become more developed and industrialized, the United States has lost its once dominant position in the world economy, as we will see in chapter 5. The old theories of comparative advantage and protectionism no longer seem as logical as they once did. The patterns of trade have shifted, and the United States is rapidly becoming a deindustrialized nation. Services now account for 70 percent of the

U.S. Gross National Product. Many believe the United States has become a nation of hamburger flippers, stockbrokers, software developers, and insurance salespeople.

One result of all this is that the United States has now, for the first time since 1914, become a debtor nation. To understand the significance of that simple fact and how it relates to the present international financial crisis, we will need to take a brief excursion into the world of international finance. It is an intricate and complex world—a world of exchange markets, "strong" and "weak" currencies, balance of payments, debts and defaults, gold, and arbitrage. It is a world understood by only a very few people. These days even the gnomes of Zurich are perplexed.

Notes

1. See Wassily Leontief, "Factor Proportions and the Structure of American Trade: Further Theoretical and Empirical Analysis." *Review of Economics and Statistics* 38 (November 1956), pp. 386–407.
2. See Raymond G. Vernon, "The Product Cycle Hypotheses in a New International Environment." *Oxford Bulletin of Economics and Statistics* 41 (November 1979), pp. 255–267.
3. See Paul R. Krugman, *Strategic Trade Policy and the New International Economics* (Cambridge: MIT Press, 1988).
4. See Michael E. Porter, "The Competitive Advantage of Nations," *Harvard Business Review* (March–April 1990).
5. *U.S.A. Today,* Feb. 14, 1986.
6. *U.S.A. Today,* Nov. 7, 1986.
7. *Wall Street Journal,* June 19, 1986.
8. For a concise discussion of the recent GATT round, see *The Economic Report of the President, 1990* (Washington, D.C.: U.S. Government Printing Office, 1990).
9. *Economic Report of the President, 1990.*
10. "GATT Brief," *The Economist,* 21–27 April 1990, pp. 85–86.
11. *Dollars and Sense,* March 1986, p. 14.
12. Thomas Riddell, Jean Shackelford, and Steve Stamos, *Economics: A Tool for Understanding Society,* Instructor's Manual (Reading, Mass.: Addison-Wesley, 1982), chp. 13.
13. *Dollars and Sense,* March 1986, p. 15.

3

The Mysterious World of International Finance

I t is relatively easy, as we have just seen, to understand how and why nations engage in international trade, but since barter is not generally practical, there has to be a system to pay for and account for international transactions. That means someone has to decide (and everyone has to agree) what will be acceptable to all nations as a medium of exchange to be used as the international currency. Moreover, since every nation has its own currency, there has to be some way to determine the exchange value of each currency in terms of some standard unit of account. This is the role of international finance.

Economists are fond of pointing out that it doesn't make sense to compare a household budget to the budget of a nation. The reason is that the flows of income are not the same. Since incomes flow in and expenditures out, households have to try to keep their flows of spending equal to their expenditures—that is, they have to "live within their means." Governments, on the other hand, don't have that problem. Since they can always raise additional income by increasing taxes or by borrowing from their own citizens, governments can (and usually do) consistently run budget deficits.

However, when we begin to look at the economy from an international perspective, everything changes. So far as international transactions are concerned, a nation's economy functions exactly like a household's. Expenditures roughly have to equal income or problems will soon follow. Internationally, budgets have to balance.

The Balance of Payments Accounts

Nations keep track of their international financial position by statistically analyzing their international expenditures and income flows. The result is known as the *balance of payments* account, which is a simple double-entry accounting system involving debits and credits—just like any household or business accounting system. Since double-entry bookkeeping requires that the debits and credits must always balance, the issue is not one of balance, because by definition the balance of payments accounts must always balance. For example, the import of a good on one side of the ledger is matched by the outflow of money to pay for the good on the other side. Instead of balance, the issue is one familiar to students of economics: it is a question of maintaining equilibrium. Over time imports cannot exceed exports because the country would run out of money to pay for foreign goods.

To understand this, look at table 3–1, a hypothetical, summarized version of the U.S. balance of payments accounts. In it you can see that there are debits and credits that can happen to the accounts in any given year. Typical transactions that give rise to debits and credits are shown in table 3–2. The balance of payments accounts are divided into five different categories, each of which tracks a different type of transaction.

The first two categories constitute the *current account,* which shows the value of sales of merchandise and services (imports and exports), flows of income from investments abroad, and the income payments to foreign investors. The current account data is what is generally referred to in the financial press because it reflects the *balance of trade,* which is simply the difference between exports and imports and is a large part of the current account. Overall balance of payments figures are often confused with balance of trade data. Actually the trade data is only part of the larger balance of payments picture.

Investment income is included in the current account because it is a *flow* of annual income payments. It includes, for example, interest and dividend payments on stocks and bonds, or profits from more direct investments, such as building factories or buying real estate.

The *capital account* measures annual additions to foreign invest-

Table 3–1
Hypothetical Summary Balance of Payments for the United States
(billions of $)

	Debit (payments)	Credit (receipts)	Net
1. Goods and services	−350	+220	−130
2. Investment income	−70	+90	+20
Current account balance	−420	+310	−110
3. Capital account	−25	+125	+100
4. Reserve account	0	+8	+8
5. Statistical discrepancies	0	+2	+2
Total	−445	+445	0

Table 3–2
Positive and Negative Effects on Balance of Payments Accounts

Positive Effects (credits)	Negative Effects (debits)
1. Any receipt of foreign money.	1. Any payment to a foreign country.
2. Any earning on an investment in a foreign country.	2. Any investment in a foreign country.
3. Any sale of goods or services abroad (export).	3. Any purchase of goods and services abroad (import).
4. Any gift or aid from a foreign country.	4. Any gift or aid given abroad.
5. Any foreign sale of stocks or bonds.	5. Any purchase of stocks or bonds from abroad.

ments and is, therefore, an addition to capital stock rather than a flow. The difference between flow and stock is a subtle but important part of understanding how the balance of payments accounting system works. In a household, budget flows are the paycheck, and stocks are the accumulated assets, either financial or real. Flows of income add to the stock if there is a surplus, and they reduce it if there is a deficit.

The *reserve account* merely measures net additions to or deductions from a country's reserve assets which result from international transactions. It is, theoretically, the account that makes the others balance. Nations accumulate reserves in the form of foreign currencies if they sell more abroad than they buy, or in gold if they mine it or buy it, or in deposits with the International Monetary Fund, which serves as the central banks' bank.

Statistical discrepancies are included partly because the accounts must by definition balance, but, more importantly, because the gathering of balance of payments data is, at best, an exercise in statistical fantasy and is not in fact very accurate. (In 1988 the statistical discrepancy in the U.S. balance of payments accounts amounted to around $11 billion.) But, like most economic statistical data, it is useful not so much for the actual numbers involved but because such data allow us to discern trends that tell us a lot about how things are going and where.

Now, by looking again at table 3–1, we can begin to understand how balance of payments accounting works and why it is so important. In this hypothetical year, in its current account, the United States exported some $220 billion worth of goods and services, and it imported $350 billion. So, obviously, it ran a balance of trade deficit of $130 billion. Since, in this householdlike world, a country can't spend more than it earns unless the difference is borrowed or comes out of savings, something has to happen to balance the deficit. (However, as we will see in the following chapter, the United States has some special spending privileges, because the U.S. dollar is the key international currency.)

Also, in its current account for that year the United States earned more from its investments abroad ($90 billion) than foreigners earned from their U.S. investments ($70 billion). The net difference of $20 billion paid for part of the trade deficit. The current account was, nonetheless, in deficit.

The rest of the deficit consisted of a considerable excess of net receipts from foreign investments made in the United States compared with U.S. foreign investments made abroad ($125 billion versus $25 billion). This almost balanced the accounts, but not quite. A $10 billion deficit remained which in essence had to be paid by drawing down by $8 billion U.S. savings. That meant accumulations of foreign currencies were spent, gold was sold, or funds were withdrawn from the U.S. "savings account" with the International Monetary Fund. The rest was covered by a $2 billion statistical discrepancy in the United States favor. The net balance of payments is of course, zero, which is what it must be according to the prevailing rules of the game.

The Theory of Balance of Payments Adjustment with Floating Exchange Rates

Now, if you were a doctor of international economics looking at this chart (table 3–1) on your patient, the U.S. economy, what would be your diagnosis? Clearly the accounts balance, so the accountants are satisfied, but even with this sketchy data we can see that there are some equilibrium problems, so this won't satisfy the economists.

The country is running a huge trade deficit, covered only by a small net flow of investment income and a very large flow of new foreign investments, and it is even being forced to draw down its reserves. Is this something that can continue forever? Maybe, maybe not—it all depends on the discipline of the international financial system. On the surface, with the limited data we have, it would appear that any country that is buying more than it is selling and depending on foreign investors to make up the difference is courting problems. What happens if, for some reason, foreign investors decide the United States is not such a good place to invest after all and withdraw their investments? As you can probably imagine, economic theory has an answer to all of these questions: exchange rates should automatically adjust any balance of payment disequilibrium.

Every country in the world has a currency with a rate at which it exchanges for another country's currency. (Look at table 3–3 for some examples.) If the value of a currency has increased, it is called appreciation; a decrease is depreciation. For example, between 1984 and 1987 the U.S. dollar depreciated against the Japanese yen. In 1984 the market rate of yen per dollar was 251.1 yen; by 1987 it had depreciated to 123.5 yen. We look at the exchange rate from the flip side: instead of each dollar buying 251.1 yen in 1984, we can say each *yen* buys .004 *dollars*. But by 1987 each yen bought .00809 dollars. So while the dollar depreciated from 1984 to 1987, the yen appreciated, buying almost twice as many dollars as before. By March of 1990 the dollar had appreciated to a value of 157.20

Table 3–3
Foreign Exchange Rates[a]

Country/currency	1987	1988	1989
1 Australia/dollar[b]	70.137	78.409	79.186
2 Austria/shilling	12.649	12.357	13.236
3 Belgium/franc	37.358	36.785	39.409
4 Canada/dollar	1.3259	1.2306	1.1842
5 China, P.R./yuan	3.7314	3.7314	3.7673
6 Denmark/krone	6.8478	6.7412	7.3210
7 Finland/markka	4.4037	4.1933	4.2963
8 France/franc	6.0122	5.9595	6.3802
9 Germany/deutsche mark	1.7981	1.7570	1.8808
10 Greece/drachma	135.47	142.00	162.60
11 Hong Kong/dollar	7.7986	7.8072	7.8008
12 India/rupee	12.943	13.900	16.213
13 Ireland/punt[b]	148.79	152.49	141.80
14 Italy/lira	1,297.03	1,302.39	1,372.28
15 Japan/yen	144.60	128.17	138.07
16 Malaysia/ringgit	2.5186	2.6190	2.7079
17 Netherlands/guilder	2.0264	1.9778	2.1219
18 New Zealand dollar[b]	59.328	65.560	59.354
19 Norway/krone	6.7409	6.5243	6.9131
20 Portugal/escudo	141.20	144.27	157.53
21 Singapore/dollar	2.1059	2.0133	1.9511
22 South Africa/rand	2.0385	2.2773	2.6215
23 South Korea/won	825.94	734.52	674.29
24 Spain/peseta	123.54	116.53	118.44
25 Sri Lanka/rupee	29.472	31.820	35.947
26 Sweden/krona	6.3469	6.1370	6.4559
27 Switzerland/franc	1.4918	1.4643	1.6369
28 Taiwan/dollar	31.753	28.636	26.407
29 Thailand/baht	25.775	25.312	25.725
30 United Kingdom/pound[b]	163.98	178.13	163.82
Memo			
31 United States/dollar[c]	96.94	92.72	98.60

[a] Averages of certified noon buying rates in New York for cable transfers. Data in this table also appear in the Board's G.5 (405) release.

[b] Value in U.S. cents.

[c] Index of weighted-average exchange value of U.S. dollar against the currencies of 10 industrial countries. The weight for each of the 10 countries is the 1972–76 average world trade of that country divided by the average world trade of all 10 countries combined. Series revised as of August 1978 (see *Federal Reserve Bulletin*, vol. 64, August 1978, p. 700).

(.0064)d/y as the yen depreciated. The point is that rates of exchange fluctuate widely depending on economic circumstances within, and transactions between, the two countries. And they affect all of us in a very direct way.

Calculating Foreign Prices: The Divide or Multiply Decision

Some people have a talent for converting one currency into another; others are openly confused. Assume, for example, you are a German importer of French wine. Let's say a case of wine costs Fr 1,415, and one French franc is worth .29730 German marks. How many marks does the case of wine cost? Some currency whizzes can, in their heads, say a franc is roughly worth 30 percent of a mark and so they will need about 400 deutsche marks. The less confident, however, may have to multiply it out:

$$\text{Fr } 1415 \times .29730 \, \frac{DM}{Fr} = DM \; 420.68$$

But what if you had been given the reciprocal of the .29730 exchange rate—that is, what if you were told there were 3.36361 francs for each deutsche mark? Then, to calculate the price of a case of French wine in German currency we would divide:

$$\text{Fr } 1415 \div \frac{3.36361F}{DM} = DM \; 420.68$$

To check whether you multiply or divide, be sure the currency units cancel:

$$\text{Fr } 1415 \times .29730 \, \frac{DM}{Fr} \; \Rightarrow \; \text{the "Fr's" cancel, leaving you with the}$$

DM price.

$$\text{Fr } 1415 \times 3.36361 \, \frac{Fr}{DM} \; \Rightarrow \; \frac{Fr^2}{DM}, \; \text{a nonsensical term so you}$$

know you must divide:

$$\text{Fr } 1415 \div 3.36361 \, \frac{Fr}{DM} = \text{Fr } 1415 \times \frac{1}{3.36361} \, \frac{DM}{Fr} \; \Rightarrow \; DM \; 420.68$$

Exchange rates come to your attention a little more dramatically if you are on a vacation or a business trip in a foreign country. If you traveled to Tokyo in 1984, a hotel might have cost you 31,375 yen a night, or $125 (divide 31,375 yen by the 1984 exchange rate of 251.1). In 1987 the same charge of 31,375 yen would show up on your credit card as $254 (31,375 yen divided by 123.5). Thus, if the hotel price did not change, you had to give up nearly twice as many dollars to sleep in the same room. In March 1990 the price might have been $199. Such exchange rate fluctuations like this happen all the time. What causes them?

Within the country, when we make purchases of goods or services there is only one currency involved, so the process is fairly simple. You hand over the money to someone, and that person will sell you what you want. The price you pay is, generally speaking, determined by the supply of the product that is available at the time and people's demand for it.

But when you buy an imported product, a much more complicated exchange process is triggered. If, for example, you buy a Japanese automobile you pay for it in dollars, and that's all you have to think about. However, the Japanese auto producer can't pay bills in dollars and so needs yen. Somewhere along the line your dollars have to be changed into yen so the Japanese auto producer can be paid in domestic currency.

This exchange takes place in the foreign exchange market, which is why foreign money is called foreign exchange. The amount of yen that a dollar will buy depends on a number of factors, but mostly it's a matter of how many yen Americans in general want compared to how many dollars the Japanese want. In 1988 the United States wanted (imported) $89.8 billion worth of Japanese products, but the Japanese wanted (imported) only $37.7 billion worth of U.S. goods. So, the U.S. trade deficit with Japan was $52.1 billion dollars, as can be seen in figure 3–1.

This is five times the size of the trade deficit with Japan ten years earlier. Now, when the Japanese are selling more in the United States than the United States is selling in Japan, Americans also demand more yen than dollars. And because of this excess demand for yen it would seem to follow that the price of yen is going to go up, which is another way of saying that Americans will get fewer yen per dollar, which is another way of saying that the value of the dol-

Millions of U.S. $

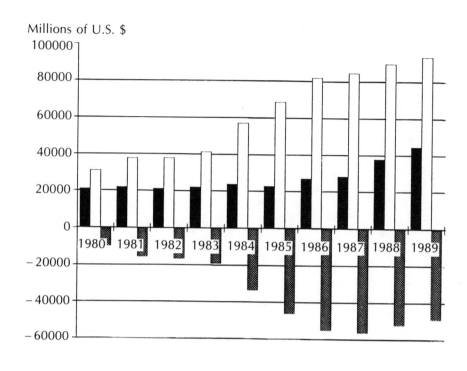

■ Exports to Japan
□ Imports from Japan
▨ Balance

Source: U.S. Department of Commerce, *U.S. Foreign Trade Highlights 1988,* and *Survey of Current Business,* April 1990.

Figure 3–1. *U.S.-Japanese Trade Flows, 1980–1989*

lar will fall. Note in figure 3–2 that in the 1980s each dollar was buying fewer yen.

When the dollar is down against the yen, imports from Japan are costing more in the United States, but exports to Japan are costing the Japanese less. So the United States sells Japan more at lower prices; Japan sells the United States less at higher prices.

Americans both lose and gain in this process. Americans pay higher prices for the Hondas and the Sonys, but the fact that the Japanese goods are becoming more expensive means that American

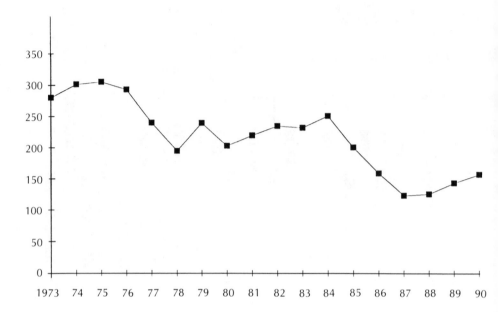

Source: International Monetary Fund, *International Financial Statistics*, various years.

Note: End of period market rates; 1990 is for March only.

Figure 3–2. *Yen/Dollar Exchange Rates, 1973–1990*

consumers should switch to domestically produced goods and that more jobs will be created in the United States. For the Japanese it's the opposite: lower prices for the American blue jeans and airplanes at the expense of less employment. So exchange rate fluctuations affect everybody in a very direct way.

As we have seen, the price of one country's goods in relation to another's depends on the rate of exchange between their currencies. If rates of exchange are left to fluctuate freely according to the laws of supply and demand, then they simply reflect the reciprocal demand for goods and services. This is because the demand for foreign currencies (foreign exchange) is a *derived demand,* derived from the demand for imports and exports.

When two countries are trading, there is not just one but two markets involved: the *product market* and the *foreign exchange market*. This complicates the process considerably. To see why, let's examine a simple case of a trade between the United States and Japan. Since there are two countries involved, the process is doubly complicated, which is one of the reasons international economics is so difficult to understand.

First, as we just saw, everything depends on which side of the border one is on. U.S. producers want dollars for their products, since they can't pay their bills in yen; for the same reason Japanese exporters want yen, not dollars. So when the products are exchanged, dollars and yen must also be exchanged. This means American demand for Japanese products is also the American demand for yen, and the Japanese demand for American products is the Japanese demand for dollars. If, as is usually the case, the United States is demanding more Japanese exports (imports to the United States) than the Japanese are demanding U.S. exports (Japanese imports), then there is more demand for yen than there is demand for dollars, and the price of yen in terms of dollars should rise accordingly. Looked at another way, the Americans are supplying more dollars than the Japanese are supplying yen, so the price of dollars, in yen, should fall accordingly.

For example, assume the United States exports fish to Japan, and the Japanese export cars to the States. As shown in the top of figure 3–3, if the demand for American-caught fish in Japan increases while the demand for cars stays the same, the dollar will appreciate because the Japanese will need more dollars to pay for the fish. Conversely, if Americans demand more Japanese-made cars (without an accompanying change in demand for U.S. exports), the United States will be selling dollars for yen to buy their Hondas and Toyotas. The dollar will then depreciate.

Thus, the supply of dollars is derived from American demand for Japanese exports (we are willing to supply our dollars in order to buy yen), and the demand for dollars comes from Japanese purchases of American goods.

If the demand for Japanese exports is greater than the demand for U.S. exports, then the supply of dollars will exceed demand. But as every economist knows, supply cannot exceed demand for long before the price will begin to fall.

So the dollar begins to depreciate—instead of a level of 200 yen

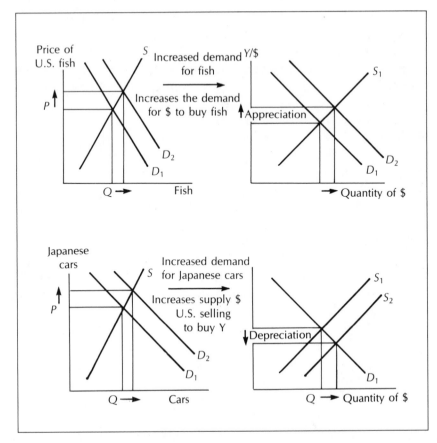

Figure 3–3. *Currency and Goods in U.S.-Japanese Trade*

for each dollar, the price falls until the supply of dollars meets demand at the equilibrium price of 150 yen per dollar. This is shown in figure 3–4.

But this lower value of the dollar will have positive effects on the U.S. trade balance. Now fish from the United States are cheaper for the Japanese to buy. And since the value of the dollar is going down, the value of the yen must be going up, making Japanese cars more expensive in the United States.

The end result of this price adjustment should be balanced trade. A deficit in traded goods should generate an excess supply of dollars until the price of the dollar falls to the point where foreigners want to buy now cheaper American goods. Conversely, a trade surplus

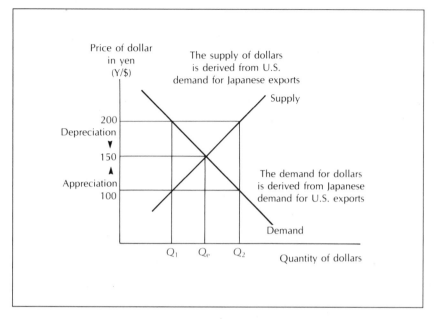

Figure 3–4. *Supply and Demand of Foreign Exchange*

signals demand for a currency. This drives the price up, making that nation's goods more expensive, bringing balance in the goods market. Neither nation should have a deficit or surplus over time.

We can therefore conclude that a trade deficit should cause depreciation, and a trade surplus should prompt appreciation. Theoretically, under a freely floating system, a change in the value of the currency will change the international price of the good, and will work to clear markets at an equilibrium price.

Exchange Rate Systems

This floating exchange rate system was the mechanism for creating balance in global markets from 1973 to 1985. As figure 3–5 shows, exchange rates have fluctuated considerably over that period. However, rates did not adjust sufficiently to bring trade into balance—for reasons to which we will return shortly.

Before the floating exchange rate system was instituted, the world economy operated under fixed rate regimes: the gold stan-

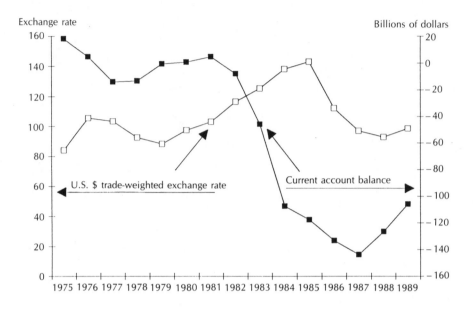

Source: *Federal Reserve Bulletin,* various years.

Figure 3–5. *Trade-Weighted Exchange Rate versus the U.S. Current Account*

dard, and later the Bretton Woods system. Under a fixed rate system, money stocks rather than foreign exchange prices are adjusted. Consider the workings of the gold standard, under which each country's currency was anchored in terms of gold. Assume that under this system, France is running a balance of payments deficit with Great Britain. Since the French exchange rate is fixed to the price of gold and can't depreciate, making British goods more expensive, the French somehow have to import less to balance trade. This would be accomplished through the rules of the international trading game under gold: a balance of payments deficit is matched by an outflow of gold to cover the gap, and a surplus is compensated by an inflow of gold. Since national money supplies are tied to the gold stock, in France, the deficit country, the money supply would fall. Prices would decline, and both the British and the French would buy more of the now cheaper French goods. Conversely, since the money stock in Britain would rise, so would prices, and people would turn away from more expensive British goods until trade between the two countries was in equilibrium. In this way, not only did the system automatically promote balance, but gold provided a noninflationary anchor to global money supplies.

Although this system worked relatively well from 1880 until World War I, as more countries began to industrialize, the global demand for gold outstripped mining capabilities. The scarcity of money in the system (called the liquidity constraint) caused its collapse under pressures from World War I and World War II. Following World War II a new international system was instituted that preserved the automatic internal adjustment mechanism of the fixed rates, but relieved the liquidity constraint of tying the world's money to gold. Instead all currencies were pegged to the U.S. dollar—which was "as good as gold" in settling accounts. However, as we will later see, the special position of the dollar also created the conditions for the fixed exchange rate dollar system to collapse.

A fascinating aspect of international finance is the way pressures in the workings of the international system force revisions in theory. The difficulties of the fixed exchange regime in practice pushed the floating system into place. This *freely flexible exchange rate system* was in place from 1973 to 1985, and it worked fairly well until around 1982 when the U.S. current account deficit began to grow at an alarming rate, as can be seen in table 3–4. Concerned that things were getting out of hand, the Group of Five (the major industrialized countries, including the United States, Japan, West Germany, the United Kingdom, and France) met at the initiative of U.S. Secretary of the Treasury James Baker III at the Plaza Hotel in New York and agreed to begin (again) managing exchange rates. This agreement—the Plaza Agreement—was a momentous change in international economic policy.

Managing exchange rates requires participating countries to intervene in the foreign exchange markets whenever any country's balance of payments appears to be moving toward disequilibrium. In order to understand more clearly how this works, consider any market—say, wheat in the commodities market. Anyone who owns enough wheat can control wheat prices by entering the market and supplying wheat anytime the price of wheat begins to rise. This has the effect of stabilizing or destabilizing wheat prices, depending on the goal of the seller.

Since the foreign exchange market is simply a market for a com-

Table 3–4
U.S. International Transactions

International Transactions	1970	1975	1980	1985	1986	1987	1988	1989
Current Account	2331	18116	1533	-112682	-133249	-143700	-126548	-105878
Exports	42469	107088	224269	245935	223367	250266	319251	361872
Imports	-39866	-98185	-249749	-338083	-368425	-409766	-446466	-475120
Net investment	6233	12787	30387	25931	21647	22283	2227	123694
Net military transactions	-3354	-746	-2577	-3557	-4576	-2857	-4606	-792
Net travel & transactions	-2038	-2812	-997	-9832	-8031	-7324	-2633	-5662
Other services, net	2330	4854	7794	12351	18547	17909	20335	25487
Remittances & other unilateral transfers	-3443	-4868	-7593	-15426	-15778	-14212	-14656	-14276
Capital account								
Total Net U.S. Assets Abroad	9337	-39703	-86118	-32628	-99628	-76218	-82110	-125707
U.S. official reserve assets	2481	-849	-8155	-3858	312	9149	-3566	-25293
Other U.S. government assets	-1589	-3474	-5162	-2821	-2024	997	2999	1037
Private assets	-10229	-35380	-72802	-25950	-97954	-86543	-81543	-101451
Total foreign assets in the U.S.	6359	15670	58112	130012	221605	219299	219299	196671
Foreign official assets	6908	7027	15497	-1083	35594	38882	38882	7369
Other foreign assets	-550	8643	43615	131096	185011	180418	180418	189303
Special drawing rights	897	na	1152	na	na	na	na	na
Statistical discrepancy	-219	5917	25322	15298	11308	-10641	-10641	34914

modity (money) and is subject to the laws of supply and demand, it can be controlled (or manipulated) by anyone who holds large amounts of currency. This process is shown in figure 3–6. At price P_x, the demand for dollars exceeds the current supply; therefore there is a tendency for market forces to push the price even higher, toward the equilibrium price, P_e. If the United States and/or its trading partners don't want that to happen (because, for example, it would make U.S. exports more expensive), they can intervene in the market and supply (sell) an amount *AB* of additional dollars. This has the effect of keeping the price of the dollar stationary, at P_x. In this case, this also means that the dollar is undervalued (it is "weak") in terms of other currencies, and the United States would run a balance of payments surplus represented by the distance between points *A* and *B* in figure 3–6. On the other hand, if the exchange price of dollars were P_m, then the dollar is overvalued, and the United States would be running a balance of payments deficit (since the dollar is too strong) in the amount of *AB* in this example.

Since the objective of managing exchange rates is (theoretically)

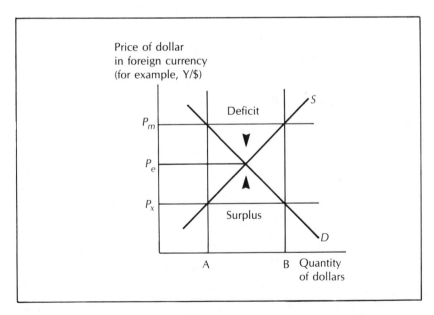

Figure 3–6. *Managed Exchange Rates*

to achieve balance of payments equilibrium, the monetary authorities—under a managed system—attempt to intervene in the market
and cause exchange rates to bring the system into equilibrium.
Under a free-flexible system this should happen automatically.
Management of exchange rates is advocated by some when factors
such as protectionism or uncertainty prevent the system from
achieving the market-clearing price. Critics of managed exchange
rates argue, however, that the costs of intervention (central banks
must sell currencies against market trends) aren't worth uncertain
benefits.

If the world were simple, then trade between nations could be
balanced and everyone would benefit equally from the international
trade process. But in economics things are seldom as simple in practice as they appear in theory. Neither the free-flexible system of the
1973–85 years nor the attempts at managing the system since have
brought about international trade equilibrium.

Two Factors in Exchange Rate Determination
and Balance of Payments Adjustment

Before turning to consider the seemingly intractable problem of contemporary global imbalances, it is useful to highlight two factors
that underlie adjustment between countries: prices in goods markets
and prices in financial markets. To illustrate, let's initially assume
that two countries, Spain and Portugal, are in equilibrium; then
Spain becomes involved in a hotly contested political election, and
the incumbent increases the money supply to grease votes. Inflation
results. What happens to Spain's international payments profile?

Since prices in Spain are higher than those in Portugal, Spaniards
will import cheaper Portuguese goods, resulting in a balance of payments deficit. If Spain is under a flexible exchange rate system, the
increased demand for Portuguese goods will generate an increased
demand for escudos. As the demand for Spanish pesetas conversely
falls, the Portuguese escudo will appreciate and the peseta will
depreciate. Since the stronger value of the escudo will make Portuguese goods more expensive, the Spanish will cut back their imports,
and international payments will settle back to equilibrium. If the
Spanish were under a fixed exchange rate system, instead of the

price of foreign exchange adjusting, the country would have to export gold or dollars to pay for the imports, and the money supply and the imbalance would be resolved.

The important point to remember is that differences in prices will, with free trade, precipitate balance of payments adjustment. But prices of goods and services are not the only determinant of exchange rate movements and balance of payments adjustment. In addition to merchandise trade, financial instruments such as stocks and bonds are increasingly traded internationally. The price of such capital, the interest rate, is the second key determinant of international adjustment. Let's say a country, like the United States, has high real interest rates because the government must borrow money to finance burgeoning federal deficits. If interest rates in the United States then exceed those in, say, Japan, the Japanese (or other foreign investors) will purchase U.S. assets. But to do so, they need dollars. This increased demand would push the value of the dollar up under a flexible exchange rate system. Under a fixed exchange rate system, the flow of gold would cause money supplies to readjust and interest rates would equalize.

Understanding these two determinants of international adjustment—goods prices and asset prices—provides the key to untangling the complexity of contemporary international finance. Quite simply, we see that the goods market and the capital market have gone in different directions internationally and a single price for foreign exchange cannot balance them both. That is, given the nation's recent debt-driven macroeconomic policy, the United States is running a balance of payments deficit as it consumes more than it produces. Thus, the dollar should depreciate for balance. But to finance internal deficits, U.S. interest rates have exceeded global rates. This creates a demand for dollars, keeping the value of U.S. currency too high. The U.S. trade balance isn't adjusting automatically because the demand for high interest assets is working in the opposite direction. In the next section we investigate the specifics of this dollar dilemma.

The Paradox of the Strong Dollar

Since 1982 the United States has been running gigantic trade deficits. In 1987 the merchandise trade deficit peaked at $159.5 billion, while the current account reached a deficit of $143.7 billion. This is, to say the least, historically unprecedented (see figure 3–5).

Given the theoretical considerations we have just examined, it would seem that under such circumstances the value of the dollar would *fall* and that accordingly U.S. exports would be cheaper, imports more expensive, and the trade imbalance should be corrected. But this hasn't happened. The reason it hasn't is an integral part of the present international financial crisis.

Let's look first at the data. Figure 3–5 compares the current account with the value of the dollar (as weighted against a selected group of foreign currencies) and clearly shows that between 1980 and 1985 while the trade deficit became larger, the dollar became *stronger*. This, of course, is the opposite of what should—theoretically—have occurred.

Whenever a nation runs a trade deficit, there has to be a compensating flow in one or more of the other accounts to balance the accounts. That is, the difference has to be made up by earnings from foreign investments, or by net flows of new investments, or by borrowing from reserves.

By looking at the U.S. balance of payments history shown in table 3–4, we can see the paradoxical events that have occurred to make the dollar strong even in the face of a large trade deficit. First of all, in the current account, income from U.S. investments abroad generally helped reduce the net effects of the merchandise deficit over the period 1979–82 (this is also shown in figure 3–7). That income averaged around $30 billion over that period.

Also, in the capital account, large annual (incremental) increases in foreign investment in the United States, coupled with *decreases* in U.S. investment abroad, provided a huge U.S. surplus in the investment account. This annual inflow of new private investment (shown as capital inflow of private assets), which amounted to $125 billion in 1985, more than anything increased foreign demand for the dollar and kept it strong when, in the face of a large trade deficit, it should have been weak.

There are several reasons for this unprecedented shift in the patterns of investment. Domestic federal government deficits have pressured capital markets. Foreign investors also seem to feel that the U.S. economy is a "safe haven" for investments, compared with

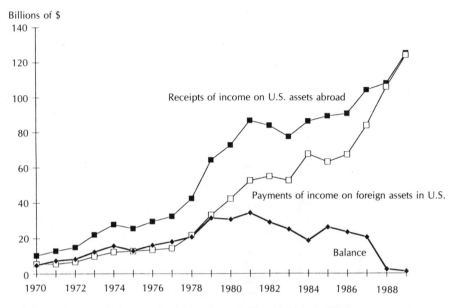

Billions of $

Receipts of income on U.S. assets abroad

Payments of income on foreign assets in U.S.

Balance

Source: *Survey of Current Business,* June 1988 and March 1990.

Figure 3–7. *U.S. Investment Income, 1970–1989*

other options. This is partly because of the sheer size of the U.S. economy and partly because of the political and economic uncertainty and turmoil in much of the rest of the world.

Another reason is that the rate of inflation in the United States has been relatively low since 1982. This means that the real rate of return (inflation adjusted) on investments in the United States has remained relatively high. Also, especially during the 1982–84 period, as shown in figure 3–8, interest rates in the United States were high compared with the rest of the world. Even as rates have fallen during 1985–86, the *real* rate of interest (interest rate minus inflation rate) remains high by historical standards.

So the primary reason the U.S. dollar has remained strong is that investors have confidence in the U.S. economy, interest rates have remained high, and inflation is low. Now, the question is, what does this unexpected, unprecedented, and paradoxical turn of events mean? There are three important issues here, all of which are analyzed in more detail in later chapters.

Percent

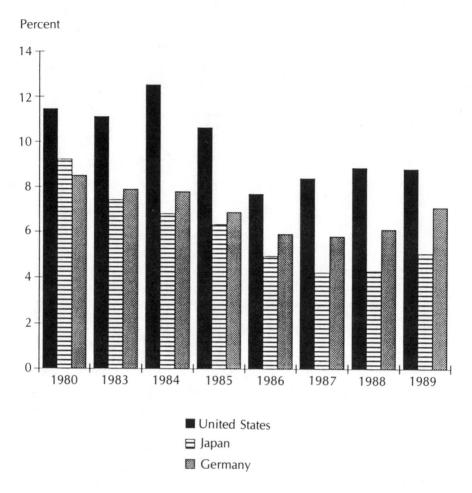

Source: International Monetary Fund, *International Financial Statistics,* May 1990.

Figure 3–8. *Government Bond Yields*

The Emerging Financial Crisis

To begin with, there is the question of the increasing fragility of the international financial system. One important result of the massive inflows of foreign investment over the past several years is that they have financed much of the U.S. *internal* deficit (the U.S. national debt). If there were a sudden loss of confidence in the U.S. economy due to, say, a developing world debt default, these funds could be withdrawn almost overnight. This would almost certainly precipitate a rapid drop in the value of the dollar and a financial panic, if not a total collapse of the U.S. economy and with it, a collapse of the international economy.

Second, the world economy now finds itself between the proverbial "rock and a hard place." Developing countries are now facing an external debt burden that exceeds $1 *trillion*. If they are to have even the most remote chance of repaying it, they must be able to earn foreign exchange by exporting to the industrialized nations. This means the United States *must* continue to run a huge trade deficit; it must continue to buy the exports of the Third World. But this, in turn, means the U.S. trade deficit must continue to be financed by foreign investments from the other industrialized countries, which also means that the U.S. economy will continue to enjoy the benefits of cheap imports, a lower inflation rate, and an internal deficit financed by someone else's savings. In many ways this is a case of being able to have your cake and eat it too. The price, however, is losing the U.S. industrial sector's dominance and the millions of jobs that are associated with it to foreign competition.

Finally, the dramatic and ironic shift of roles in the international economy means that the United States has—already—become a debtor nation for the first time since 1914. There is nothing inherently wrong with being a debtor country. Historically, *developing* countries have borrowed from more advanced countries—as the United States did during the 1800s—to finance investments in capital stock which then stimulate productivity and growth, ideally at a rate that provides a rate of return higher than the interest on the loans. If that happens, then the loans can be repaid and everyone gains. But for the most developed, richest, and most productive economy in the world also to be a debtor nation is, to put it mildly, somewhat unusual.

A nation, like a household, becomes a net debtor whenever it spends more than it earns—that is, incurs obligations in its capital account that exceed its net income from exports and the net inflow of foreign investments. By accepting foreign investments, a nation incurs an obligation to pay a stream of income to investors over a long period of time, indefinitely in the case of direct investments. Because of compounding, portfolio investments (such U.S. Treasury bonds) tend to grow at an increasing rate, and the outflow worsens over time.

One result of such a staggering external debt is that it will engender an estimated outflow (on current account) of some $100 billion annually in interest and dividend payments to other countries. This—if present trends continue—would push the total current account deficit into the $200–$300 billion range, which would, in turn, cause the external debt to double to $2 trillion by 1993.

The reason for this unsettling turn of events is that while U.S. investment abroad has declined dramatically since 1982, foreign investment in the United States has been increasing rapidly. As shown in figure 3–9, total (accumulated) U.S. foreign investment abroad exceeded foreign investments in the United States until 1984. By 1989 foreign assets in the United States exceeded U.S. investments abroad by more than $650 billion. Incrementally, the annual inflow of investments made in the United States began to

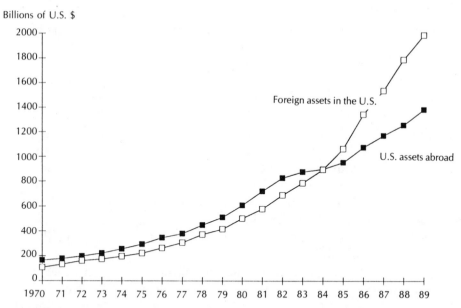

Source: *Survey of Current Business,* June 1986, 1988, and *Federal Reserve Bulletin,* May 1990.

Figure 3–9. *International Investment Position of the United States, 1970–1989*

exceed the annual outflow in the summer of 1982. This is shown in figure 3–10.

Since new investments typically yield a lower rate of return in the early stages (as new factories are built, and so on), it took some time for the outflows on the new investments in the United States to exceed the inflows from the more mature U.S. investments abroad, but, as we have seen, that did begin to occur by 1985. What this means is, first, that as larger and larger shares of the U.S. internal national debt are owned by foreign interests, more and more U.S. resources will have to flow abroad to service the debt. And this will mean that the benefits of cheaper imports currently enjoyed by the United States will no longer be possible. The United States will be forced into austerity programs and a general reduction of its standard of living just to pay its debts—in much the same way that the Third World countries are now being forced to do.

Moreover, it means that the United States has now exchanged roles with Japan and some of the Western European countries. A bilateral investment profile of Japan and the United States is pre-

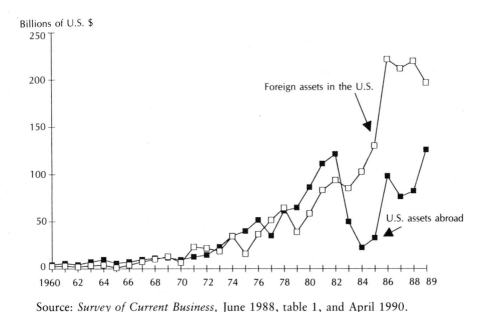

Source: *Survey of Current Business,* June 1988, table 1, and April 1990.

Figure 3–10. *Annual Net Flows of Foreign Investment, 1960–1989*

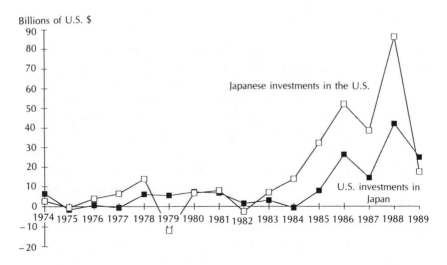

Billions of U.S. $

Source: *Survey of Current Business,* March issue, various years, "U.S. International Transactions by Area."

Figure 3–11. *Bilateral Investment Profile: United States and Japan, 1974–1989*

sented in figure 3–11. Japan is now the world's largest creditor nation, the United States the largest debtor. It should be clear by now that it is logically inconsistent for one country to sustain the position of being the world's largest spender *and* the world's largest debtor at the same time.

Much will depend on how the international financial community continues to perceive the role of the United States in the world economy and, especially, the role of the U.S. dollar as the world's key international currency. Since the Western world decided at Bretton Woods to make the U.S. dollar the medium of exchange for international transactions, the strength of the U.S. economy—and the U.S. dollar—has become the paramount issue in the world economy. The reasons why this is so crucial to the world economic balance of power and to continued financial stability is the topic of the following chapter.

4

The Historical Evolution
of the International Monetary System

I n order to understand the current international monetary system and its problems, one must realize that, for practical purposes, all international financial transactions are inextricably linked to the U.S. dollar. As the dollar goes, so goes the international financial system.

Many people still think that the U.S. dollar is somehow related to gold. Indeed, until 1971, that was the case. Throughout history, gold has played a major role in the international financial system.

In the "golden days" of international trade, if a country was running a balance of trade deficit (importing more than it was exporting), then, according to the prevailing rules of the game, some kind of financial transaction had to occur to compensate for the difference. Historically, that was accomplished by transferring gold reserves from the country that was buying more than it was selling to the country that was selling more than it was buying.

Therefore, while the gold standard was in place, the only way it was possible for a country to buy more abroad than it sold was for it to pay for the trade deficit with gold reserves, which were often literally shipped between countries to pay for trade imbalances. However, if the selling country was willing to accept payment in the buyer's own currency, then this gold transfer was not necessary. And therein lies a tale.

The Discipline of International Finance

In addition to facilitating and financing international trade, the international financial system plays a disciplinary "policing" role.

Within a country, monetary and other government authorities are able to adjust monetary and fiscal policies to the end of maximizing economic growth, maintaining full employment, and minimizing inflation. Normally, this is done by manipulating government spending, taxes, interest rates, and the supply of money. However, when a country engages in international trade, it must give up some of these options and submit to the discipline of international finance. This has interesting and complicated implications.

Virtually all countries engage in international trade because of the perceived and real benefits discussed in chapter 2. So most nations have no choice but to accept the discipline of international finance. If a country cannot maintain balance in its international accounts (that is, if it cannot balance import purchases with export sales), then, unless it can mine gold and sell it to pay for trade deficits, it must initiate appropriate policies to make its own economy conform to the rules of the international financial game. That is, it must make itself more competitive in international markets. Often, this is a paradoxical case of the tail wagging the dog.

Consider, for example, the common case of a country running a large balance of trade deficit. Assuming it doesn't have enough gold to pay for the difference, then its only option is to do something to increase its export sales or to decrease its import purchases. The conventional wisdom says that the way to increase exports is to put into place appropriate monetary and fiscal policies to lower its rate of inflation, thereby making its products cheaper relative to competitors'. This, in turn, should increase its export sales to the rest of the world.

However, to reduce its rate of inflation, a nation must slow down its economy by decreasing government spending, raising taxes and interest rates, and decreasing the money supply. Taken together, these policies will generally slow down economic growth and reduce the rate of inflation. But, at the same time, unemployment will increase. For most countries, this is a high (and not generally politically feasible) price to pay. In essence, they are trading off more domestic unemployment for the jobs generated by the export sector and the benefits of lower-priced imported goods. Whether such a trade-off makes economic sense depends on the extent to which any given economy is involved in international trade as compared to how well it can be self-sufficient using its own resources.

The Special Case of the United States

Needless to say, such adjustments are not popular, especially in the underdeveloped countries, which are often highly dependent on imports and can ill afford to lower their standard of living, but these adjustments have been the reality of the international financial system for a long time. Only one country in the world is exempt from such discipline: the United States of America. Understanding why this is the case is crucial to understanding the current international financial situation.

The United States emerged from World War II not only as a military victor, but as an economic victor as well. It was by far the strongest economic power in the world and had, by 1945, accumulated some $25 billion in gold reserves, almost 75 percent of the world's gold supply. This of course meant that the United States was in a very powerful position to reorganize the international financial system to serve its own best interests. God was clearly not up to the task of providing the necessary liquidity to finance world trade. The price of gold had been set at thirty-five dollars an ounce by President Roosevelt in 1933, but the general price level had almost doubled since then, so gold was a very underpriced commodity, scarce even for commercial uses. Therefore, everyone realized that a new system was needed.

So, with the war winding down and victory apparent, the monetary authorities of the leading Allied nations gathered at Bretton Woods, New Hampshire, in 1944 to work out a new international monetary arrangement. The delegation from Great Britain, headed by economist John Maynard Keynes, argued that an international central bank should be established. It would monitor trade imbalances and have the power to force deficit countries to adjust their economic policies anytime deficits became out of line. But turning over the power to control domestic economic policy to an international institution was more than most countries could accept. The United States, in essence, vetoed any such plan.

Out of that meeting came one of the more dramatic historical examples of what is sometimes referred to as the Golden Rule: "Whoever has the gold makes the rules." The gold standard was replaced with the *dollar standard,* and the United States was accordingly exempted from the traditional discipline of international finance.

Under the dollar standard, the United States, since it had most of the world's gold supply anyway, agreed to make the dollar "as good as gold," redeemable on demand by any central bank at the rate of thirty-five dollars an ounce. This meant that the dollar became the accepted medium of exchange for international transactions. This seemingly routine event was to have far-reaching implications for the international financial system, certainly far beyond what anyone would have imagined at the time.

Since the dollar was now "as good as gold," the rest of the world could, and did, use dollars instead of gold for settling international payments, for international transactions in general, and for their own reserves. The system was generally acceptable to most of the Bretton Woods participants (with the notable exception of France). Dollars were more liquid than gold, they didn't have to be stored or shipped (a very cumbersome and expensive process), and, most important, dollar deposits earn interest while gold simply gathers dust in a bank vault.

The new system did not, however, exempt anyone (except the United States) from the discipline of international finance. Instead of gold, dollars now provided that discipline. All countries' currencies were now tied to the dollar instead of gold. Only the dollar was pegged to gold, at the rate of thirty-five dollars an ounce. Trade imbalances now had to be settled in U.S. dollars. The Bretton Woods conference had made the dollar the world's key currency, and the stage was set for an unprecedented series of developments, not the least of which is the present international debt crisis.

Also at the Bretton Woods conference a quasi-international bank, the International Monetary Fund (IMF), was established to monitor trade discipline and to provide temporary loans to countries with balance of payments problems. Such loans were conditional on deficit countries "getting their house in order" promptly—in other words, slowing down their inflation rate, stimulating their export sector, and/or reducing imports if they were running trade deficits. Funds for the IMF operation were provided by contributions from member nations whose voice (vote) in its operations was proportional to their contribution. The United States had the controlling vote. Thus, it was no coincidence that the headquarters of the IMF was located in Washington, D.C.

The Evolution of the Dollar Glut

The new system worked well for a number of years. So long as the United States held a large percentage of the world's gold supply, other countries were willing to accept dollars in payment for international transactions. Under such conditions, the United States could run trade deficits at will and simply pay for the difference with dollars. But in the early years of the agreement, this didn't happen because the United States was consistently running trade surpluses. (This, in fact, caused a dollar shortage, which these days is hard to imagine.)

How did we move from a dollar shortage to a dollar glut? And what does this have to do with anything anyway? Understanding the historical significance of this requires a brief look at the data.

First, you will recall from the previous chapter that balance of payments accounts must always be in balance. Or, to put it another way, total dollar expenditures abroad by the United States must equal total dollar receipts for the rest of the world. This means that if the United States is selling more abroad (exports exceed imports), then it must also provide the means to finance this. (Where else would a country get the dollars to purchase U.S. goods?)

In the years just following World War II, the United States (in the process of helping to rebuild Europe through the Marshall Plan and other aid programs) was running huge export surpluses and was at the same time providing the wherewithal to pay for them.

If we slightly rearrange and summarize the balance of payments accounts over the period, it is easy to see how this happened. Look first at table 4–1. Here we see that the United States ran a huge balance of trade surplus of $31.9 billion during the 1946–49 postwar period as it furnished much-needed capital goods to the war-damaged countries of Europe. But remember, balance of payments accounts must always balance. Therefore, something had to happen in the other accounts to offset this large credit item. In this case, the credits in the current account were largely balanced by debits in the capital account in the form of loans and grants made to the European countries under the Marshall Plan. If these loans had not been made, it would have been impossible to run this large surplus. During this early period, this caused no special problem with the inter-

Table 4–1

U.S. Balance of Payments, 1946–1949

(billions of $)

Export of goods and services (excluding military transfers)	+67.0
Import of goods and services	−35.1
Excess of exports	+31.9
Means of financing excess exports:	
U.S. private capital (long- and short-term)	−2.9
U.S. private remittances	−2.5
U.S. government financing:	
Loans	−11.7
Grants (excluding military transfers)	−13.1
Liquidation of gold and dollar assets	−4.8
Errors and omissions	+3.1
Total net financing	−31.9

Source: U.S. Department of Commerce, *Survey of Current Business,* various issues.

Table 4–2

U.S. Balance of Payments, 1950–1957

(billions of $)

Export of goods and services (excluding military transfers)	+156.3
Import of goods and services	−134.4
Excess of exports	+21.9
Means of financing excess exports:	
Private capital (net)[a]	10.8
Remittances	−4.7
U.S. government grants and loans (net)	−20.0
Total financing	−35.5
Excess of financing over export balance	−13.6
Increase in foreign U.S. balances and short-term dollar claims (net)	+8.6
Purchases of gold from U.S. (net)	+1.7
Errors and omissions (net)	+3.3
Total	+13.6

Source: U.S. Department of Commerce.

[a]U.S. capital outflow, less long-term foreign investment in the United States.

national monetary system since the United States was easily able to make these loans. In fact, if anything, it had a positive effect on the U.S. economy by creating jobs.

Table 4–3

U.S. Balance of Payments, 1958–1965

(billions of $)

Export of goods and services (excluding military transfers)	+ 241.1
Import of goods and services	– 202.3
Balance on current account	+ 38.8
Private capital (net)[a]	– 28.1
Remittances and pensions	– 5.5
U.S. government grants and loans (excluding military grants)	– 23.8
Balance on capital and unilateral transfer accounts	– 57.4
Deficit	– 18.6
Means of financing deficit:	
Changes in short-term liabilities to foreigners, gold reserves, and foreign exchange balances, and U.S. gold tranche position in IMF	+ 22.8
Errors and omissions	– 4.2
Total	+ 18.6

Source: U.S. Department of Commerce, *Survey of Current Business,* various issues.

[a] U.S. capital outflow, less accumulation of foreign-owned nonliquid assets in the United States.

Now let's see how the situation began to change. This is clearly shown in table 4–2. During the 1950–57 period, the United States not only financed its export surplus but overfinanced it, so that the rest of the world began to accumulate dollar balances to the tune of $8.6 billion by the end of that period. At the same time, the United States began to lose some gold as part of the dollar balances were cashed in. This was a clear indicator of trouble ahead but was not considered by most economists to be a serious problem at the time. However, as we can see in table 4–3, the situation began to change rapidly around 1958.

During the 1958–65 period, the United States still maintained a balance of trade surplus but at the same time continued granting loans and foreign aid and investing capital abroad. These far exceeded the trade surplus, so large dollar balances began to be accumulated by the rest of the world. This was the beginning of the so-called dollar glut, which is still with us and remains one root of the international financial crisis.

The Rise of the Eurodollar Market

By the early 1960s, another significant event occurred that was to have far-reaching implications: the development of the so-called *Eurodollar* market. Eurodollars are dollars deposited in any bank—not necessarily in Europe—outside the United States and kept there, denominated in dollars. European banks, many heavily involved in foreign trade transactions, found it convenient to begin accepting dollar deposits and using them in their day-to-day business. This avoided bothersome exchange transactions and earned them interest as well. Since the dollar was backed by gold, this seemed logical to everyone concerned.

There was one catch, however, which later turned out to be a catch-22—the *reserve requirement*. U.S. banks are required to maintain a percentage of their deposits as reserves. This requirement limits the extent to which they can expand their asset base by loaning out deposits and keeping only a portion of them as reserves. By controlling this reserve requirement, the Federal Reserve Bank (the U.S. central bank) can maintain some control over the U.S. money supply. An increase in the reserve requirement, for example, causes an anti-inflationary contraction of the money supply and is a powerful, but not often used, monetary policy tool. But foreign banks, in general, have no such requirement, which means that Eurodollar deposits can be expanded infinitely through a multiple expansion process. Thus European banks could make profits by lending all their Eurodollars, while U.S. banks had to keep a portion out of circulation in the Federal Reserve. In addition, European banks are allowed to pay interest on very short-term deposits, while U.S. banking laws require that a deposit be held for at least thirty days before interest can be paid.

Meanwhile, the 1960s was a period of rapid expansion of U.S. multinational corporate activities all around the world. Many multinational corporations (MNCs), which routinely move large sums of surplus funds between countries, found Eurodollar deposits to be a very attractive option compared with holding their surpluses in U.S. banks. Accordingly, large sums moved into the Eurodollar market.

All this, in essence, created an entirely new money supply, based on and denominated in dollars, which did not exist before. This had two effects. One was that the U.S. banking authorities lost control of a large portion of the U.S. money supply, which reduced their ability to control inflation with monetary policy, one of the primary macroeconomic policy tools. And second, it further made the U.S. dollar the cornerstone of the international monetary system.

These days Eurodollar deposits amount to more than $2 *trillion* (nobody knows quite how much for sure), which is equal to the basic U.S. money supply itself. One half of the U.S. dollars in existence are outside of any kind of control whatsoever by the U.S. banking authorities, which makes it easier to understand why the entire world maintains a lively interest in the health of the U.S. economy.

The Demise of Gold

The other relevant (and unexpected) developments of the 1960s were that the United States continued to run balance of trade deficits and that its gold supply began to dwindle. Although, in theory, anyone should have been willing to accept dollars in payment for international trade transactions (given that the dollar was supposed to be as good as gold, convertible on demand), some countries (such as France) were beginning to doubt the long-term viability of a system that substituted green pieces of paper for gold.

U.S. gold reserves fell from a high of $25 billion in 1950 to $10 billion in 1970. During the same period, dollar claims against the U.S. gold supply increased from around $5 billion to $70 billion (see figure 4–1). Clearly, it no longer made any sense at all to say that the dollar was convertible to gold on demand since the potential dollar claims against the U.S. gold supply were seven times larger than could be honored.

Faced with a crisis of confidence, on August 15, 1971, President Nixon cut the link between the dollar and gold. The United States would no longer honor its pledge to redeem dollars for gold. This meant that the rest of the world was left holding $70 billion that were worth only what the U.S. government said they were worth. Surprisingly, most foreign governments accepted this as an inevitable reality and continued to use dollars as reserves and as the international medium of exchange. There was no alternative. This, then, was the final step in establishing the international financial system

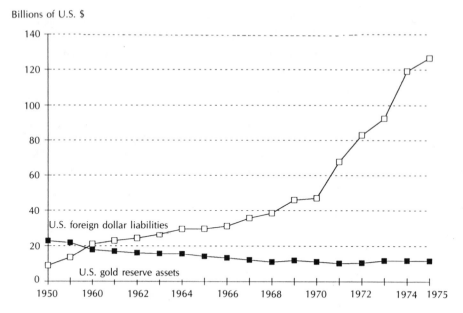

Billions of U.S. $

Source: International Monetary Fund, *International Financial Statistics Yearbook 1989.*

Figure 4–1. *U.S. Gold Reserve Assets and Dollar Liabilities, 1950–1975*

as a dollar system. Gold eventually became just another commodity that could be bought and sold on the commodity markets at whatever price it would bring.

By the end of 1971 the United States was experiencing a major balance of payments problem. The current account deficit was $1.4 billion, and the trade deficit came to $2.2 billion. The Nixon administration responded to this situation on December 18, 1971, by signing the historic Smithsonian Agreement.

This agreement formalized the results of President Nixon's New Economic Policy (NEP), which had been announced and instituted in August 1971. The NEP, in addition to halting the convertibility of the dollar into gold, provided for a 10 percent tax on the value of all imports and the *floating* of the dollar. ("Floating" means, in effect, that the United States would neither buy nor sell currency on the foreign exchange markets, while exchange rates would be left at their own natural level or be influenced by the intervention of other governments.)

Floating the dollar and cutting its link to gold violated the established guidelines of the IMF. So, in essence, this agreement represented the collapse of the Bretton Woods system.

Petrodollar Recycling

By 1973, with the dollar firmly entrenched as the world's key currency, the stage was set for the beginning of what was to be the most serious crisis ever faced by the international monetary system. Interestingly, what happened was as much a political problem as an economic one.

Outraged by the United States' support of Israel during the Yom Kippur War, OPEC placed an embargo on oil sales to the United States and later, when the embargo was relaxed, raised the price of oil from $1.30 a barrel in 1970 to $10.72 in 1975 and to $28.67 by 1980. Since virtually all oil transactions are carried on in dollars and because, at the time, the United States was dependent on OPEC for almost 50 percent of its oil imports, this sent an inflationary shock through the United States and the rest of the world.

Having no short-run alternative, the United States and the rest of the world paid OPEC's price. The result, among other things, was one of the most massive transfers of wealth in history. Hundreds of billions of dollars were transferred to the Middle East, which was in turn faced with the ironic and paradoxical problem of what to do with this windfall. Clearly, their own economies couldn't absorb such an injection of funds without risking runaway inflation, so the OPEC countries had no alternative but to look for other places to invest them.

In spite of the problems caused by the oil shock, the U.S. economy was still the strongest in the world, so the only logical thing for the dollar-rich OPEC nations to do was to cycle the oil revenues back into American and European banks. The details of this are shown in table 4–4. Now it was the U.S. and European banks that were faced with a paradoxical dilemma: billions in new deposits, and, with a recession going on in the United States (caused in part by the higher oil prices), nowhere to put them to work. Since banks must pay interest on deposits, it follows that they can only survive if they can loan out those deposits at rates higher than those they

Table 4–4

OPEC International Placements, 1976–1983

(billions of U.S. $)

Type of Placement	1976	1977	1978	1979	1980	1981	1982	1983
U.S. bank deposits	1.9	0.4	0.8	5.1	− 1.3	− 2.0	4.6	0.9
Other investments	9.2	6.9	− 0.4	1.9	18.4	19.8	8.1	− 10.4
Eurocurrency bank deposits	11.2	16.4	6.6	33.4	43.0	3.9	− 16.5	− 11.9
Other bank deposits	− 0.9	1.2	0	2.09	2.6	2.5	− 0.4	0
Other placements[a]	21.0	20.9	18.6	19.7	37.5	40.7	18.2	11.6
Total	42.4	45.8	25.6	62.1	100.2	62.9	14.0	− 9.8
Bank deposits as a percentage of total deposits	28.8	39.3	28.9	65.2	44.2	3.8	—	—

Source: For U.S. placements and other bank deposits: Bank of England *Quarterly Bulletin,* March 1985; for Eurocurrency placements: U.S. Department of the Treasury, Office of International Banking and Portfolio Investments, and Bank of England *Quarterly Bulletin,* March 1985.

[a] Other placements include those in OECD countries, international organizations, and developing countries. The last include net flows of concessional assistance, syndicated Eurocurrency credits, bond issues, and direct investment.

have to pay depositors. This elementary fact explains much of the present economic crisis.

Most developing countries were desperate for outside development capital, especially since they too are mostly dependent on imported oil and were having to pay more than before for these imports. Therefore, they were prime candidates for loans from U.S. and European commercial banks. So, in what at the time seemed to be a logical process (capital moving to where it is needed), the underdeveloped countries were only too willing to absorb the banks' excess funds. Everybody was happy. Bankers lined up at the doors of finance ministers' offices with loan money in hand. The cycle was complete. Almost.

Now called "petrodollar recycling" (see figure 4–2), what had happened was that the Middle Eastern countries had shipped the oil to the rest of the world, which in turn had sent along the dollars to pay for it to the Middle East. The OPEC countries then deposited those same dollars back in U.S. and European banks, which in turn loaned them to the capital-poor developing countries. Unfortun-

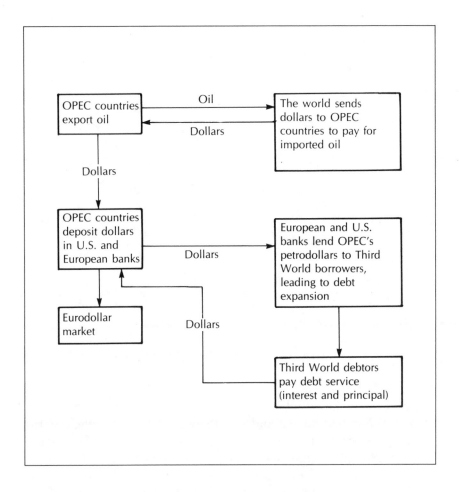

Figure 4–2. *Petrodollar Recycling*

ately, as everyone now knows (in hindsight), there the cycle stopped, and the seeds of the present debt crisis were planted.

The Oil Price Shock of 1973–1974

The system of floating exchange rates was severely challenged by the shock of the 1973–74 OPEC oil embargo. The dramatic rise in the price of a barrel of oil (see figure 4–3) severely disrupted the international monetary system. Since oil prices rose over 73 percent in

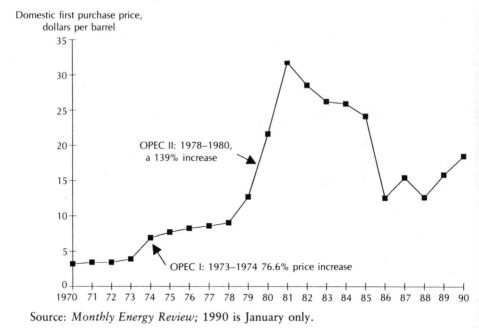

Source: *Monthly Energy Review;* 1990 is January only.

Figure 4–3. *Crude Oil Prices, 1970–1990*

one year, the value of oil imports pressured the balance of payments in both the industrialized and developing world. Nevertheless, the recycling of petrodollars took place without the catastrophic disruption and disequilibrium that many experts predicted, although the tremendous flow of petrodollars to Europe helped stimulate the rapid growth and expansion of the Eurodollar market, which was to change fundamentally the character of the international monetary system.

By the middle of the 1970s, chronic balance of payments problems plagued most developing nations, particularly large oil importers. These balance of payments deficits placed greater and greater pressure upon the International Monetary Fund for adjustment loans and assistance, and it rapidly became clear that the IMF was increasingly being called on to perform a function far different from its original goal of assisting nations with their short-run balance of payments problems and economic stabilization policies and programs.

These chronic balance of payment deficits reflected long-term structural problems by the middle 1970s. Most developing nations were facing steady deterioration of their terms of trade, an outflow of capital, and the economic shocks of the first OPEC oil embargo and subsequent quadrupling of oil prices. This required new loans to pay for oil imports and to adjust to declining exports caused by the U.S. recession of 1974–75. The spread of inflation and general economic instability from advanced industrial nations to the developing nations became more evident during this period than ever before.

The Flight of Capital: 1975–1985

One of the more significant and persistent trends that evolved in the midst of the resulting debt explosion was the growth of *capital flight*—the transfer of money from one country to another by private individuals or firms. It has been estimated that from 1976 to 1985, over $198 billion fled the larger underdeveloped nations. This represents about 50 percent of the total money borrowed over the same period. It is estimated that about $62 billion of this money has been deposited in foreign banks and about half of this in U.S. banks (see table 4–5). Many experts argue that the years of continued economic austerity and declining economic growth generated conditions that actually invited capital flight. Certainly, hyperinflation and constant devaluations encouraged it.

As illustrated in figure 4–4, capital flight has considerably increased the growth in the foreign dept of many major debtor nations. Argentina's capital flight from 1976 to 1985 represented 62 percent of its debt growth. Mexico's and Venezuela's debt growths from capital flight were 71 percent and 115 percent, respectively, for the same period.[1]

A Morgan Guaranty Trust Company analysis of capital flight revealed that without capital flight, Mexico, for example, would have had a total foreign debt of only $12 billion in 1985 compared with its actual debt of $96 billion (see figure 4–5). The same study tracked the steady growth of savings deposits in the United States (due in part to the inflow of foreign deposits) and compared it to the dramatic decline of domestic savings in Mexico and Argentina (see

Table 4–5
Estimated Net Capital Flight: Cumulative Flows, 1976–1985
(billions of $)

	Total	1976–82	1983–85
Latin America			
Argentina	26	27	(1)
Bolivia	1	1	0
Brazil	10	3	7
Ecuador	2	1	1
Mexico	53	36	17
Uruguay	1	1	0
Venezuela	30	25	6
Other countries			
India	10	6	4
Indonesia	5	6	(1)
Korea	12	6	6
Malaysia	12	8	4
Nigeria	10	7	3
Philippines	9	7	2
South Africa	17	13	4

Source: Morgan Guaranty Trust Company.

Note: Numbers in parentheses represent capital inflows. Figures might not add due to rounding.

figure 4–6). It was clear that unless something could be done to stem the outflows of capital, there was little hope of ever resolving the debt problems.

Over the twelve-year (1973–85) second stage of the debt crisis, both the IMF and the private commercial banking system were drawn into roles and responsibilities never imagined. This has fundamentally changed the character of the international financial and monetary system.

The International Monetary Fund

Of particular concern for the developing nations that were forced to go to the IMF for loans and economic assistance was the IMF's conditionality requirement. From its inception in 1944, the International Monetary Fund had as its primary responsibility the job of

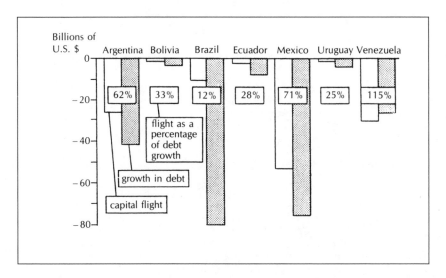

Source: Morgan Guaranty Trust Company.

Figure 4–4. *How Capital Flight Adds to Latin America's Growing Debt, 1976–1985*

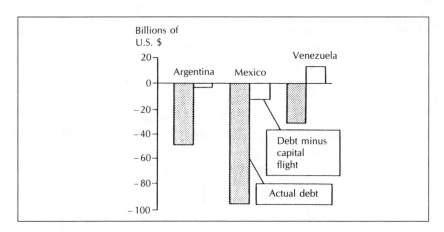

Source: Morgan Guaranty Trust Company.

Figure 4–5. *The Debt Picture in Mexico, Venezuela, and Argentina If There Had Been No Capital Flight, 1985*

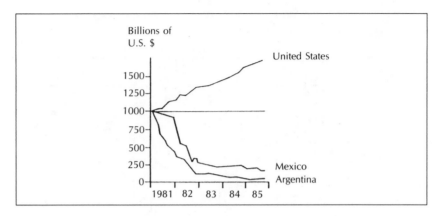

Source: Morgan Guaranty Trust Company.

Figure 4–6. *Domestic Savings Deposits in the United States, Mexico, and Argentina, 1981–1985*

assisting nations in resolving temporary balance of payments problems. Through loans and economic policy recommendations, the IMF helped countries adjust to periods of balance of payments disequilibrium. But by the middle of the 1970s, the problems became increasingly complicated, larger in magnitude, and more interrelated. As the IMF's loan capability was dwarfed by the borrowing needs of the developing countries, the private commercial banks stepped in to fill the void. Yet the IMF continued to play a major role in the international monetary system, mostly now as a disciplinarian as well as a lender of last resort.

When a nation requests a loan from the IMF, a team of economic experts is sent into the country to analyze that country's economy and its balance of payments problems. Before approving a loan, the IMF generally requires that the country agree to a set of comprehensive economic policies and targeted economic goals in order to qualify for the loan. The IMF feels this "conditionality" requirement is necessary in order to ensure that the country will get its own economic house in order, which also signals the commercial banking community that the country is taking the kinds of measures deemed necessary to enable it to make good on its debt obligations. So, in effect, the IMF loan approval becomes a prerequisite for a debtor country to obtain more loans from private commercial banking sources.

Typically, the IMF's analysis of a country's balance of payments problems concludes that the country needs to expand its exports, reduce its imports, curb its rate of inflation, and cut its domestic deficit by decreasing the level of government spending. If the country can properly stabilize its economy, then, the argument goes, it will be easier to attract private foreign investment and reduce the flight of capital. Although this analysis and strategy seem logical, there are predictable costs and consequences.

First, the IMF normally demands that a country's domestic deficit be significantly reduced. This requires a country to reduce its level of government spending, particularly for agricultural subsidies, price supports, and projects in the public sector. Implicit in the IMF's strategy is a philosophy that views the state's role in the economy as inefficient. There is a clear bias toward free enterprise as the primary mechanism for generating economic growth and stability. But for an already underdeveloped country to cut back on its social spending and reorder its priorities means not only a reduction in its standard of living but also an increased potential for political instability.

In addition to spending cuts, the IMF usually requires that a tight monetary policy be implemented to bring down excessive rates of inflation. This will decrease inflation but usually at the short-term cost of reduced economic growth. A contractionary fiscal policy in conjunction with a tight monetary policy often induces a decline in economic growth.

Moreover, to improve the balance of payments disequilibrium, the IMF usually requires a nation to produce a trade surplus, by increasing exports and/or by decreasing imports. Normally, this means a planned devaluation of the country's currency. A devaluation makes the country's exports more price-competitive and its imports more expensive to its citizens.

It follows in IMF logic that the earnings from increased exports could then be used to service the country's debt obligations. In extreme cases, a country is expected to reduce its imports significantly to generate the required trade surplus. While such action may create a trade surplus, it is a double-edged sword. Reducing needed imports has serious consequences for a developing nation. A country's imports of capital goods are vital for forming and maintaining the productive base of the country. That is the primary reason for a nation's being involved in international trade in the first place. (We should also remember that the reduction in imports in part explains falling exports from the United States.)

The IMF assumes that a nation can achieve economic growth and stability after a temporary period of adjustment and austerity. If this program works, it will provide the environment necessary not only to attract foreign investment but also to enlist the capital resources of its own private investors. But any way one looks at them, the IMF's programs and policies have exacted a high social and economic cost from debtor nations. The continuing economic austerity from IMF-imposed policies has produced political tensions and social unrest in many nations.

The Call for a New International Economic Order

In the early 1970s, many prominent leaders of the developing nations began to argue that their countries' problems were in fact structural in nature, and that the OPEC oil price shock merely worsened an economic crisis already in the making. This point of view was well represented at the United Nations. In April 1974, at the sixth special session of the United Nations, the General Assembly drafted and passed two related resolutions. The first called for the establishment of a New International Economic Order (NIEO). The second outlined a program of action to implement it.

On December 12, 1974, during the Twenty-ninth Session of the General Assembly, the call for the NIEO was reaffirmed, and the Charter of Economic Rights and Duties of States was adopted. It stated, in part:

> We, the Members of the United Nations,
>
> Having convened a special session of the General Assembly to study for the first time the problems of raw materials and development, devoted to the consideration of the most important economic problems facing the world community,
>
> Bearing in mind the spirit, purposes and principles of the Charter of the United Nations to promote the economic advancement and social progress of all people,
>
> Solemnly proclaim our united determination to work urgently for THE ESTABLISHMENT OF A NEW INTERNATIONAL ECONOMIC ORDER based on equity, sovereign equality, inter-

dependence, common interest and cooperation among all States, irrespective of their economic and social system which shall correct inequalities and redress existing injustices, make it possible to eliminate the widening gap between the developed and the developing countries and ensure steadily accelerating economic and social development and peace and justice for present and future generations, and, to that end declare:

(1) The greatest and most significant achievement during the last decade has been the independence from colonial and alien domination of a large number of peoples and nations which has enabled them to become members of the community of free peoples. Technological progress has also been made in all spheres of economic activities in the last three decades, thus providing a solid potential for improving the well-being of all peoples. However, the remaining vestiges of alien and colonial domination, foreign occupation, racial discrimination, apartheid and neocolonialism in all its forms continue to be among the greatest obstacles to the full emancipation and progress of the developing countries and all the people involved.

(2) The present international economic order is in direct conflict with current developments in international political and economic relations. Since 1970, the world economy has experienced a series of grave crises which have had severe repercussions, especially on the developing countries because of their generally greater vulnerability to external economic impulses.

(3) All these changes have thrust into prominence the reality of interdependence of all the members of the world community. Current events have brought into sharp focus the realization that the interests of the developed countries and those of the developing countries can no longer be isolated from each other, that there is close interrelationship between the prosperity of the developed countries and the growth and development of the developing countries, and that the prosperity of the international community as a whole depends upon the prosperity of its constituent parts.

The well-reasoned grand design of the NIEO was predicated on a collective recognition that fundamental structural change was needed and on a belief that there was the political will to implement change. This change would have required that the advanced industrial countries trade short-run concessions for their own and everyone's long-term best interests. But economic stagnation in the advanced industrial nations, particularly the United States, and general indifference effectively prevented any serious consideration of the U.N. resolution.

Meanwhile, the system of floating exchange rates and continuous petrodollar recycling functioned during the mid-1970s in the midst of declining economic growth and spiraling inflation. This period of stagflation contributed further to the world's balance of payments problems.

For the developing nations, the continued high level of interest rates made their annual trek to the bank and the IMF that much more expensive. Their balance of payments problems were worsened by a slowdown in world trade and economic growth. Their exports and foreign exchange earnings fell.

For all developing nations, the early 1980s marked the beginning of major balance of payments problems. As table 4–6 demonstrates, after 1980 their capital account was negative every year. In 1984 it reached a low of negative $34.6 billion—a dramatic change compared with a capital account *surplus* of $37.5 billion in 1978. As the developing nations' capital accounts began to decline, the current account balance soon followed. The table includes OPEC nations, so one should not be surprised at the current surplus of $31.8 billion in 1980 which followed the OPEC price increase of 1979.

As the recession became worse in the major advanced nations, the demand for petroleum decreased. This resulted in a softening of oil prices and a decreased demand for oil exports from developing nations. By 1982, in the depth of the recession, the developing nations' current account deficit reached a crushing $89.5 billion.

In addition, independent (non-OPEC) producers such as Mexico, Great Britain, and Norway began to place larger and larger supplies of petroleum on the world market. The decline in demand coupled with increased supply set into motion forces that would eventually lower the price of oil and weaken OPEC itself. Also, several OPEC nations broke ranks and produced greater amounts of petroleum than they had agreed to in order to generate desperately needed revenues to fund large domestic spending programs and debt obligations. This decline in oil prices began in 1982, when oil was selling for $33.47 a barrel. By 1983 oil prices had fallen to $29.31 a barrel, and by 1985 to $25 a barrel, before the collapse in 1986 to $12.50. This process (shown in figure 4–3) set the stage for even more serious international problems in oil-producing nations.

Table 4–6

Current and Capital Accounts of Developing Countries, 1978–1984
(billions of U.S. $)

Year	Current Account	Capital Account
1978	− 32.1	+ 37.5
1979	+ 10.0	+ 32.5
1980	+ 31.8	+ 15.7
1981	+ 45.5	− 6.9
1982	− 89.5	− 5.2
1983	− 59.9	− 8.1
1984	− 35.1	− 34.6

Source: World Bank, *World Development Report,* 1985.

Table 4–7

*Percentage Change in Gross Domestic Product of Developing
Countries and Industrial Countries, 1978–1985*

Year	Developing Nations	Industrial Nations
1978	5.1	4.0
1979	4.5	3.3
1980	4.6	1.3
1981	3.0	1.4
1982	1.7	− 0.4
1983	0.5	2.5
1984	4.0	4.7
1985	3.2	2.8

Source: International Monetary Fund, *World Economic Outlook,* April 1986.
Note: Adjusted for inflation.

It is also important to note that in the 1978–83 period, *both* the developing *and* the advanced nations entered a period of economic stagnation, as shown in table 4–7. For developing nations, growth of gross domestic product (GDP) was 5.1 percent in 1978; it dropped to 3 percent in 1981, and fell to an abysmal 0.5 percent by 1983. The industrial nations did not perform any better. In 1978, they were growing at an average of 4.0 percent. This fell to 1.4 percent by 1981, a negative 0.4 percent in 1982, and a still low 2.5 percent in 1983.

Mexico's debt crisis focused worldwide attention on an international financial problem that had been brewing for many years.

But few were willing to acknowledge its magnitude until it reached the crisis stage. All of a sudden, the global debt crisis was added to the seemingly unending list of global economic problems. It suddenly became clear that not only was Mexico in trouble, but so were Argentina, Brazil, Chile, Venezuela, Peru, Nigeria, the Philippines, Turkey, Poland, Romania, and many others—most of the under-developed world. But the major Western countries' governments were so preoccupied with their own stagnating economies that they did not confront the wide-ranging long-run implications of the crisis.

The Reagan administration's response was to facilitate the extension of additional loans by the IMF and private commercial banks to enable the debtor countries to meet their obligations. If this meant that they would face domestic economic austerity, then, the United States argued, that would be necessary until global economic growth and the recovery of the advanced nations could improve the trading environment for developing nations.

Fortunately, some recovery occurred. By 1984 world trade had expanded at a rate of 8.5 percent, and world output grew at a rate of 4.2 percent. For developing nations 1984 brought growth rates of 4.1 percent and an increase in exports of 8.0 percent, compared with 4 percent for the period 1981–82. But even with the recovery continuing through 1984 into 1985, it became obvious that the international economic problems weren't going to go away. Part of the problem, clearly, was the continued strong dollar and the free-flexible exchange rate system.

The Plaza Agreement and Tokyo Summit

At the initiative of Treasury Secretary James Baker III the United States invited the four other largest industrial nations (Great Britain, France, West Germany, and Japan) to New York to discuss the exchange rate problem. At this meeting at the Plaza Hotel in September 1985, the Group of Five agreed to return to an informal system of managed exchange rates. The objective was to bring down the value of the dollar through coordinated macroeconomic policies.

Yet, in spite of the "Plaza Agreement," the major problems—the U.S. trade deficit and the huge Third World debt—remained and were two of the primary issues on the agenda of the Tokyo Summit in May 1986. The other issues were the pace of industrial world growth, the strength of the U.S. dollar, the possibility of policy coordination, high interest rates, and the U.S. federal budget deficit.

Though overall world industrial growth was increasing, most summit participants continued to express concern over the slowing growth in the United States and Japan. The Reagan administration took the position that Japan and West Germany should stimulate their economies to speed up their economic growth rates and increase their demand for imports—U.S. exports. Japan and West Germany didn't agree.

The major issue at the Tokyo Summit was policy coordination. Since each nation's economy had started to converge (with declining interest rates, continuing real growth, and lower inflation), it was possible to begin thinking seriously about coordinating economic policies. But since unemployment rates and trade deficits varied considerably among countries, the prospects for workable economic policy coordination appeared to be remote, and there was no formal agreement.

The summit participants did, however, acknowledge the fact that another year had gone by without a Third World debt crisis (except, of course, for the unique case of Mexico). Declining interest rates and oil prices had brought an easing of the debt problem for most developing nations. Also, the summit group endorsed a plan developed by U.S. Treasury Secretary Baker to aid debtor countries by generating an additional $29 billion in loans, with $9 billion from the IMF and the World Bank conditional on another $20 billion coming from the private commercial banks, the total to be spread among seventeen countries.

At the conclusion of this summit, there appeared to be a renewed spirit of cooperation and a determination to work toward a more coordinated set of economic policies that would simultaneously promote and protect the interests of each individual nation while considering the consequences and ramifications on the group as a whole. But beyond some coordinated interest rate reductions, little had been accomplished.

In the wake of the crash of the U.S. stock market on October 19, 1987, efforts at international cooperation were renewed—if not by choice, by necessity. One of the precipitating events of Black Monday, when the Dow Jones plunged 508 points, was widening

U.S. trade deficits. The trade deficits signaled that the U.S. dollar would have to fall, some thought on the order of 25 percent, to correct the trade imbalance. This made Japanese investors nervous because the value of their dollar investments—historically huge— would also drop 25 percent. American analysts were also worried because the falling dollar, in raising import prices, would promote inflation at the same time that recession was predicted due to rising interest rates to service the domestic government deficit. This intricate web of domestic and international economic repercussions created much uncertainty over the value of U.S. stocks. Investors decided to sell, and, facilitated by fast computer programs, the market rushed into a downward spiral.

Following the crash, strong pressure was brought to bear on the West Germans to lower interest rates and pump up their economy. This expansion would have the effect of increasing German demand for goods from the United States, and the lower German interest rate would direct investors toward the sliding dollar. Germany complied, somewhat unwillingly because of inflationary fears, and international markets were calmed. However, as the crash of 1987 receded into memory, efforts at cooperation were weakened. Little was accomplished at the subsequent economic summit of the Group of Seven nations (the United States, Japan, West Germany, Britain, France, Italy, and Canada), because these countries were occupied with domestic troubles.

It is clear, however, that the international monetary system that came out of the Bretton Woods conference worked smoothly from 1944 to 1971—more than a quarter of a century. As we have observed, the dollar became the key international reserve currency during this period. The IMF played the important role of facilitating adjustment and stabilization for nations experiencing balance of payments problems. But President Nixon's New Economic Policy and the Smithsonian Agreement qualitatively changed the ground rules of this system. The transition from a fixed exchange rate system to a free-floating system ushered in a new era in international monetary affairs.

The OPEC oil price shocks of the 1970s and the seemingly intractable stagflation of the period brought hard times upon the industrialized nations and oil-importing developing nations as well. The developing nations' ill-fated cry for a New International Economic Order fell upon deaf ears as stagnation forced the industrialized nations to focus on their own economic problems.

As the U.S. dollar declined in the late 1970s and then made a strong recovery in the early 1980s, the legacy of the Reagan administration's supply-side economics became more apparent. In the United States, inflation was harnessed and a recovery began in 1983. But this recovery did little to reduce severe unemployment, the awesome federal deficit, or the massive trade deficit. These dire problems came to a head in 1987 when the stock market crash made it clear that the system was fragile. The decline in oil prices and interest rates provided some relief for all nations, but the debt burden of developing nations still remained, and the debtors' time bomb was still ticking.

So the history of international finance has—for the past twenty-five years—been tumultuous. Crises have been built on crises. The key factor in all this has been the role of the U.S. economy and the U.S. dollar as the international standard of value and exchange.

There are serious problems remaining—some perhaps manageable, some not. But, above all, the escalating debt problem must be resolved if the system is to return to normal and a collapse of the system is to be avoided. This, we shall argue in the following chapters, is crucial to everyone's well-being.

Note

1. Manuel Pastor has recently presented similar figures in his excellent article surveying the causes and consequences of capital flight. See "Capital Flight in Latin America," *World Development* 18 (1990), pp. 1–18.

5
The U.S. Debt Crisis

While the Third World's debt problems form one of the three financial crises analyzed in this book, the other two crises center around the U.S. economy. These crises are *internal debt* (debt the U.S. government owes its own citizens due to government borrowing and budget deficits), and *external debt,* as shown by the flow of funds to and from other nations. These problems are made worse by the overall decline of the U.S. economy.

Over the past two decades, the U.S. economy has been troubled by inflation (partly caused by soaring fuel prices), budget and trade deficits, and stagnating growth in production. Moreover, the U.S. banking industry has made itself dangerously vulnerable to problems in the economies of Third World nations whose development attempts it has funded by loans. At the same time, U.S. industry— once the world's leader—has been plagued by both internal problems and foreign competition. To understand all this, let's take a look at two examples of the decline of U.S. economic power: agriculture and high-technology industries.

U.S. Industry: National and International Troubles

Agricultural Overproduction

For many years, the United States has been the breadbasket of the world. Abundant natural resources coupled with the world's highest level of agricultural technology permitted American farmers to produce vast quantities of food, far more than could be consumed. Indeed, one of the major problems facing every administration since World War II has been how to keep farmers from *overproducing.*

Myriad government programs ranging from price supports to surplus food storage programs had done little to stem the rising tide of surplus grains and other agricultural products. One solution, which seemed logical in a world where hunger is a constant for most people, was to encourage agricultural exports. But, as one observer put it, you can't export your problems.

Public Law 480 was enacted in 1954 to allow the government to buy up surplus crops for export. This "Food for Peace" became a pillar of U.S. foreign policy and the primary way of dealing with surplus problems. By the mid-1960s, however, surpluses had accumulated to such an extent that PL 480 exports were not sufficient to eliminate surpluses. Following the lead of PL 480, the Berg Commission of 1966, convened by President Johnson, called for restructuring agricultural production around export crops. Reduction of support prices to meet world market prices meant that farmers would be encouraged to grow more corn, wheat, soybeans, and cotton for export.

The government's orientation toward export crops shows how U.S. agricultural policy was affected by changes outside the domestic economy. During the 1950s, the U.S. was the dominant economic and military power in the world. As the largest producer of agricultural products and the world's banker, the U.S. was in a very good position to take advantage of renewed economic growth abroad. These were boom years for exports of U.S. manufactured goods. Exports of agricultural products in turn helped reduce U.S. grain surpluses.

This was an important role for farm exports to play, because exports relieved pressure on the farm price floor held up by government price supports. But by the beginning of the 1970s, agriculture was playing a second important role: it was the key to keeping the U.S. balance of payments deficit under control. . . .

In response to severe balance of payments deficits generated in part by the skyrocketing value of oil imports, the Nixon administration looked to agriculture to save the day. It was "Food for Crude," as farmers were encouraged to plant "fence row to fence row." Rather than address the root causes of the international trade deficit, successive administrations seized on agriculture (and other exports, such as arms and military equipment) as a quick fix. As a result, farmers were dragged into the chaos of the international trade and financial systems of the 1970s. Since then, any time the dollar rises or falls, farmers' fortunes swing the opposite direction.[1]

And indeed they have. According to the *Economic Report of the People:*

In 11 Midwestern farm states, land values dropped by an average of 17 percent from 1981 to 1984. The decline was 12 percent in 1984, the largest one-year decline since the Depression.

On January 1, 1985, 6 percent of family-sized commercial farms were technically insolvent (ratios of debts to assets were greater than 100), another 7 percent of all farms had debt/asset ratios over 70, and an additional 20 percent had debt/asset ratios between 40 and 70. In total, 33 percent of family-sized commercial farms were in severe financial stress.

Agricultural area bank failures have been running at 10 times the annual rate for the past 30 years. In 1984, agricultural banks accounted for 32 percent of the total of 78 bank failures in the United States, up from 13 percent of total failures in 1983.

Interest on farm liabilities in March 1985 was more than $21 billion, while total farm income averaged only $23 billion in 1983 and 1984.

More than 25 percent of all U.S. cropland, much of it highly productive, is eroding at rates exceeding the soil's regenerative capacity. This erosion rate is greater than 5 tons per acre.

Retail food prices rose by 24 percent from 1980 to the end of 1984. Only 3 percent of the increase went to farmers; the rest went to processors and distributors.

The share of U.S. farm products in the world markets has fallen from a peak of 62 percent in 1979–80 to an estimated 48 percent in 1984–85.

In 1980, the average export price per ton for Argentine wheat was $25 more than the U.S. export price. By March 1985, the Argentine price was about $30 less than the U.S. price.

Wharton Econometrics estimates that the cost of the high dollar to American farmers through loss of export markets was $4.42

billion between January 1983 and February 1985 for just corn, wheat, and soybean producers.[2]

There are two primary reasons for this ironic turn of events. One is that the demand for farm products is inelastic. The other reason is that as U.S. agricultural technology has been exported around the world, total world production has come to exceed world demand by far.

Basic economics tells us that, other things being equal, decreases in the price of a product will cause consumers to buy more of it. This is called *price elasticity.* The important question here, however, is how much more? And more to the point, how will the price change affect the total income (revenues) of the firm or, to be more specific, the farm?

In a free market without government support, as production rises, the prices of agricultural products fall, and the presumption is that farmers could sell more and increase their incomes. Not true. Why? Because the demand for agricultural products is, in general, inelastic—no matter how far food prices fall, people will only buy and eat a certain amount.

When demand is relatively inelastic, it is not responsive to changes in price. A given percentage increase in price will lead to a smaller percentage decrease in quantity purchased, while a given decrease in price will lead to a relatively smaller increase in volume of purchases. The reason behind agriculture's inelastic nature is simple: food is a necessity. If prices go up, you might cut back a little, but you still need to eat. If prices drop, you might binge a bit, but there is only so much food you can eat. So despite changes in price, your food consumption will remain more or less the same. Since the demand for farm products *is* inelastic, the decreases in prices that would accompany removal of agricultural price supports would cause farm incomes to drop precipitously. That is, since the fall in price would not be matched by an increase in quantity demanded, total revenue would fall. The number of farm bankruptcies would skyrocket. The only way out is for farmers to be able to sell more abroad. But if the inelasticity problem is the rock, then this is the hard place.

Two out of every five acres of American farmland are planted for export overseas. But as foreign competitors adopt advanced U.S. agricultural technologies, they are becoming more and more competitive. And in many cases, the United States is importing farm products. In fact, in some months of 1986, U.S. farm imports actually exceeded exports for the first time since the 1950s. U.S. farm exports fell from $44 billion in 1981 to an estimated $27 billion in 1986. If present trends continue, the United States will soon be a net importer of farm products.

Farmers have clamored for greater protection from imports. But as in other industrialized countries, the American agricultural system is among the most protected sectors of the economy. Furthermore, this approach runs counter to the Bush administration's promotion of more open trade policies. Indeed, several developing countries, called the Cairns Group, have joined forces within the GATT (General Agreement on Tariffs and Trade) to try to hold the industrial world to greater openness in agricultural trade.

The amazing and unexpected phenomenon of the United States as a net importer is caused mainly by government price supports that have kept American farm prices higher than world market prices. One of the most dramatic examples comes from—of all places—the Soviet Union. In 1983 the Soviets agreed to annual purchases of at least 4 million metric tons each of corn and wheat. But in 1985 they bought only 2.3 million tons of wheat. Concerned, the Reagan administration put through a subsidy that allows the Soviets to buy wheat selling in the United States for $110 a ton for $85 a ton, a discount of nearly 23 percent. To date, the Soviets haven't bought any at that price because they can still get it cheaper elsewhere—from U.S. allies in Australia, Argentina, and Canada.

So, even if the government completely eliminated farm aid, price supports, loan guarantees, and subsidies of all kinds, it is not likely that the United States would become much more competitive in world markets. Why? Because there would still be overproduction, and because the demand for agricultural products is inelastic. Many people in the debt-constrained Third World don't have the money to purchase food. It is ironic, to say the very least, to find that a world still plagued by famine in many areas also has too many farmers.

U.S. Performance in High-Technology Industries

Another example of declining U.S. economic power can be found in the performance of high-technology industries. The United States' lead in the high-technology sector is being challenged by Japan and by the East Asian newly industrializing countries (NICs). An article in the Spring 1990 issue of *Foreign Affairs* presented these startling facts:

> The United States dominated consumer electronics from Thomas Edison's invention of the phonograph in 1887 through the 1970s. American firms now control less than five percent of this market, despite the fact that sales in consumer electronics tripled over the last decade.
>
> The U.S. share of the color television market fell from 90 percent in 1970 to 10 percent twenty years later.
>
> Despite the fact that two Americans discovered the integrated circuit, in 1986 the Japanese held 65 percent of the memory products market share, with Americans trailing at 30 percent.
>
> Research in an IBM lab in Zurich on superconductors has yet to be commercialized by any American firm; the Japanese have already developed a prototype.[3]

Furthermore, as can be seen in figure 5–1, the United States' share of world exports of microelectronics declined from 21.2 percent in 1980 to 17.2 percent in 1989, while Japan's share rose from 15.2 percent to 25.2 percent. In telecommunications, the U.S. share also falls, from 12.4 percent to 10.7 percent, while the Japanese share nearly triples. The performance of the East Asian NICs is most impressive, expanding from a world market share in telecommunications of 2.6 percent to overtake the United States with 13 percent of world export markets in 1989.

The decline in U.S. global shares is not surprising, however, when we see in figure 5–2 that the United States has not increased spending on research and development as rapidly as has its competitor Japan. As we will see later in this chapter, much of the reason for the decline in research and development and in the competitiveness of U.S. industry overall can be traced to the public and private mountain of debt in the United States. The competitive edge of high-technology industries is being eroded by foreign competition, and the balance of economic power is rapidly shifting. This becomes clearer if we examine the overall U.S. trade position in more detail.

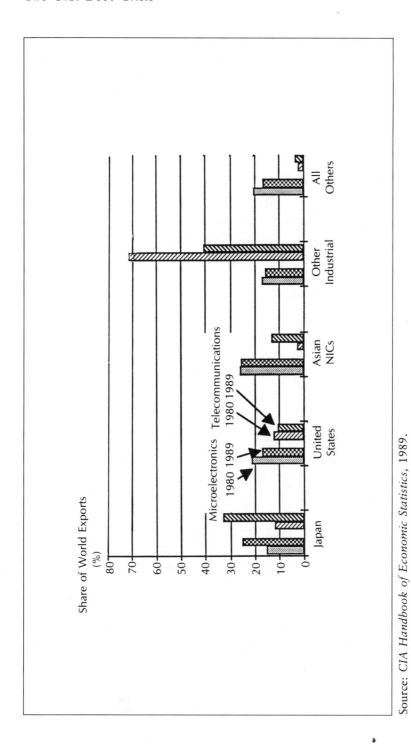

Source: *CIA Handbook of Economic Statistics,* 1989.

Figure 5–1. *Export Shares in Microelectronics and Telecommunications*

Percent of GNP

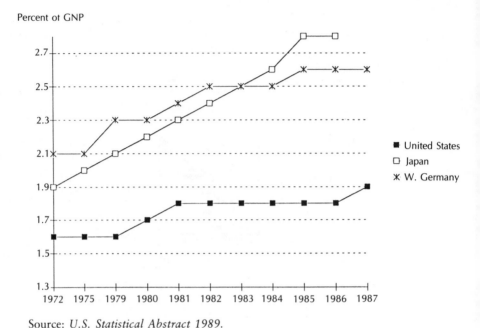

Source: *U.S. Statistical Abstract 1989.*

Figure 5–2. *Nondefense R & D Expenditures*

The U.S. Trade Deficit

From the early 1900s until 1971, the United States maintained a trade surplus. It sold many more goods and services abroad than it bought. As is shown in figure 5–3, some small current account deficits began to occur in the 1970s, but they were mostly due to the higher cost of oil imports. Then, between 1982 and 1984, the bottom dropped out, and the current account deficit plummeted. Figure 5–4 shows how the merchandise trade deficit (which, unlike the current account, does not include trade in services and investment income) marched steadily downward from 1982 through 1987. The balance of world economic power began to shift away from the United States to Japan, Western Europe and, to a lesser extent, to the newly industrialized countries, especially Brazil, South Korea, and Taiwan. As figure 5–5 illustrates, the U.S. share of total exports of the "Big Three" (the United States, West Germany, and Japan) *dropped* from 17.34 percent in 1960 to 12.58 percent in 1989,

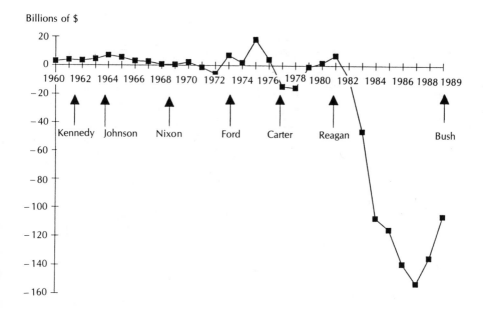

Source: International Monetary Fund, *International Financial Statistics Yearbook 1989* and June 1990.

Note: Remember, the current account equals exports minus imports of goods and services (including income on investments abroad) plus unilateral transfers.

Figure 5–3. *U.S. Current Account Balance, 1960–1989*

while Japan's share grew rapidly. West Germany increased over the period as well.

Tables 5–1 and 5–2 illustrate the changing composition of U.S. international trade over the 1965–89 period. As late as 1975, agricultural products, industrial products, and capital goods exports far outweighed imports in these sectors. Automotive imports were roughly balanced by exports, and agricultural exports were four times petroleum imports. So in the 1970s the United States was largely trading food and industrial products for oil and raw material imports.

Overall, U.S. merchandise exports grew from around $115 billion in 1976 to an estimated $361.9 billion in 1989. But over that decade U.S. imports grew from $124 billion to $475.1 billion. Put differently, 1989 imports exceeded exports by some $113 billion, or 31 percent.

Billions of $

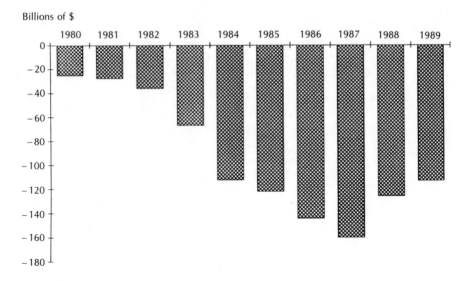

Source: International Monetary Fund, *International Financial Statistics Yearbook 1989* and June 1990.
Note: Remember, merchandise trade is the export minus the import of goods, not including services or investment income.

Figure 5–4. *U.S. Merchandise Trade Deficit, 1980–1989*

By the early 1980s change was rapid. Agricultural exports leveled off, petroleum imports actually declined, but industrial imports exceeded exports by 1985, capital goods imports (mostly machinery) nearly doubled between 1980 and 1985, and automotive imports more than doubled during the same five-year period. This was the end of an era. The United States became a *net importer* of industrial products, with no corresponding increase in agricultural exports to make up the difference. U.S. employment in the manufacturing sector dropped from over 21 million in 1979 to around 18 million in 1985. Roughly 3 million jobs were lost to foreign competition.

A key factor in this strange scenario is that much of the problem is not just a question of good, old-fashioned competition between U.S. and foreign manufacturers. Rather, it is a result of U.S. multinational corporations' shifting their own production facilities abroad to take advantage of lower labor costs and less restrictive environmental protection regulations.

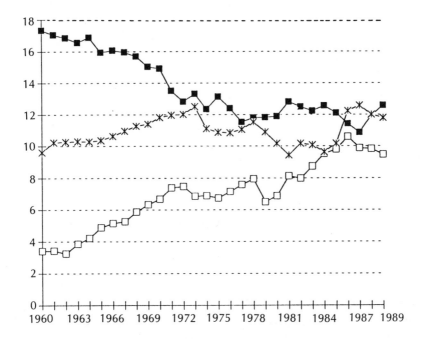

Source: International Monetary Fund, *International Financial Statistics Yearbook 1989* and June 1990.

Figure 5–5. *Major Powers' Share of World Exports, 1960–1989*

Table 5–1
U.S. Merchandise Exports by Product Group, 1965–1989

Year	Total	Agricultural	Industrial	Capital	Automotive	Exports
1965	26.5	6.3	7.6	8.1	1.9	2.6
1970	42.5	7.4	12.3	14.7	3.9	4.3
1975	107.1	22.2	26.7	36.6	10.8	10.7
1980	224.3	42.2	64.9	74.2	17.5	25.4
1985	212.4	29.4	58.3	73.6	22.9	28.3
1989	361.9	41.4	97.8	130.1	34.6	63.4

Source: U.S. Department of Commerce.
Note: Military shipments are excluded. Figures may not add exactly due to rounding.

Table 5–2

U.S. Merchandise Imports by Product Group, 1965–1989

(billions of U.S.$)

Year	Total	Petroleum	Industrial	Capital	Automotive	Other
1965	21.5	2.0	9.1	1.5	0.9	8.0
1970	39.9	2.9	12.3	4.0	5.7	15.0
1975	98.2	27.0	23.6	10.2	12.1	25.3
1980	249.8	79.3	54.0	31.2	27.9	57.4
1985	335.1	50.4	61.2	62.8	65.0	95.7
1989	475.1	50.2	122.4	113.2	86.1	103.2

Source: U.S. Department of Commerce.

Note: Figures may not add exactly due to rounding.

Now the trade deficit takes two forms. First, there are products in which the United States is simply no longer competitive: cameras, stereo components, videocassette recorders, television sets, and the like, which are almost all produced now in other countries. But the more important trend is that many intermediate products are now being produced abroad by U.S. companies and then imported to the United States, thus worsening the trade deficit crisis. This process is called *outsourcing* or *export platforming*.

There are many examples. A *Business Week* study found that 75 percent of some IBM computers are produced abroad.[4] More obvious are finished goods, such as the Dodge Colt, which is produced in Japan by Mitsubishi and imported to the United States by Chrysler. Such goods marketed by U.S. firms accounted for some $13 billion of the $60 billion U.S. trade deficit with Japan in 1985. A U.S. Department of Commerce study concluded that imports of finished products produced abroad *by U.S. firms* accounted for $50 billion of U.S. imports in 1983.[5] That's 19 percent of total U.S. imports, or more than four times the U.S. merchandise trade deficit for that year. So the United States has become a debtor nation, a net importer instead instead of a net exporter, and primarily a producer of services rather than manufactured goods. Meanwhile, problems of inflation, unemployment, and minimal growth of GNP have challenged government economists. The government has taken very different approaches to these woes during the administrations of Jimmy Carter, Ronald Reagan, and George Bush. Although some problems (most notably, inflation) have improved, others remain serious.

Government Efforts

The Carter Years:
Stagflation and the Decline of the Dollar

As we saw in chapter 4, the dollar was in decline from 1977 to 1980. The Carter administration's preoccupation with fighting inflation brought about a change in monetary policy in 1979 when Paul Volcker was appointed chairman of the Federal Reserve. Volcker initiated a tight monetary policy that was designed to attack the viruslike inflation of the period and slowly strengthen the ailing dollar. But the economy responded poorly, as is shown in table 5–3. This eventually caused Jimmy Carter to lose the 1980 election and set the stage for some dramatic economic changes under the stewardship of Ronald Reagan.

In 1979 OPEC took advantage of the growing demand for imported petroleum and the political context of the Iranian revolu-

Table 5–3
U.S. Economic Data, 1977–1981

Year	Current Account (billions)	Trade Deficit (billions)	Real GNP	Inflation[a]	Unemployment	Dollar Index (1973 = 100)
1977	$ – 14.5	$ – 31.0	4.7%	6.8%	7.0%	93.1
1978	– 15.4	– 33.9	5.3	9.0	6.0	84.2
1979	– 0.9	– 27.5	2.5	13.3	5.8	83.2
1980	+ 1.8	– 25.5	– 0.2	12.3	7.1	84.8
1981	+ 6.3	– 29.9	1.9	10.2	7.5	100.8

Source: *Economic Report of the President,* February 1986.
[a]As measured by the consumer price index.

tion to impose once again a major price shock on the international monetary system. The impact on the United States was especially severe because of U.S. reliance on petroleum imports.

Back in 1973 U.S. dependence on imported petroleum represented 34.8 percent of total U.S. petroleum consumption. Despite the 1973–74 OPEC embargo and the eventual quadrupling of oil prices, the U.S. appetite for imported oil grew to 46.5 percent of its petroleum demand by 1977. At this peak level of dependency, the United States was importing a total of 8.5 million barrels a day from all nations.

Even after the implementation of conservation policies by the Carter administration, the United States was, by 1979, still importing just under 8 million barrels of petroleum daily, about half of that from OPEC (see table 5–4). In 1979 the United States was spending $63 billion annually on oil imports. This *increased* to almost $83 billion by 1980, as table 5–5 shows.

The near doubling of oil prices sent the U.S. economy into a

Table 5–4

U.S. Dependence on Petroleum Imports, 1973–1989

(thousands of barrels/day, average annual rate)

Year	Arab OPEC Nations	All OPEC Nations	All Nations
1973	914	2,991	6,025
1974	752	3,277	5,892
1975	1,382	3,599	5,846
1976	2,423	5,063	7,090
1977	3,184	6,190	8,565
1978	2,962	5,747	8,002
1979	3,054	5,633	7,985
1980	2,549	4,293	6,365
1981	1,844	3,315	5,401
1982	852	2,136	4,298
1983	630	1,843	4,312
1984	817	2,037	4,660
1985	470	1,821	4,286
1986	1,160	2,828	5,439
1987	1,272	3,053	5,914
1988	1,837	3,513	6,587
1989	2,210	4,099	7,120

Source: Energy Information Administration, *Monthly Energy Review,* January 1990.

Table 5–5
Cost of U.S. Energy Imports, 1975–1988
(billions of $)

1975	28.325
1976	36.384
1977	47.153
1978	44.763
1979	63.077
1980	82.924
1981	81.360
1982	65.409
1983	57.952
1984	60.980
1985	53.917
1986	37.310
1987	44.220
1988	41.042

Source: Energy Information Administration, *Monthly Energy Review*, January 1990, p. 11.

three-year period of stagflation—simultaneous inflation and recession—which plagued the United States from 1979 through 1981. The oil price increase brought higher interest rates, soaring inflation, declining economic growth, and increasing unemployment. Moreover, the oil import bills of all industrialized nations increased, as did those of the oil-importing developing nations. And OPEC, once again, was faced with the financial challenge of prudently allocating oil revenues for internal development and investing the surplus in European and U.S. banks and government securities.

As a consequence of the higher oil prices, and many other factors such as declining trade, spiraling inflation, compounding past loans, and rising interest rates, the oil-importing developing nations increased their demand for loans from the IMF and now, more importantly, from private commercial banks (including many banks in the United States). The IMF's limited loan capability was not sufficient to meet the avalanche of credit demand. So the private commercial banks stepped in to meet the demand for credit. Flush with petrodollar deposits and facing limited demand for credit in their own countries (because of the prolonged recession), they were only too happy to oblige. With tight U.S. monetary policy, interest rates were at record highs, so bankers faced the pleasant prospect of making extremely profitable loans to developing nations with little risk.

The Reagan Years: Budget Deficits, Trade Deficits, and the Strong Dollar

In January 1981 Ronald Reagan became president. The new policy prescriptions of the Reagan administration were to have far-reaching consequences for the international financial system in general and the debt crisis in particular.

Reagan had campaigned on a platform of supply-side economics. His goals were to reduce taxes and government spending, which, the theory suggested, would generate a burst of economic growth and output sufficient to reduce inflation, decrease unemployment, and balance the budget. In addition, Reaganomics emphasized the continuation of free-floating exchange rates and strongly supported free trade against increasing demands for protectionism.

The supply-side economic program was accompanied by a very tight monetary policy between 1981 and 1983. This policy induced the worst recession since the 1930s and finally broke the back of inflation but only at a very high social and economic price: two years of severe unemployment and declining economic growth, coupled with historically high budget and trade deficits (see table 5–6).

By 1982 the economy began to recover, but by then the seeds had been sown. The high interest rates of this period caused the dollar to recover and become strong once again as foreign investment flowed in. But this was to have far-reaching implications. The strong dollar directly contributed to the U.S. trade deficit because it made U.S. exports more expensive and imports comparatively cheaper. Furthermore, the effects of the overvalued dollar are likely to be long-term in nature. Even as the dollar falls to a more competitive rate, firms that failed when they couldn't sell their dollar-inflated goods abroad won't be able to contribute to redressing the trade balance. Closed firms simply don't export.

But while U.S. exports of manufactured goods had fallen, exports of dollars continued to be high. Banks remained only too happy to loan Third World nations funds they desperately needed to develop economically and improve their standards of living. Unfortunately, these loans brought the banks a vulnerability they hadn't anticipated.

Table 5-6

The Reagan Economic Record, 1981–1989

Year	Growth in Real GNP	Inflation	Unemployment	Budget Deficit (billions)	Trade Deficit (billions)	Dollar Index (1973=100)	Prime Rate
1981	1.9	10.3	7.5	−78.9	−27.9	100.8	18.8
1982	−2.5	6.2	9.5	−127.9	−36.4	111.7	14.8
1983	3.6	3.2	9.5	−207.8	−67.1	117.3	10.8
1984	6.8	4.3	7.4	−185.3	−112.5	128.5	12.0
1985	3.4	3.6	7.1	−212.3	−122.1	132.0	9.9
1986	2.7	1.9	6.9	−221.2	−145.1	103.3	8.3
1987	3.7	3.6	6.1	−149.7	−159.5	90.6	8.21
1988	4.4	4.1	5.4	−155.1	−127.2	88.0	9.32
1989	2.9	4.8	5.2	−152.0	−114.87	94.2	10.87

Source: *Economic Report of the President*, 1990.

Notes: Although President Bush assumed office in 1989, data for that year are included for the lagged effects of Reagan's policies. Inflation is based on changes in the consumer price index. The trade deficit is merchandise trade. The trade balance for 1989 is from *International Financial Statistics*, November 1990. The dollar index is a multilateral trade-weighted value of the U.S. dollar.

The Vulnerability of the U.S. Banking System

What does it matter if U.S. banks are so heavily exposed to Third World debtor nations? It matters because the risks, consequences, and potential costs to the banks and the U.S. economy are of primary importance to the survival of the international financial system.

In a December 1982 presentation before the House Banking, Finance, and Urban Affairs Committee, Mr. Donald Regan, then U.S. treasury secretary, pointed out the disastrous consequences to the Western banking system and the global economy if there were a default by even one of the major borrowers or by a series of the smaller ones. What follows is a telling excerpt from his testimony.

> The American citizen has the right to ask why he or his government needs to be concerned with debt problems abroad. With high unemployment at home, why should we be assisting other countries, rather than, say, reducing taxes or increasing spending domestically? Why should he care what happens to the international financial system?
>
> One way to look at this question is to ask what the implications are for workers in Providence, Pascoag, or Woonsocket if foreign borrowers do not receive sufficient assistance to adjust in an orderly way. What if they are late in making interest payments to banks, or can't pay principal, and loans become nonperforming or are written off as a loss?
>
> If interest payments are more than ninety days late, the banks stop accruing them on their books; they suffer reduced profits and bear the costs of continued funding of the loan. Provisions may have to be made for loss, and as loans are actually written off, the capital of the bank is reduced.
>
> This in turn reduces the banks' capital asset ratio, which forces banks to curtail lending to individual borrowers and lowers the overall total they can lend. The reduction in the amounts banks can lend will impact on the economy. So will the banks' reduced ability to make investments, which in everyday language includes the purchase of municipal bonds which help to finance the operations of the communities where individual Americans work and live. Reduced ability to lend could also raise interest rates.
>
> I want to make very clear, Mr. Chairman, that we are not talking here just about the big money-center banks and the multi-

national corporations. Well over 1,500 U.S. banks, or more than 10 percent of the total number of U.S. banks, have loaned money to Latin America alone. They range in size from over $100 billion in assets to about $100 million. Those banks are located in virtually every state, in virtually every Congressional district, and in virtually every community of any size in the country. Those loans, among other things, financed exports, exports that resulted in jobs, housing and investment being maintained or created throughout the United States.

If the foreign borrowers are not able to service those loans, not only will U.S. banks not be able to continue lending abroad, they will have to severely curtail their lending in the United States. Let me illustrate this point as graphically as I can. A sound, well-run U.S. bank of $10 billion in assets—not all that large today—might have capital of $600 million. It is required by the regulators to maintain the ratio of at least $6 in capital to every $100 in assets. What happens if 10 percent, or $60 million of its capital, is eroded through foreign loan losses? It must contract its lending by $1 billion. Now realistically, the regulators will not force it to contract immediately, but they will force it to restrict its growth until its capital can be rebuilt.

The new result in either event is $1 billion in loans that can't be made in that community—20,000 home mortgages at $50,000 each that can't be financed, or 10,000 lines of credit to local businesses at $100,000 each that can't be extended.

And of course, this reduction in lending will have negative effects on financing of exports, imports, domestic investment, and production in individual cities and states around the United States, be it in shipping, tourist facilities, farming, or manufacturing. The impact will not only be on the banks—it will negatively affect the individual as well as the economic system as a whole. Higher unemployment and a reduction in economic activity, with all they entail for city, state, and federal budgets, would be a further result. None of this is in the interest of the U.S. citizens.[6]

Many U.S. bankers shared these sentiments. In 1983 commercial bankers pulled back and began to reassess their situation. They reduced their new foreign loans and overall debt exposure even further. The beginning of the recovery in 1983 and the decline in inflation and oil prices generated widespread economic optimism. If the major industrial nations could generate economic growth, developing nations could increase their exports and earn the necessary foreign exchange to service their debts without having to borrow large amounts of new money. The decrease in interest rates also provided some debt relief and breathing space for many nations.

From 1983 through 1985 the consensus was that most debtor nations could manage to keep up with their obligations if they would simply discipline themselves while the global recovery continued. The only perceived danger zones were the nations suffering from declining oil revenues because of declining oil prices. The drop in inflation and interest rates, and the recovery itself, were felt by most to be enough for even these countries to manage their debt obligations.

But, as shown in tables 5–7 and 5–8, the U.S. money-center banks were precariously exposed to the Third World debtor countries. In 1984 such loans to just the six most troubled debtor countries represented 179 percent of their primary capital (shareholders' equity). However, this has been reduced somewhat since then. For example, the U.S. banks' exposure to Mexico alone was 33 percent in 1982 at the time of the first crisis, but by 1986 it had been reduced to 23 percent. This, however, is still an unprecedented level of exposure to just one very financially troubled country.

By now it should be clear that the external shocks of two OPEC oil price increases and the tight monetary policy of the United States contributed much to the evolution of the debt crisis. Bankers were willing to provide the loans, but very little has been said about their eagerness to do so. It has been documented that the banking community aggressively pursued and often pushed these loans on developing nations in what was at times almost a frenzied pace and surrealistic atmosphere. The volume of loans generated high profits for the banks. There were promotions and raises for people who obtained and negotiated the loans. Power, prestige, and privilege all seemed to gravitate toward those involved in this dynamic process.

The excitement of making gigantic loans in the billions by coordinating the telex drew even the most reserved bankers into the debt expansion game. In addition, the early 1980s was a period of rapid deregulation of the U.S. banking system. There was little government control over the frantic pace of aggressive lending. To verify this, in his book *The Money Mandarins* (1986) Howard Wachtel shares the story of S.C. Gwynne, a twenty-five-year-old with a mas-

Table 5-7

Exposure of Major U.S. Banks to Six Troubled Developing Countries, March 1984
(billions of $)

	Mexico	Brazil	Venezuela	Philippines	Argentina	Chile	Six-Country Total	Six-Country Total as a Percentage of Shareholders' Equity[a]
Bank of America	$ 2.7	$ 2.5	$1.5	$0.5	$0.3	$0.3	$ 7.8	150.9%
Citicorp	2.9	4.8	1.4	1.2	1.7	0.5	12.5	206.7
Chase Manhattan	1.6	2.7	1.2	0.8	0.5	0.5	7.4	212.7
Manfacturers Hanover	1.9	2.2	1.1	1.3	0.4	0.7	7.8	268.5
Morgan Guaranty	1.2	1.8	0.5	0.8	0.3	0.3	4.9	143.3
Continental Illinois	0.7	0.5	0.4	0.4	0.1	0.3	2.4	129.9
Chemical	1.4	1.3	0.8	0.4	0.4	0.4	4.6	196.7
Bankers Trust	1.3	0.7	0.4	0.3	0.2	0.3	3.3	177.6
First Chicago	0.8	0.7	0.2	0.2	0.2	0.2	2.4	126.9
First Interstate	0.7	0.5	0.1	0.1	0.1	0.1	1.5	70.8
Security Pacific	0.5	0.5	0.1	0.2	0.1	0.1	1.6	88.8
Wells Fargo	0.6	0.5	0.3	0.1	0.1	0.1	1.7	129.8
9 money centers	14.5	17.5	5.9	4.2	3.5	53.2	179.2	

Source: Becker Paribas, *Banking Industry Review*, August 1984; *The Costs of Defaults*, by Anatole Kaletzsky, © 1985, The Twentieth Century Fund, New York.

Note: Shows cross-border risks (loans denominated in dollars). Exposures in most cases are from published company reports; some are estimates based on conversations with bank managements. (Data are as of March 31, 1984. Figures may not add exactly due to rounding.)

[a]Includes common and preferred.

Table 5-8
Exposure of U.S. Banks to Third World Debtors, June 1984

	209 Major Banks		Top 9 Banks		Next 15 Banks		Next 185 Banks	
	Billions	Percentage	Billions	Percentage	Billions	Percentage	Billions	Percentage
Mexico	25.8	30.4	14.3	41.9	5.1	33.0	6.4	18.2
Brazil	24.1	28.5	15.7	46.0	5.0	31.9	3.5	9.9
Korea	12.1	14.2	6.2	18.2	3.2	20.7	2.6	7.5
Venezuela	11.0	12.9	7.6	22.1	2.0	13.1	1.4	3.9
Argentina	8.7	10.3	5.7	16.6	1.9	12.4	1.4	3.9
Chile	6.3	7.5	3.6	10.5	1.3	8.0	1.5	4.1
Philippines	5.3	6.3	3.7	11.0	1.1	6.8	0.5	1.5
Colombia	3.3	4.0	2.3	6.9	0.6	3.3	0.5	1.4
Total	96.6	114.0	59.1	173.3	20.2	129.5	17.8	50.9
Total capital	84.7		34.1		15.6		35.0	

Source:: American Express Economics based on Federal Financial Institutions Examination Council, *Country Exposure Lending Survey*, June 1984; *The Costs of Default*, by Anatole Kaletsky, © 1985, The Twentieth Century Fund, New York.

ter's degree in English and only eighteen months of banking experience. Gwynne describes his experience:

> The world of international banking is now full of aggressive, bright, but hopelessly inexperienced lenders in their mid-twenties. They travel the world like itinerant brushmen, filling loan quotas, peddling financial wares, and living high on the hog. Their bosses are often bright but hopelessly inexperienced twenty-nine-year-old vice presidents with wardrobes from Brooks Brothers, MBA's from Wharton or Stanford, and so little credit training they would have trouble with a simple retail installment loan . . .
>
> As a domestic credit analyst, I was taught to develop reasonable asset security for all loans unless the borrower was of impeccable means and integrity. As an international loan officer, I was taught to forget about that, and instead to develop a set of rationales that would make the home office feel good about the loan, even though, technically, it was unsecured.[7]

Profligate and irresponsible lending by the banks calls into question who should bear the burden of resolving the debt crisis in the Third World. But as will be shown in the next chapter, banks have been able to use their political power to pass much of their share onto developing countries.

The Legacy of the Reagan Era

By the mid-1980s, it was apparent that the United States had lost control of monetary discipline. One leading business magazine called it the "Casino Society"—and the government, corporations, and consumers all hold precariously high stakes. Because the Reagan administration both cut taxes, which caused a fall in revenues, and expanded spending, particularly in the military sector, the federal deficit of the United States took a nosedive in the 1980s. This is shown in figure 5–6, which makes clear that by the mid-1980s the deficit of the U.S. government surpassed $200 billion annually. To put this figure in context, this *yearly* government shortfall is about twice the size of the *total* external debt accumulated *over time* by state and private agents in Mexico.

Because the government must borrow money to finance these

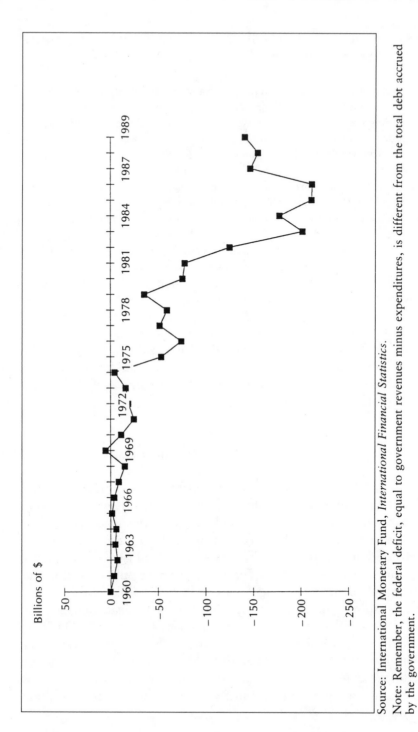

Source: International Monetary Fund, *International Financial Statistics.*
Note: Remember, the federal deficit, equal to government revenues minus expenditures, is different from the total debt accrued by the government.

Figure 5–6. *U.S. Federal Deficit, 1960–1989*

massive deficits, the gross outstanding debt of the United States reached nearly $3 trillion in 1989, as figure 5–7 shows. The total accumulated debt of all Third World nations in 1989 was "only" a third of this.

Beyond the magnitude of the debt, what is most worrisome is its burden: the increase in debt as a percentage of GNP and the effects of servicing it—that is, paying the interest. Debt musts be repaid; in figure 5–8 we can see that by 1989 the federal government owed an amount equivalent to 55 percent of the Gross National Product. To service this debt a higher interest rate had to be offered. For example, in 1989 bond yields in the United States were 8.50 percent; in Japan they were only 5.05 percent. So it's not surprising that Japanese investors wanted to buy U.S. bonds with higher yields, bidding up the dollar in the process. With a stronger dollar, however, U.S. export industries are less competitive, and the U.S. trade deficit suffers. In addition to the effect on exchange rates, deficit-driven high interest rates also affect productivity. As the federal deficit puts upward pressure on interest rates, funds for research and investment become more scarce, compromising the future productivity of the U.S. economy as well. As a percent of GDP the United States is already investing less than Japan and West Germany (see figure 5–9). It is a simple fact that if we don't invest, our productivity will fall and we will all experience a decline in our standard of living.

But the government is not alone in the debt game; corporations and households have also participated. Total corporate debt has risen dramatically in the 1980s, as can be seen in figure 5–10. An increase in corporate debt is not in itself alarming: it makes good business sense to borrow money, invest it, and repay the loan out of enlarged profits. The danger in the ballooning corporate debt of the 1980s, however, is that it largely was not incurred to expand the plant and equipment in the United States. Rather, this debt was taken on in an elaborate game of corporate finance. Firms found that instead of issuing stock to raise funds they could raise capital by selling bonds—the promise to pay interest and principal at some point in time. Since interest is tax-deductible for corporations while dividends on stock are not, firms found it profitable to pay higher interest rates to those willing to hold their bonds. Driving the debt wagon was the desire for cash to engage in takeovers of other firms. Firms also used junk bonds to finance the repurchase of their

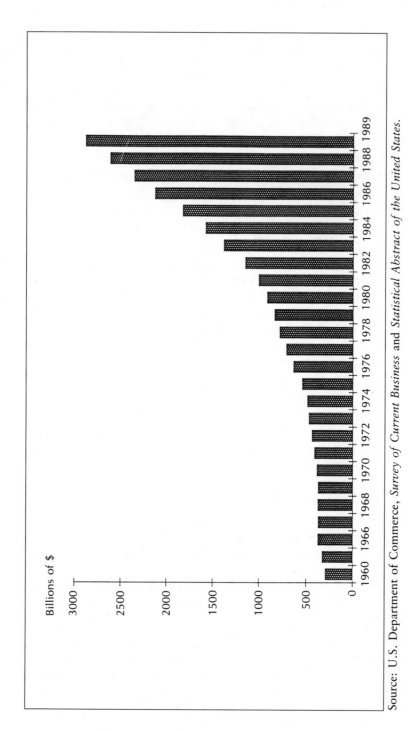

Source: U.S. Department of Commerce, *Survey of Current Business* and *Statistical Abstract of the United States.*

Figure 5–7. *Gross Outstanding Federal Debt of the United States, 1960–1989*

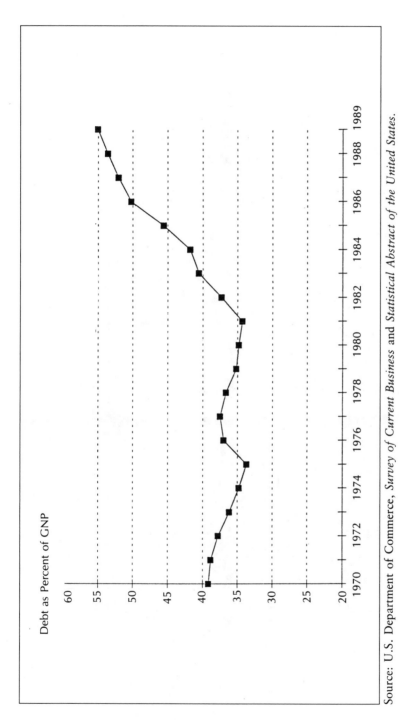

Figure 5–8. U.S. Gross Federal Debt As a Percentage of GNP

Source: U.S. Department of Commerce, *Survey of Current Business* and *Statistical Abstract of the United States.*

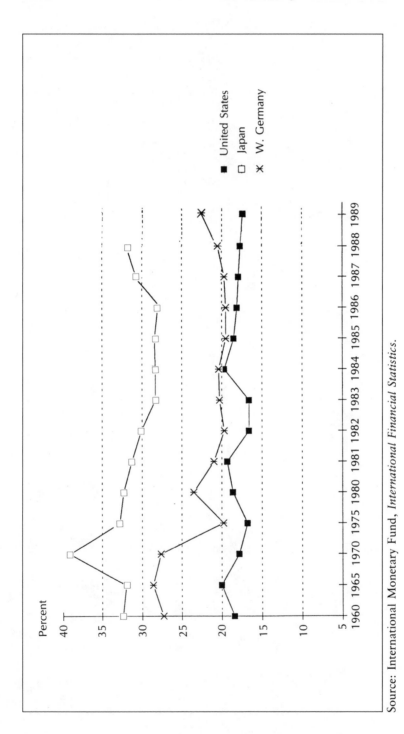

Figure 5-9. *Investment As a Percent of GDP*

Source: International Monetary Fund, *International Financial Statistics.*

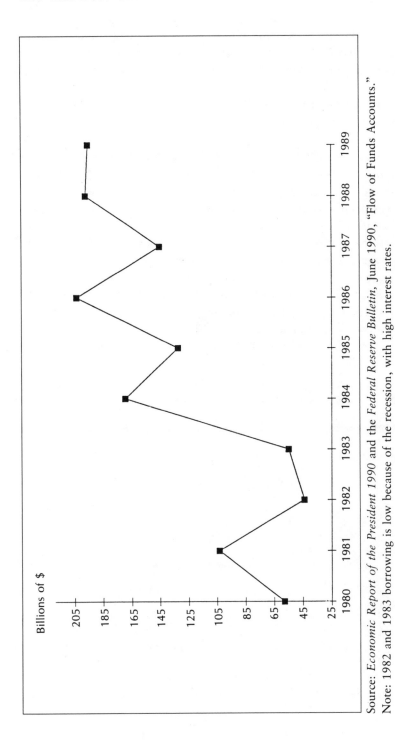

Source: *Economic Report of the President 1990* and the *Federal Reserve Bulletin*, June 1990, "Flow of Funds Accounts."

Note: 1982 and 1983 borrowing is low because of the recession, with high interest rates.

Figure 5–10. *Total Corporate Debt in the United States, 1980–1989*

stock—to take it off the public market in order to protect the firm from a hostile takeover.[8] The upshot of all this financial maneuvering is that corporate America has a huge debt to pay. *The Economist* noted that in the 1950s and 1960s, pretax debt costs to corporations were sixteen cents on every dollar of income; in the 1980s interest service ate fifty-six cents of each dollar of income.[9] In firms throughout the country, subsidiaries are being sold to provide the cash for ballooning interest payments on this debt. Firms have gotten "leaner and meaner"—which mostly means that cutbacks have been made in long-range projects that lack immediate payoffs. Thus, research and development has suffered, and these short-term horizons are likely to constrain competitiveness for years to come.

Corporations won't be the only group pressed to pay the bills in the future: consumer debt has also risen dramatically. As figure 5–11 shows, total household borrowing in the United States burgeoned in the 1980s. According to economist Robert Pollin, some of this is explained by real estate and other speculative investments made by the wealthier in America.[10] However, he argues, the primary cause of household debt accumulation is that the less affluent

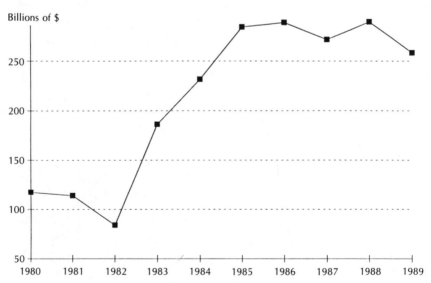

Source: *Economic Report of the President 1990* and the *Federal Reserve Bulletin,* June 1990, "Flow of Funds Accounts."

Figure 5–11. *Total Household Borrowing in the United States*

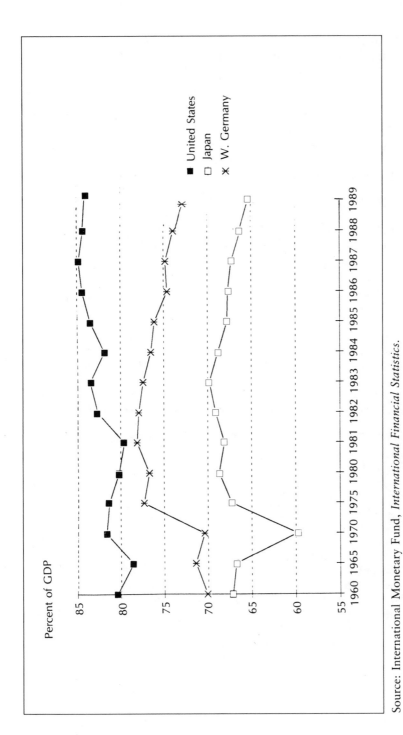

Figure 5–12. *Consumption As a Percent of GDP*

Source: International Monetary Fund, *International Financial Statistics.*

have been borrowing simply to maintain living standards. Pollin shows that despite the entry of women into the labor market, real household income stagnated at 2.6 percent below the 1973 level. Rather than cut back on consumption, households borrowed to keep afloat. As we can see in figure 5–12, in the United States, consumption as a percent of gross domestic product (GDP),[11] rather than declining to adjust to more austere national and international economic conditions, increased over the decade. But with investment declining and productivity likely to fall, the high-paying jobs necessary to pay off the consumer debt won't be easy to find. Just like the Third World nations that we will study in the next chapter, the United States faces in the future lower incomes and continued transfers of money to the rest of the world to pay for having splurged beyond its means.

Notes

1. Center for Popular Economics, *Economic Report of the People* (Boston: South End Press, 1986), chap. 7, "Trouble in Farm Country," pp. 93–114.
2. Ibid.
3. These points are made in B.R. Inman and Daniel F. Burton, Jr., "Technology and Competitiveness: The New Policy Frontier," *Foreign Affairs* 69(Spring 1990).
4. John B. Judis, *In These Times,* July 23, 1986, pp. 7–8.
5. Ibid.
6. Statement of Donald T. Regan, as secretary of the treasury, before the House Banking, Finance, and Urban Affairs Committee, Washington, D.C. (Congressional Record, Dec. 21, 1982).
7. Howard M. Wachtel, *The Money Mandarins* (New York: Pantheon Books, 1986), pp. 107–108.
8. For a clear overview of junk bonds see Tim Wise, "Junk Bond Overdose," *Dollars and Sense,* March 1990.
9. "How to Handcuff a Central Bank," *The Economist,* May 5, 1990.
10. Robert Pollin, "Borrowing More, Buying Less," *Dollars and Sense,* May 1990.
11. Gross national product refers to the income received from all factors of production (such as capital and labor) no matter where they are located in the world. Gross domestic product refers to all income produced within a country, including that generated by nonresidents.

6
The Developing World
Debt Problem

A nyone not living in a cave knows that the international financial system is facing a developing world debt problem of
unprecedented proportions. Third World countries now owe over
$1 trillion to the more industrialized countries. One-third of that is
owed to U.S. banks. If this debt cannot be repaid, the consequences
will be far-reaching and irreversible. A default by even one of the
major debtors would, most likely, cause a panic, a run on the banks,
and a collapse of the international financial system as we know it.

The magnitude of the numbers is staggering. As figure 6–1
shows, the foreign debt of the developing nations increased from
$135.5 billion in 1974 to over $1.2 trillion in 1990. Between 1978
and 1986, total developing world debt has doubled. The growth of
long-term debt for developing nations between 1970 and 1987 was
staggering. Between 1973 and 1980, the average annual increase in
external debt was 21.3 percent.

The debt has now reached the point that many of the developing
nations are having to borrow money just to cover the interest payments on their loans. For example, non–oil-exporting developing
nations paid over $450 billion in interest payments on their foreign
debt between 1978 and 1985. During the same period these nations
borrowed approximately $535 billion. This was happening in a
period when GDP growth rates for developing nations were declining from an average of 5.5 percent in the 1973–80 period to an average of 3 percent during 1980–85, and per capita growth rates (which
include population growth) had decreased from 3.4 percent to 0.9
percent during the same time periods.

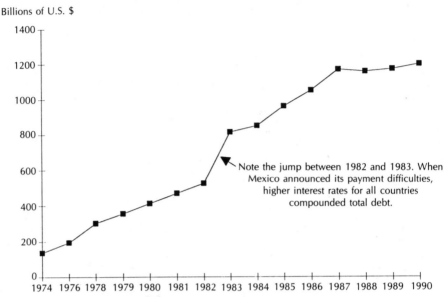

Source: World Bank, *World Debt Tables 1988–89;* data for 1989 and 1990 are estimates.

Figure 6–1. *Total Debt of Developing Nations, 1974–1990*

Other indicators of the severity of this crisis and its impact upon developing nations are the changes in their ratios of debt to Gross National Product (GNP), debt service to exports, and interest payments to GNP. These indicators are summarized in table 6–1. For example, the ratio of debt to GNP nearly tripled from 1974 to 1984, increasing from 13.9 percent in 1974 to 40.8 percent in 1984. Debt service payments, the sum of interest and the portion of principal due, represented 8.5 percent of exports in 1974, but by 1986 represented 28.6 percent of exports. Another way to think about this is that more than one-quarter of export earnings desperately needed for investment were going right back to industrial country banks. In 1974 interest payments were only 0.6 percent of GNP but grew to almost 3.3 percent by 1984.

It should be clear by now that it is possible to parade an endless list of statistics to dramatize the point that the problem exists, it is real, it has great magnitude and scope, and it has very serious consequences for both the developing and the industrialized countries. How and, more importantly, why did this happen?

Table 6–1

Debt Indicators for Developing Countries, 1974–1990

(percentages)

Year	Total Debt/ Export of Goods and Services	Total Debt/ GNP	Total Debt Service/Export of Goods and Services	Interest/ Export of Goods and Services	Interest/ GNP
1974	72.2	13.9	8.5	2.9	.6
1976	92.6	16.4	10.1	4.0	.7
1978	110.4	19.6	15.4	5.3	.9
1979	99.9	19.3	15.8	5.9	1.1
1980	88.6	18.7	13.5	6.2	1.3
1981	93.9	19.8	14.8	7.1	1.5
1982	115	24.1	n/a	n/a	1.9
1983	176.1	39.6	24.0	13.8	3.1
1984	170.7	40.8	24.0	13.7	3.3
1985	198.2	45.6	26.9	14.5	3.3
1986	222.6	48.3	28.6	14.2	3.1
1987	212.4	49.8	26.4	11.7	2.7
1988	193.8	46.5	27.1	13.0	3.1
1989	177.7	43.4	22.4	11.7	2.9
1990	167.3	41.7	22.0	11.6	2.9

Source: World Bank, *World Debt Tables 1988–89.* The data for 1988 are estimated and 1989–90 are projected.

Causes and Origins of the Debt Crisis

There are many competing explanations of the origins and causes of the debt crisis. Some argue that it evolved as a result of poor economic policies and fiscal irresponsibility on the part of developing nations. Others focus on the external shocks of the 1970s as the principal cause, and still others emphasize the inherent instability of unregulated international capital markets. Although everyone has his or her own analysis, ours is that the cause is a combination of all these factors.

However, the fundamental problem is that the simple mechanics of the lending process demonstrate that any situation that involves a regular annual amount of borrowing and a conventional repayment schedule will soon lead to a situation in which the debt servicing (the interest and the amortization) will exceed the annual amount of new loans. This process will soon lead to a reverse capital flow (a flow of capital from the capital-poor to the capital-rich), which,

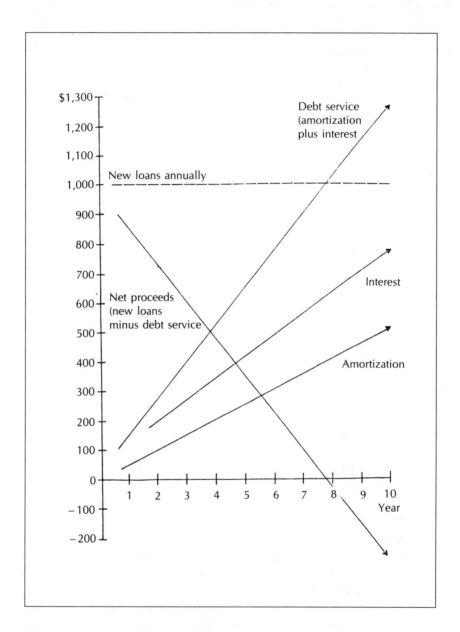

Source: *Monthly Review*, April 1985.
Net capital flow if $1,000 is borrowed each year at ten percent interest for twenty years.

Figure 6–2. *The Debt Trap*

of course, is the opposite of what one would presume to be the desired effect.

This process is shown in figure 6–2, which is a hypothetical example. Assume that a country obtains each year a new foreign loan of $1,000 to be repaid in equal installments over twenty years plus 10 percent interest on the outstanding balance. The net result is a downward trend of net proceeds (the amount left over after paying the accumulated debt service, which gets larger and larger—through paying interest on interest—making net proceeds smaller and smaller). By the eighth year, the borrowing of an additional $1,000 is insufficient even to meet the obligations on the past debt, so a reverse flow of funds back to the lending country begins, unless the rate of new borrowing is increased. Let us now turn to consider how this hypothetical example worked out in practice.

A Chronology of the Debt Crisis

Stage I: OPEC and Petrodollar Recycling, 1973–1978

Almost all analysts agree that the OPEC oil embargo and the consequent quadrupling of oil prices between 1973 and 1974 represents the first stage in the debt crisis. Non–oil-exporting developing nations had a current deficit of only $11 billion in 1973. After the oil price shock, this deficit leaped to $37 billion in 1974 and to $46 billion in 1975. Non–oil-exporting developing nations saw their oil costs soar from 6 percent of total spending in 1973 to 21 percent by 1981. This extra cost from the oil price increase alone added $260 billion to their total spending between 1973 and 1982. If interest on money borrowed to pay for the oil imports were added to this figure, it would be $335 billion.

As we saw in the previous chapter, this was a period of recycling petrodollars from OPEC nations to European and U.S. financial institutions. The price increase induced a recession and generated inflationary pressures. The recession spread throughout the major Western nations and ultimately brought about a decline in demand for developing nations' exports. Unable to earn sufficient export revenues and facing escalating oil bills, the non–oil-exporting developing nations had to go to the IMF and commercial banks to borrow money in order to settle their deteriorating balance of payments position. Given the overall demand for credit, they were indeed fortunate that the *real interest rate* was low or negative for much of the 1970s.[1]

The historic chronic balance of payments problem of developing nations was now compounded by an emerging layer of foreign debt. This in turn placed greater and greater pressure upon the IMF and later the private commercial banks to provide the additional loans necessary for them to service their debt and resolve their continuing balance of payments difficulties.

Stage II: OPEC's Price Increase
and U.S. Monetary Policy, 1979–1982

The second stage of the debt crisis began in 1979 when OPEC doubled oil prices and President Carter appointed Paul Volcker as chairman of the Federal Reserve Bank. These two seemingly unrelated events were to trigger a major expansion of the debt crisis.

Along with the second major OPEC price increase came another phase of petrodollar recycling. By 1979 OPEC petrodollar deposits totaled $62 billion and increased to $100 billion in 1980. The commercial banks, once again flush with petrodollars, were now able—and quite willing—to make even more sizable and very profitable loans to developing nations. The private commercial banks made loans to non–oil-exporting developing nations to help them pay for their oil imports. At the same time, they made sizable loans to oil-exporting developing nations, such as Mexico, so that they could more rapidly develop their petroleum sectors and diversify their economies. These megaloans were very profitable for the banks.

But the timing of the OPEC price increase, the second stage of recycling of petrodollars, and the need for most new loans to come from private commercial banks in lieu of the IMF (which was by then short on capital) placed the borrowing nations in an even more precarious position. The reasons are complex.

As can be seen in table 6–2, for the United States 1979 was a year of sluggish economic growth (only 2.5 percent) and high inflation (13.3 percent). Federal Reserve chairman Volcker's strategy for fighting inflation was to maintain a tight monetary policy as long as necessary to bring inflation down. This is observable in the movements of key monetary indicators for the period 1979–82 (see table

6–2). The rate of growth of the U.S. money supply was reduced dramatically, and interest rates increased to record highs. By 1983 this policy worked: it reduced inflation from 1979's horrendous 13.3 percent level to 3.6 percent. However, this success came at the expense of a deep recession that resulted in unemployment rates that averaged 9.5 percent in both 1982 and 1983. As a consequence of contractionary monetary policy, interest rates soared. The prime rate hit 18.8 percent in 1981. Since these high interest rates came at a time when inflation was beginning to abate, one result was higher real interest rates for borrowers including those in the Third World. This was good news for bankers because their real earnings were now higher, but it was the beginning of the end for the debtor nations. The higher interest rates drove the value of the dollar higher because investors bought high-yielding U.S. bonds. The stronger dollar made it more difficult for the indebted developing nations to service their debt burdens since they now needed even larger revenues from export earnings to pay their predominantly dollar-denominated debts.

For the United States the strong dollar was a mixed blessing. On one hand it stimulated the purchase of imports and made U.S. exports less competitive, driving up the already large trade deficit shown in table 6–2. But the higher interest rates attracted foreign investment capital to the United States. Facing rapidly growing annual budget deficits and a soaring public debt, American fiscal authorities were pleased that foreign capital was flowing to the country and helping to finance its increasing internal deficits. Little did anyone realize that the United States was, even then, on the way to becoming the largest debtor nation in the world.

Thus, the 1979–82 period was characterized by increasing oil prices, increasing real interest rates, a strong dollar, and a declining demand for exports from the Third World. Each of these factors contributed to the debt expansion in this stage of the evolution of the crisis.

In retrospect, it is now clear that tight, anti-inflationary U.S. monetary policy worsened the debt-expansion cycle. Moreover, the emergence of private commercial banks as the primary source of international lending was also notable. One result of this was more borrowing of short-term money at variable interest rates.[2]

Private debt as a percentage of total debt increased from 50.9

Table 6–2
U.S. Economic Data, 1973–1990

Year	Real GNP (% change)	Unemployment (%)	Inflation (%) (CPI)	Budget Deficit (in Billions U.S. $)	Merchandise Trade Balance (in Billions U.S. $)	Dollar Index (Real trade-weighted)	Change in M1 (%)	Average Prime Rate (%)	Average Discount Rate (%)	Average Federal Funds Rate (%)
1973	5.2	4.9	8.8	−14.8	0.9	98.8	5.5	8	6.40	8.70
1974	−0.5	5.6	12.2	−4.6	−5.5	99.2	5.4	10.8	7.8	10.5
1975	−1.3	8.5	7	−45.1	8.9	93.9	4.9	7.8	6.3	5.8
1976	4.9	7.7	4.8	−66.4	−9.4	97.3	6.6	6.8	5.5	5
1977	4.7	7	6.8	−44.9	−31.1	93.1	8.1	6.8	5.5	5.5
1978	5.3	6	9	−48.8	−34	84.2	8.3	9	7.5	7.9
1979	2.5	5.8	13.3	−27.6	−27.5	83.2	7.2	12.6	10.3	11.2
1980	−0.2	7.1	12.3	−59.5	−25.5	84.8	6.6	15.2	11.8	13.4
1981	1.9	7.5	10.2	−57.9	−27.9	100.8	6.5	18.8	13.4	16.4
1982	−2.5	9.5	6	−110.6	−36.4	111.7	8.8	14.8	11	12.3
1983	3.5	9.5	3.6	−195.4	−67.2	117.3	9.8	10.8	8.5	9
1984	6.8	7.7	3.5	−183.6	−114.1	128.5	5.8	12	8.8	10.2
1985	3.4	7.1	3.6	−212.3	−122.1	132	11.9	9.9	7.7	8.1
1986	2.7	7	1.1	−221.2	−145.0	103.3	8.2	8.33	6.33	6.81
1987	3.7	6.2	4.4	−149.7	−159.5	90.6	8.4	8.22	5.66	6.66
1988	4.4	5.8	4.4	−155.1	−127.2	88	9.6	9.32	6.2	7.57
1989	2.9[a]	5.4	4.6	−152.0	n/a	94.2	3.3	10.87	6.93	9.21
1990	n/a	n/a	n/a	−123.8[a]	n/a	n/a	n/a	n/a	n/a	n/a

Source: *Economic Report of the President,* January 1989 and 1990.
[a] Preliminary estimates.

percent in 1970 to 64.6 percent in 1982, and the debt service ratio (export earnings as a percentage of interest and principal payments in a given year) increased from 14.7 percent in 1970 to 20.5 percent in 1982. The major factor here is the changing role of private banks. Their large-scale involvement in meeting the credit needs of Third World nations had now placed them in a new and unexpectedly vulnerable position in the international monetary system. But it was not until Mexico's near economic collapse in 1982 that the Western governments and bankers realized that there was in fact a large-scale debt crisis that transcended the case of Mexico to include numerous other Third World nations.

As we will discuss in the next chapter, Mexico was rescued from the 1982 crisis. This rescue effort—along with the accumulated experience of rescheduling debt—gave governments and bankers valuable on-the-job training. It was also a signal to the international financial community that everybody needed to reassess their roles and positions in the debt game. After 1982 the banks reduced the rate of new loans and improved their capital position by reducing their *loan exposure abroad*.[3] This was wise, since as the percentage of potentially nonperforming loans increases in comparison to its capital, the bank becomes increasingly vulnerable should the debt not be repaid in full or repudiated—that is, not paid at all. Recall, for example, our discussion of the vulnerability of the U.S. banking system in chapter 5.

Stage III: Shortsightedness and Muddling Through, 1983–1989

While the banks were adjusting their loan exposure to the Third World, the developing countries were learning to live with a virtual standstill in new lending. From 1983 to 1986 there was some feeling that the situation would improve as a result of lower world interest rates and the reduced exposure of industrial country banks. Such debtor countries as Argentina and Brazil had successfully instituted new growth-oriented economic programs and were beginning to meet some of their debt obligations. However, although an immediate crisis was averted, Third World debt has proved to be an intractable problem for sustainable, long-run development.

Of immediate concern to policymakers in both Argentina and Brazil were extraordinary high inflation rates. In 1984 annual price

Reprinted by permission: Tribune Media Services.

inflation in Argentina was approximately 700 percent; Brazil's reached 300 percent. Though there are a variety of sources of inflation in a developing country economy, such as wage push or supply bottlenecks, the debt crisis compounded them in at least two ways. Unable to borrow abroad after the Mexican crisis, the countries took to printing money to finance overblown government budgets. In addition, to promote exports to earn dollars in order to meet their debt service obligations, they devalued their exchange rates regularly. But when you devalue to make your exports cheaper, imports become more expensive, pressuring the general price level up.

Both Argentina's and Brazil's new programs were unique. Each nation created a new currency (in Argentina the *austral,* and in Brazil the *cruzado*), and used wage and price controls to harness their rapid rates of inflation and more evenly distribute the costs and consequences of economic adjustment. In addition, the decline in interest rates and oil prices eased the pressures on each nation, as did the global economic recovery. After major devaluations, both nations' export sectors boomed, and so did their economic growth rates. Most notable was Brazil under the democratic leadership of President José Sarney. It registered real GNP growth rates of 8.4 percent in 1985 and an estimated 7 percent for 1986, and in 1985 it generated a trade surplus of $13 billion, while reducing its inflation rate from 225 percent in 1985 to just 80 percent in 1986.

Yet in spite of this incredible turnaround of the economy, permanent gains have yet to be realized. Ultimately the cruzado and austral plans collapsed. In Brazil, since prices were fixed after workers were given a boost in wages, consumers went on a buying spree—until producers were unwilling to supply at unprofitable prices and consumer imports pressured the balance of payments. Domestic fiscal adjustment did not take place, and international debt service was suspended.

By 1989 inflation reached 3,400 percent a year in Argentina and about 1,300 percent in Brazil. As soon as families received their paychecks at the beginning of the month, they rushed to the supermarket to purchase staple goods, since more than 50 percent of the value of their wages would be eroded by the end of the month. With money losing value so quickly, a joke went around in hyperinflationary Latin American countries that it is cheaper to travel by taxi than by bus—on the bus you pay on the way in; in a taxi, on the way out. In March 1990 the newly elected government of Fernando Collor de Melo imposed a radical shock plan on the Brazilian economy to contain inflation. One aspect of this program was to freeze all assets in excess of U.S. $2,000. Whether the package has the credibility over time to reverse inflationary expectations is closely tied to a resolution of the country's external debt problem. But it is politically difficult to make payments to foreigners when a decade of economic shocks have left the nation impoverished.

Attempts at Managing the Debt

The International Response to the Third World Debt Crisis

The response to the debt crisis by the international financial community—commercial banks, multilateral organizations such as the World Bank, the IMF, and industrial country governments—can be broken down roughly into three stages: austerity, adjustment with growth, and debt reduction. Immediately following the realization in 1982 that countries such as Mexico could not service their debt, the primary international actor in country adjustment became the International Monetary Fund. If a country found itself unable to meet its scheduled interest and principal payments, the lender of last resort was the IMF. But there was a price to pay at the IMF window: very strict belt tightening in the economy. In exchange for new funds and the rescheduling of commercial bank loans, developing countries had to sign a letter of intent stipulating certain conditions. This "conditionality," as we saw earlier, generally included a sharp decline in the rate of growth of the money supply to rein in inflation, paring down government spending to reduce domestic deficits, selling off state-owned enterprises on the assumption that private concerns are more efficient, reducing wages to cut the cost of production, and devaluing the currency to promote exports. Thus, IMF packages were broadly designed to cut the consumption of goods and services by consumers and governments, releasing the surplus for exports to earn dollars to service external debts.

For most countries, however, the recession created by the cut in the money supply and the decrease in government spending was politically insupportable. Social unrest erupted throughout the debtor countries as poor people, already on the margin of existence, could not have their consumption depressed further. New investment in developing countries slowed dramatically. The plan, in practice, was unworkable. Economies in recession did not produce enough new goods and investment for exports. And, paradoxically, those who were capable of generating a surplus were caught in a web of protectionist measures imposed by industrial countries that were experiencing their own recessions.

In October 1985 then secretary of the treasury James Baker introduced a plan that recognized that developing countries must be able to grow if they are to meet their international obligations. This program of "adjustment with growth" included an expansion of international lending, $9 billion to come from the World Bank and $20 billion to follow in new lending from commercial banks. Conditionality similar to that of the IMF programs would also be imposed.

Although the realization that developing countries had to grow to generate a surplus was very important, the mechanism of new lending was ill-conceived. Commercial banks saw no reason to pour more money into debtor nations. For the countries themselves, the amount projected was too small—indeed, the $29 billion, if given only to Brazil, wouldn't have matched even a third of that country's debt.

While the Baker plan was virtually declared stillborn, the international financial market continued to muddle through, providing a few innovative mechanisms to reduce debt. A secondary market for debt emerged, in which banks could buy and sell debt obligations at a discount. For example, if speculators thought that Peru might see a turnaround in the future, they could buy Peruvian debt at twenty cents on the dollar of book value. Ironically, developing countries used such secondary markets to buy back their own debt at huge discounts. If Argentine debt is selling at 10 percent of face value, the government can pay only ten cents to retire each dollar of outstanding debt. Indeed, in 1989 the Philippines retired $1.3 billion of loans at a 50 percent discount.[4]

Much attention has also been given to debt equity swaps, particularly in Chile. The idea is interesting and has been used with some success. Let's say a U.S. multinational corporation wants to open a factory in Santiago. It can go to the secondary market and purchase Chilean government debt at fifty cents on the dollar. In turn, the Chilean government pays the multinational pesos to build the factory for the full (or discounted) amount of the obligation. Everyone seemingly wins. The corporation gets cheap funds to buy local supplies and pay wages, the government retires outstanding debt (and no longer has to pay interest on it), and the country gains jobs and potential exports. Indeed, in Chile approximately 10 percent of the national external debt has been retired using such a scheme.

There have been other variations on the debt for equity swaps, including "debt for nature" exchanges. International environmental organizations have used secondary market discounts to purchase huge tracts of rain forest to be maintained as preserves. Such schemes, however imaginative, are not costless. The process can be inflationary if new money is printed to pay the investing corporation, and some nations worry about an influx of foreign ownership. Furthermore, the allure of discounted funds doesn't work in every country. Even at steep discounts most multinational corporations are not interested in setting up operations in destitute or unstable countries.

The Brady Plan

A critical lesson of these market-oriented approaches is that a reduction of the face value of the dollar-denominated debt had to take place. Financial markets recognized that most developing countries cannot export enough to garner the hard currency to pay dollar-denominated debt. The international financial community recognized this in March 1989 with the announcement of a new initiative by Treasury Secretary Nicholas Brady calling for debt reduction. The concept of officially recognized debt reduction constitutes a radical break from prior rhetoric. In exchange for voluntarily reducing the outstanding value of loans, banks would receive, via a multilateral agency such as the World Bank or the IMF, a guarantee on the remaining portion of the debt. Thus, banks could trade off bad debts with little likelihood of repayment for guaranteed debt, absorbing themselves the reduced value of their assets. Like the earlier plans, however, the plan also includes austerity measures to be taken by developing countries. Despite the important recognition of the need for debt reduction, the Brady Plan is a far cry from resolving the Third World debt problem. The magnitude of the problem has had far-reaching economic effects, and debt reduction without growth-oriented measures will leave many developing countries where they are—stagnating and poor.

The Impact of the Debt Crisis

The debt crisis has brought many changes to the international monetary system. But the most critical effect of all has been the historic transfer of resources *from* debt-plagued developing nations *to* the advanced industrial nations. For the process of genuine economic development to occur, it is necessary for a developing nation to have capital resources for investment. If a country does not have sufficient domestic savings and investment, it is necessary to fill this gap if progress is to occur. Historically, this has been achieved through grants, aid, loans, and direct private foreign investment from multinational firms. But loans must be repaid, and foreign investment will earn a profit. Eventually, as we stated at the beginning of this chapter, this will create a capital *outflow* as a direct function of the development process.

What is crucial is that a nation wisely use its external capital inflows to develop its economy productively. In order to progress, a developing country must generate sufficient growth to pay for the costs of capital resources, *and* have enough economic surplus left to reinvest in its domestic economy and provide for the social and economic needs of its population.

If the vast majority of its economic surplus is used to service loans and pay profits to foreign capital, then there will be little left for domestic uses. The chronic balance of payments problem, worsened by the debt crisis, has placed a squeeze on most developing nations' scarce resources. As larger proportions of these resources are used for debt service, these nations' internal development needs and priorities suffer and are neglected at high political costs. In the 1980s we reached a historic transition with respect to the process, direction, and magnitude of capital resource transfers from developing to advanced nations.

The Resource Transfer Flow

There are several ways of measuring the reverse transfer stream of resources from the developing world back to industrialized countries. This trend has been analyzed in detail by Harold Lever and Christopher Huhne in their book *Debt and Danger* (1985).[5] Lever and Huhne define the resource flow as the current account deficit plus net investment income, including interest. In the development process it is not unusual for a growing country to have a current account deficit since machines and other capital goods are necessary for investment and growth. The current account deficit is then a measure of the additional resources coming into the country. Net investment income, including interest, shows the financial cost of present and past investments by foreigners—that is, the price for having imported needed investment goods. Together the current account deficit and net investment income indicate the direction and magnitude of resource flows in the international economy. Lever and Huhne determined that although there was a small net flow of capital from the industrial countries to the developing countries up until 1983, the trend reversed in 1984 when $29.3 billion flowed *back to* the more developed nations. From table 6–3 and figure 6–3 we can see that the resource flow for all indebted developing nations

Table 6-3

Resource Flow to and from Debtor Countries, 1978–1991

(Billions of U.S. $)

	1978	1979	1980	1981	1982	1983	1984	1985	1986	1987	1988	1989	1990	1991
Net debtor countries:														
Current account deficit	56.8	61.7	77	112.6	106.1	56.8	31.1	34.7	49.2	15.6	20.3	31.2	36.4	38.9
Net investment income including interest	−14.7	−21.1	−30.3	−44.2	−50	−52.9	−60.4	−60.8	−60.9	−62	−66	−71	−66.3	−67.8
Resource flow	42.1	40.6	46.7	68.4	56.1	3.9	−29.3	−26.1	−11.7	−46.4	−45.7	−39.8	−29.9	−28.9
Exports	235.7	310.7	402.5	412.9	375.7	375.1	413.7	408	392.8	476.8	555.4	615.8	663.4	727.5
Resource flow/exports	17.86	13.07	11.60	16.57	14.93	1.04	−7.08	−6.40	−2.98	−9.73	−8.23	−6.46	−4.51	−3.97
Fifteen heavily indebted countries:														
Current account deficit	24.7	24.5	28.7	50	50.8	15.3	1.5	0.2	17.2	9.1	9	10.7	13.3	15.4
Net investment income including interest	−8.3	−12.1	−17.3	−26.2	−35.9	−35.4	−38.6	−37.3	−33.7	−32.5	−35.4	−39.5	−35.2	−36.3
Resource flow	16.4	12.4	11.4	23.8	15.4	−19.4	−36.7	−36.3	−15.9	−22.8	−25.5	−27.9	−20.9	−20
Exports	69.1	94.8	128	127.3	112.5	111.3	123.2	119.3	100	113.8	128.6	139.8	146.4	161
Resource flow/exports	23.73	13.08	8.91	18.70	13.69	−17.43	−29.79	−30.43	−15.90	−20.04	−19.83	−19.96	−14.28	−12.42

Source: *IMF World Economic Outlook*, May 1990 and April 1986.

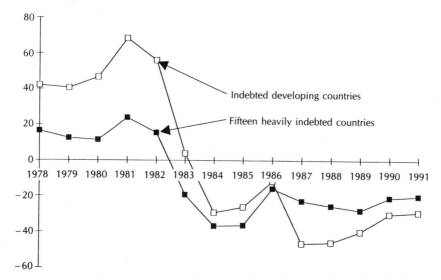

Source: *IMF World Economic Outlook,* May 1990 and April 1986; 1979–82 data for indebted countries from Harold Lever and Christopher Huhne, *Debt and Danger* (New York: Atlantic Monthly Press, 1985), table 3.

Note: Resource flow = current account deficit minus net investment income including interest.

Figure 6–3. *Resource Flow to and from Indebted Developing Countries, 1978–1991*

went from a positive $68.4 billion in 1981, to $3.9 billion in 1983, to a *negative* $29.3 billion in 1984. This was followed by a negative resource flow of $26.1 billion in 1985 to $46.4 billion in 1987. As figure 6–4 shows, on average from 1984 to 1990 this negative resource flow was 6.48 percent of indebted developing countries' exports. Thus, instead of importing capital critical to growth, developing countries are exporting needed resources back to industrial countries.

Two other measures of the reverse flow of resources from the third to the first world are the concepts of *net flows* and *net transfers* used by the World Bank (see figure 6–5). *Net flows* captures the change in debt stock in a year. From annual disbursements (the drawing on a multiyear loan commitments to a country), net flows subtracts amortization, the payment of principal on loans. Thus net

Percent of exports

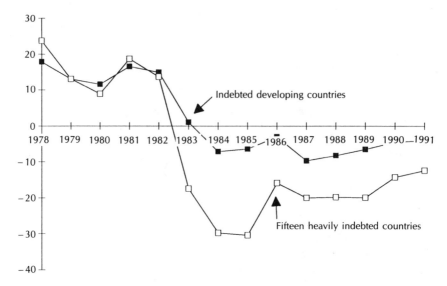

Source: *IMF World Outlook,* May 1990 and April 1986; 1979–82 data for indebted countries from Harold Lever and Christopher Huhne, *Debt and Danger* (New York: Atlantic Monthly Press, 1985), table 3.

Figure 6–4. *Resource Flow As a Percent of Exports*

flows describes whether developing countries are receiving much new lending compared with their repayments on past loans. *Net transfers* subtracts interest payments from net flows. Another way of defining net transfers is to take disbursement of debt and subtract the principal and interest payments that constitute debt service. As figure 6–6 shows, net flows of debt to developing countries declines dramatically after the debt crisis explodes in 1982. While in 1981 flows to developing countries were more than $80 billion a year, by 1988 they were barely $20 billion. Because the flow of net lending had slowed to a trickle, when we subtract interest payments we see that net transfers become negative in 1983. By 1989 developing countries were sending $51.6 billion a year back to the industrialized world. From 1982 through 1989 debt service payments of interest plus principal by debt-burdened countries equaled 133.7 percent of the total debt stock in 1982. The interest and principal payments of

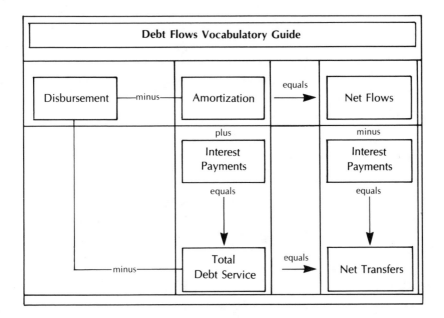

Source: Adapted from the World Debt Tables 1990.

Figure 6–5. *Debt Flows Vocabulary Guide*

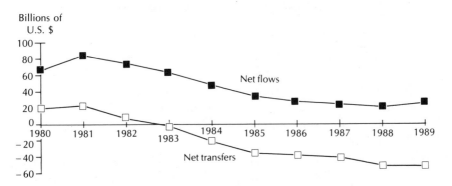

Source: World Bank, *World Debt Tables 1989–90*, vol. 1.
Note: Net flows (disbursements minus principal payments) minus net transfers equals interest.

Figure 6–6. *Net Flows and Net Transfers, All Developing Countries, 1980–1989*

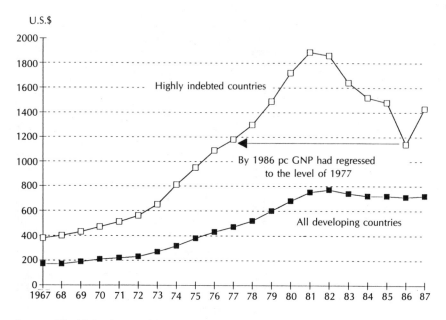

Source: World Bank, *World Debt Tables 1988–89*.

Figure 6–7. *Per Capita GNP in the Developing World, 1967–1987*

these countries averaged 35.24 percent of their exports each year from 1982 through 1989. That is to say, over one-third of their earnings from exports, which could have been invested for growth, were transferred back to the industrialized countries.

The costs of the debt crisis and the reverse transfer of wealth are visible throughout the developing world. After the explosion of the crisis in 1982, per capita growth in Gross National Product ground to a halt in the developing world. As can be seen in figure 6–7, the highly indebted countries suffered a radical decline in living standards. From 1983 to 1986 per capita GNP fell, on average 11.2 percent a year. Thus, in contrast with the healthy average annual improvement in per capita GNP of 12.25 percent a year prior to the debt crisis, people were becoming worse off as each year passed. One of the countries that suffered most was Argentina, where inflation-adjusted per capita GDP was $2,862 in 1988—down from $3,359 in 1980. From figures 6–8 and 6–9 we can see that a key factor in the decline of growth was the fall in per capita investment and in the

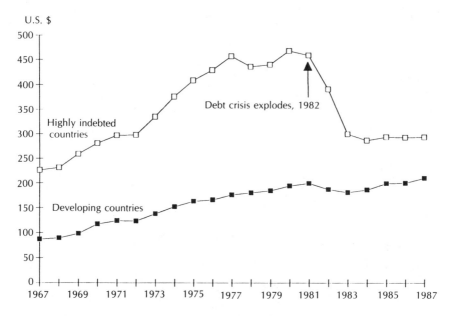

Source: World Bank, *World Debt Tables 1988–89.*

Figure 6–8. *Gross Domestic Investment Per Capita, 1967–1987*

value of imports. For a country to grow it must invest—but the finances for investment were flowing out of the developing world. The drop in per capita gross investment was most startling, falling from a high of $468 per person in 1980 to $287 in 1984. By 1987 investment had only recovered to the 1971 level. Much of the machinery critical for investment in the Third World must be imported. From figure 6–9 we can see that in order to promote a surplus in the balance of payments to service debt, developing countries suppressed imports. In contrast to the rapid growth of imports in the 1970s, imports fell and then flattened out in the 1980s. Developing countries will be paying for this decade of lost development for years to come. Throughout the Third World, infrastructure is in disrepair; schools are running triple sessions daily, open without adequate books or writing supplies; and firms are forced to make do with antiquated machinery.

Another victim of the debt crisis has been the environment. Pressured to export to service debt, countries such as Brazil introduced

Billions of U.S. $

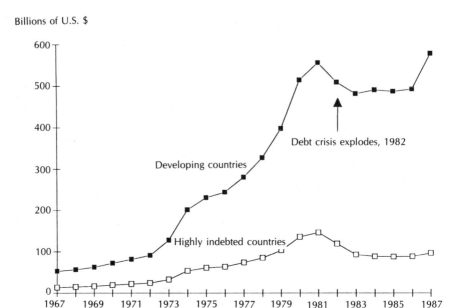

Source: World Bank, *World Debt Tables 1988–89*.

Figure 6–9. *Value of Merchandise Imports, 1967–1987*

incentives in the 1970s and early 1980s for industries such as timber, resulting in deforestation. Little attention has been paid to externalities such as industrial pollution in the drive to earn dollars to service debt. For example, Cubitão, a city in the state of São Paulo, was designated the most polluted city in the world. In one week three babies were born without fully developed brains because of the toxins the mothers breathed. Although Cubitão has tried to reduce emissions, in practice it is difficult to impose additional pollution control costs on firms when the country so desperately needs the export earnings to service debt. Even in the domestic sector, the environment has suffered. When countries have been forced to live under austere state cutbacks, funding for the environment seems less pressing than feeding malnourished and starving children. As the world has become more concerned with the environmental impact of economic activity, the term *sustainable development* has crept into our vocabulary. This criterion promotes policies that make future generations at least as well off as present generations. Though environmentally sound policies are critical to the long-run health of our planet, developing countries under the burden of debt unfortunately find it hard enough to keep present generations alive. Nevertheless, because pollution of the atmosphere knows no national boundaries, it is a cost we shall all bear.

All this would suggest that the debt crisis is far from over. In spite of some temporary calm throughout the late 1980s, policymakers and bankers can ill afford to ignore the problem. The international financial system is clearly not working for the long-term interests of either the advanced or the developing nations. How much longer can this go on? What can be done to solve this festering debt crisis? In the next chapter we address these questions in the context of one of the more serious cases—Mexico.

Notes

1. The real interest rate is the difference between the nominal interest rate and the rate of inflation. If you borrow money at a 15 percent annual interest rate, but the inflation rate is 5 percent per year, the real interest rate that you pay is 15 percent minus 5 percent, or 10 percent.
2. The interest rate most commonly used for international loans is the London interbank offered rate, or LIBOR, which varies daily. Most international loans are made at 7/8 of a percentage point above the LIBOR rate.
3. Loans to developing nations can be stated as a percentage of primary capital or its equity held by shareholders.
4. "Brady's Bazaar," *The Economist*, May 12, 1990, p. 77.
5. Harold Lever and Christopher Huhne, *Debt and Danger: The World Financial Crisis* (New York: Atlantic Monthly Press, 1985).

7
The Mexican Debt Crisis:
A Case Study

The International economic situation strongly influences the problems of Mexico and Latin America. Our countries are suffering from an unprecedented financial and economic crisis. The rise in interest rates, the contraction of international trade and the protectionist measures adopted by industrialized nations constitute obstacles to our recovery. These factors also aggravate the social inequalities in the region and threaten the political stability of several Latin American nations . . . . It is Mexico's conviction, more and more generalized throughout the world, that in order to overcome the international crisis, the present framework of international economic relations must be modified toward a more cooperative structure in which national economic policies will be in tune with a global need to expand trade and reduce interest rates . . . . We are realistically facing the necessary internal reordering of our economies. What is required is that industrialized nations carry out coherent economic policies that avoid the transfer of costs of recovery to developing nations, and which set the basis for a more equal world economic order.

— Miguel de la Madrid,
former president of Mexico[1]

T he debt crisis of Mexico is unique compared with that of most other developing debtor nations. Mexico is an oil exporter. It has over 72 billion barrels of proven petroleum reserves. How is it possible that a nation with such vast resource wealth can be one of the world's largest debtor nations? Certainly, Mexico's debt story is different from, for example, that of Argentina or Brazil. And, therefore, Mexico, since it is a key player in the debt game, merits some special attention.

By 1989 Mexico's total foreign debt came to a staggering $102 billion dollars. As is clear in figure 7–1, this increase in foreign debt has been most rapid throughout the late 1970s and early 1980s. The

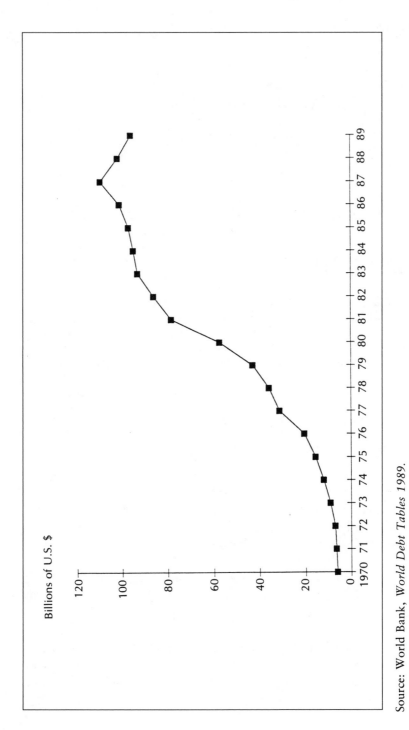

Figure 7–1. *Mexico's Total External Debt, 1970–1989*

Source: World Bank, *World Debt Tables 1989.*

total foreign debt in 1973 was less than $10 billion. It reached $50 billion by 1980. Then, in just five years, it nearly doubled. The sky-rocketing of foreign debt in the early 1980s came in a period of pro-longed economic stagnation in Mexico. During the 1980s Mexico averaged an annual growth rate of real per capita GDP of minus 1.01 percent as compared with a positive 3.5 percent in the 1970s.

What happened? By August 1982 a gradual decline in oil prices touched off a debt crisis that resulted in the rescheduling of debt and the need for additional loans to meet debt service obligations. To pay for this rescue operation, Mexico endured four years of strangling austerity that laid the groundwork for a near collapse in 1986.

Despite the 1983–86 global recovery, Mexico was worse off in 1986 that it was in 1982. Its Gross Domestic Product declined by 5 percent in 1986 alone. Inflation in that year was estimated to be over 100 percent. Underemployment (i.e., open unemployment plus people working less hours than desired or at a job less demanding than their training) was nearly 50 percent, and the population growth rate was approximately 3 percent. However, with an economic growth rate of negative 5 percent and a population growth rate of 3 percent, real per capita income fell by 6 percent. Since 1980 real wages have fallen by 50 percent, reducing the standard of living to levels of 1960.

Mexico's total public and private external debt, nearly $100 billion, required over $14 billion in debt service payments in 1986. Of this amount, interest payments alone were $10 billion. Mexico earns about 75 percent of its foreign exchange from oil exports, but the collapse of oil prices in 1986 meant that Mexico would not earn enough *even to cover the interest* on its debt. The drop in oil prices produced a major decline in anticipated oil revenues—over $5 billion in 1986. Foreign exchange reserves dwindled to approximately $2.5 billion. The peso had been systematically devalued. It reached a level of over 750 pesos to the U.S. dollar in 1986, compared with 22 pesos per dollar as recently as 1982. Mexico's domestic budget deficit in 1986 was 13 percent of GDP. Interest payments on accumulated domestic public debt required over 70 percent of the annual federal budget, compared with 15 percent in the United States.

Despite a succession of stabilization packages, Mexico's prospects for sustained, long-term growth are severely compromised. How can a semi-industrial developing nation with over 72 billion barrels of proven petroleum reserves be in such critical economic straits? It is an interesting, complicated, and unprecedented story.

Economic and Political Background: 1940–1968

Mexico's economy experienced a sustained expansion between 1940 and 1960. It averaged 7 percent annual real growth during that period. But in spite of some modernization of the nation's agricultural and industrial sectors, the Mexican development path was characterized by great social and economic inequality and by a structural dependence upon the United States for both trade and direct private foreign investment.

Politically, Mexico experienced great stability. Smooth transitions between presidents every six years were guaranteed by the dominant political party, the Revolutionary Institutional party (PRI). The PRI had for four decades successfully neutralized any genuine opposition. Its economic policies and programs contributed to the accumulation of private capital and wealth by an upper class tied to foreign capital. To maintain domestic stability, the PRI allocated resources to public works projects and some social services to maintain its political legitimacy. This model and strategy worked effectively until around 1968.

The closing years of the Diaz Ordaz administration were most notable for the Tlateloco student massacre a few days before the 1968 Olympic Games. The student demonstrations and protests, directed at the PRI, were for much-needed social and economic reforms to redress the striking inequality in the country.

Failed Ambitions for Reform: 1968–1976

President Luis Echeverria's primary goal during his 1970–76 administration was to restore confidence in the PRI and enact reforms to enhance the legitimacy of the state (for all intents and purposes, the PRI), while continuing to provide the necessary environment for the continued expansion and accumulation of capital. Though real economic growth averaged 5.7 percent during his term in office, the Mexican economy by 1976 was in a deep and serious crisis (a fact that has been largely ignored by most recent studies on Mexico's current debt crisis).

Echeverria's program of "shared development" was committed to developing the rural sector, encouraging heavy industry for employment in the urban sector, improving education, implementing programs for the redistribution of income, and enhancing the popular participation of workers and peasants. To attain these goals the president greatly expanded the state (public) sector. In 1973 legislation was passed calling for foreign investment controls. This created not only a halt to the inflow of foreign capital but a flight of capital as well. In 1973 Mexico experienced earthquakes, floods, and the OPEC oil price increase. (It is important to recall that Mexico was a net importer of oil in 1973.)

The emerging economic crisis had its roots in the adverse international economic environment and in the fiscal irresponsibility of the state sector. In the context of his goals and commitments, Echeverria spent well beyond Mexico's means. This resulted in the rapid rise of huge public deficits. These deficits were worsened by inflation, capital flight, declining foreign investment, and higher oil prices. The global recession in 1974–75 further depressed the Mexican economy, which was dependent on the U.S. market for over 66 percent of its exports.

By 1976 the economic crisis was real and severe. The growth of real GDP had fallen to 4.2 percent, compared with an average of 7 percent from 1972 to 1975. Inflation had soared to 15.8 percent, compared with the 5 percent rates of 1971–72. Public expenditures had risen to 33.6 percent of GDP, compared with 20.9 percent in 1971 when Echeverria took office. And, as a result, public sector deficits reached the level of 10 percent of GDP by 1976, compared to only 2.5 percent in 1971.

José López Portillo and Petroleum: 1976–1982

José López Portillo took over the Mexican presidency in 1976. Until the oil discovery in the following year, it appeared that his task was going to be implementing a difficult economic austerity program. But the great oil find changed the picture entirely.

The discovery of an estimated 72 billion barrels of hydrocarbon reserves in 1977 temporarily rescued Mexico's faltering economy. Prior to this windfall, most experts agreed that no president could solve the structural problems of the economy. The discovery of petroleum changed the pattern of expectations dramatically. It now appeared that petroleum exports could be used to solve Mexico's economic and social problems. The vision of new sources of revenues triggered a debate over future development strategy and economic policy. A pervasive optimism and spirit of confidence swept across Mexico. Many experts argued that Mexico could manage its oil resources and wealth in a way that would avoid the distortions and contradictions that had plagued other oil-rich developing nations such as Iran, Nigeria, and Venezuela.

The government's goals were ambitious: an annual economic growth rate of 8 percent, increased public spending, the expansion of the private sector, the expansion of tourism and the agricultural sector, and, last, the rapid development of the petroleum sector. But these goals and programs required an enormous amount of capital, which bankers flush with petrodollars were only too happy to lend. Anticipating years of steady income from oil exports, Mexico began a spending and borrowing spree that continued unabated until 1982, when the bubble burst.

From 1977 to 1981, the development and exploitation of oil reserves was the principal stimulus for economic growth; yet it was at the same time the primary source of the emerging instability. By 1981 the economy was continuing to grow—from 1978 to 1981 economic growth averaged 8.5 percent—but the internal inflationary pressures and the increasing external disequilibrium signaled the real costs of a petroleum-driven development strategy. Although exports increased by 9 percent a year between 1978 and 1981, imports increased by 24 percent a year, a rate four times higher than the previous five-year average. The exports were, of course, primarily oil and gas—2.5 million barrels per day. As the manufactured goods export sector stagnated, the relative share of petroleum exports rose from 21 percent in 1977 to 71 percent in 1981, while manufacturing fell from 46 percent to 17 percent.

This structural shift was worsened by the deepening global recession, the weakening demand in the oil market, and the rapid increase in world interest rates. The extent of the crisis was clearly visible in the deteriorating balance of payments, which registered a deficit of $13 billion in 1981. As projected oil revenues fell from $20 billion to $14 billion, Mexico's borrowing accelerated. External debt advanced to $68 billion in 1981 and to over $80 billion in 1982.

The unfavorable balance of payments position, accelerating inflation (from 29 percent in 1981 to 95 percent in 1982), and the mountain of foreign debt undermined all efforts to keep the exchange rate under control. An initial devaluation of the peso induced a panic, prompting a massive flight of capital and an erosion of confidence in the government. As is shown in figure 7–2, in 1982 the money fleeing Mexico was nearly 100 percent of the new debt incurred by the nation.

In virtual desperation, López Portillo appointed Carlos Tello to direct the Mexican central bank in September 1982. Tello immediately set into motion an economic program that included: (1) the suspension of the convertibility of the peso, (2) strict controls on imports, (3) foreign exchange controls, and (4) the nationalization of Mexico's banks. This nationalistic economic program emphasized a diversification of the economy even if it required protectionist and expansionary economic policies. Tello adopted a firm stance vis-à-vis the IMF during Mexico's loan negotiations. Tello objected to the IMF's devotion to traditional policy prescriptions requiring harsh austerity stabilization programs. However, he soon left office as a new administration took over.

Miguel de la Madrid's IMF Austerity Measures: 1983–1986

On December 1, 1982, Miguel de la Madrid was inaugurated president. Tello was replaced by Jesus Silva Herzog who, as finance minister, was put in charge of economic policy. Upon taking office, de la Madrid refused to blame Mexico's economic crisis on declining oil prices and rising interest rates as López Portillo had done during the final months of his term.

The new government set out to reverse Tello's policies and accommodate itself to the demands of the IMF. As the new economic program emerged, its essential features were: (1) a relaxation of foreign exchange controls so that the peso could float in the

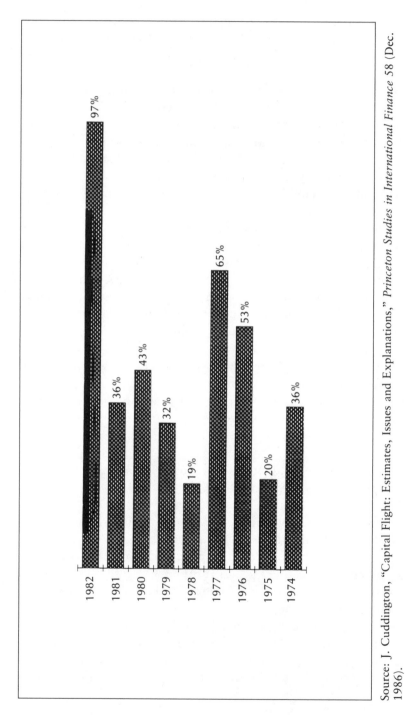

Figure 7-2. Mexican Capital Flight As Percentage of Change in Debt

Source: J. Cuddington, "Capital Flight: Estimates, Issues and Explanations," *Princeton Studies in International Finance* 58 (Dec. 1986).

open market while a temporary official exchange rate would prevent further capital flight; (2) a request to restructure $20 billion of debt due between August 1982 and December 1984 (this request was tied to a new credit of $5 billion in addition to the IMF loan request of $3.2 billion); (3) an across-the-board increase in prices of goods and services provided by the government; and (4) a commitment to reduce domestic spending drastically.

The administration of Miguel de la Madrid called for the moral regeneration of Mexico's leadership. A combination of economic belt-tightening measures and political measures to end corruption were implemented to ameliorate Mexico's economic and political crisis.

The IMF austerity measures put in place during 1983 produced some encouraging yet costly results. The public sector deficit was reduced from 18 percent of GDP to 9 percent, imports were reduced by 50 percent, and exports remained at their 1982 level of $21.3 billion. However, because of compounding, total debt service continued to grow at an increasing rate.

By fall 1984 the Mexican government reached an agreement with international bankers to reschedule its debt over a fourteen-year period. Mexico successfully followed IMF guidelines and signed an agreement with its 520 creditor banks to borrow an additional $3.8 billion. And about $12 billion in private sector debt was rescheduled.

If we carefully examine the growth of Mexico's public debt and debt service from 1973 to 1982, we can observe interesting, significant, and not commonly understood trends in new borrowing and debt service and their effect on net proceeds (the difference between new borrowing and debt service payments).

Figure 7–3 and table 7–1 show that net new borrowing increased rapidly from 1971 through 1983, as did total debt service. By 1978 debt service ($7.2 billion) exceeded new borrowing ($4.6 billion), and net proceeds became negative ($2.5 billion). In August 1982 the Mexican economy collapsed and could not meet its debt obligations. This precipitated a global recognition that there was the very real possibility of Mexico's defaulting on its foreign debt.

As is shown in figure 7–3, there were a number of critical junctures for Mexico over this ten-year period. From 1973 to 1977 new borrowing increased, as did debt service payments. However, in

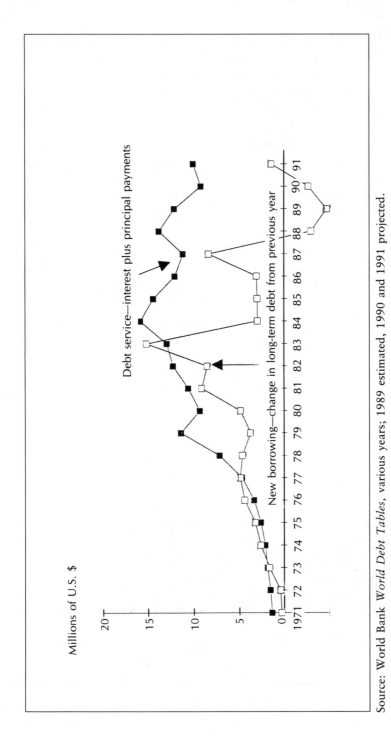

Figure 7-3. *Mexico's New Borrowing and Debt Service*

Source: World Bank *World Debt Tables*, various years; 1989 estimated, 1990 and 1991 projected.

Table 7-1
Mexican Debt Profile

Year	Total Long-Term Debt Stocks	Change From Previous Year	Long-Term Debt Interest	Long-Term Debt Amortization	Total Debt Service	Net Proceeds
1970	5966	na	283	1017	1300	−1300
1971	6416	450	311	1049	1360	−1074
1972	7028	612	353	1178	1531	−1106
1973	8999	1971	516	1354	1870	−223
1974	11946	2947	813	1310	2123	497
1975	15609	3663	1104	1509	2613	627
1976	20149	4540	1360	1985	3345	1047
1977	25227	5078	1588	3110	4698	199
1978	30487	5260	2258	4905	7163	−2533
1979	34668	4181	3364	8059	11423	−7688
1980	41215	6547	4580	4760	9340	−4493
1981	53232	12017	6117	4504	10621	−1504
1982	59651	6419	7769	4531	12300	−3781
1983	81565	21914	8140	4828	12968	2246
1984	86022	4457	10250	5656	15906	−12945
1985	88456	2434	9382	5072	14454	−11469
1986	90906	2450	7676	4433	12109	−9017
1987	98329	7423	7671	3519	11190	−2812
1988	88664	−9665	7590	6442	13832	−16807
1989	80494	−8170	7935	4222	12157	−16869
1990	77725	−2769	5657	3528	9185	−11838
1991	78849	1124	6320	3715	10035	−8611

Source: World Bank, *World Debt Tables*, various years. 1989 estimated; 1990 and 1991 projected.

1977 new borrowing began to decline, but debt service continued to increase, creating an enormous gap between incoming funds from new borrowing and funds flowing out to pay accumulated interest and amortization. The massive increase in new borrowing in 1981 was a desperate and unsuccessful attempt on the part of the Portillo administration to avert the crisis that everyone knew was coming.

But even these figures are understated, because the large increases in new borrowing give the appearance of increasing net proceeds over the 1973–77 period. However, when taken *as a percent of new borrowing,* net proceeds were low or negative almost the entire decade, as is illustrated in table 7–1. Therefore, the fact that the economy did collapse should not have been a surprise to anyone. Mexico had been running on a treadmill for at least five years before the 1982 crisis.

Looking at the evolution of Mexico's economic crisis in more conventional terms is just as revealing. Mexico's net flow of debt, shown in figure 7–4, declined precipitously after the crisis. Net transfers became negative after 1982, and remained so throughout the decade, despite a variety of rescue packages. Current account

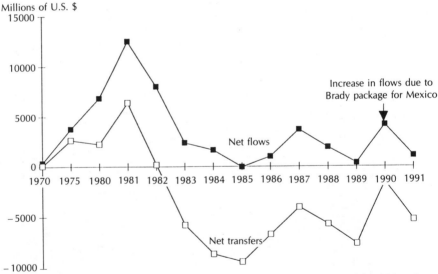

Source: World Bank, *World Debt Tables,* various years; 1989 estimated, 1990 and 1991 projected.

Figure 7–4. *Mexico's Net Flow and Transfer of Resources*

balance of payments data are supposed to measure the sustainability of a country's economic health. Looking at figure 7–5, we can see that both the merchandise trade balance and the total current account balance were negative from 1970 to 1982. By 1981 the trade deficit reached $4.2 billion, and the total current account deficit doubled from its 1981 level of $7.5 billion to $14 billion. It is not unusual for a developing country to import more than it exports to provide the inputs for growth—so long as the rest of the world is willing to lend it money to cover the shortfall. From 1977 to 1981 Mexico imported large quantities of oil-drilling equipment and services, and the financial community was only too happy to lend to this country dripping in "black gold." But beginning in 1982, both the trade balance and the total current account showed an improvement. And by 1984 the trade surplus was $12.8 billion and the current account surplus $2.5 billion.

This interesting turn of events came about because during the period 1982–84, Mexico was following IMF guidelines by reducing imports and attempting to increase exports. The global recovery that began in 1983 provided some stimulus, as did the systematic devaluation of the peso, which made Mexico's exports more competitive and imports more expensive. Mexico slowly began to adjust to moderately declining oil exports and reductions in anticipated oil revenues. But by 1986 the trade balance dropped to only $2.6 billion, and the current account deficit plunged to almost $5 billion.

In addition, capital flight continued from 1983 to 1985. Morgan Guaranty Trust Company estimated that $17 billion fled Mexico between 1983 and 1985, bringing total capital flight from 1976 to 1985 to a level of $53 billion, or *almost one-half* of Mexico's total foreign debt. Economist Manuel Pastor estimates flight for a slightly different period, 1973–87, and finds capital flight at $60.9 billion, 63.9 percent of the change in external debt.[2]

Table 7–2 summarizes the consequences of the chronic balance of payments deficit. By 1982 Mexico's net payment to foreign capital was over $13 billion—26 percent of the total for Latin America. (Payment of foreign capital is calculated by adding freight and insurance payments to dividends, interest, and royalties.) Between 1976 and 1982, Latin America's total *net* payment to foreign capital was $145 billion; of this Mexico alone had paid around $40 billion over that six-year period. This chronic balance of payments disequilib-

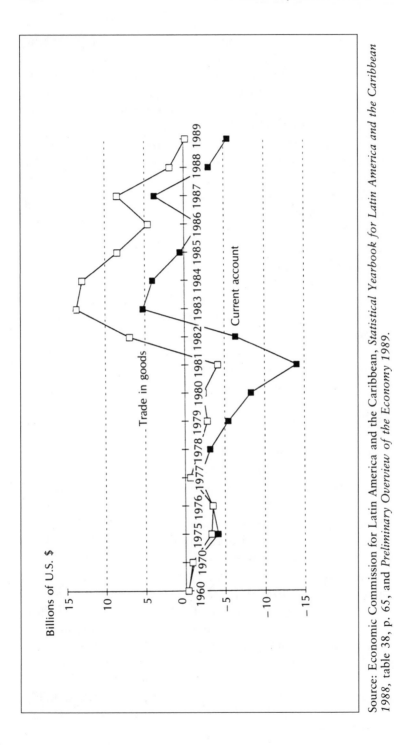

Source: Economic Commission for Latin America and the Caribbean, *Statistical Yearbook for Latin America and the Caribbean 1988*, table 38, p. 65, and *Preliminary Overview of the Economy 1989*.

Figure 7–5. *Mexico's Trade Balance*

rium in the face of the debt crisis fueled a vicious cycle and worsened the social and political contradictions that emanated from it.

As we have pointed out earlier, in the late 1970s private commercial banks began to play a larger role in international lending to sovereign states. The changing composition of Mexico's debt reflects this reality. As a percentage of its total foreign debt, Mexico's debt obligations to private commercial banks increased to almost 92 percent by 1983, whereas debt from official sources decreased to a low of just over 8 percent.

Moreover, as Mexico became more and more dependent on private sources of credit, the terms of borrowing also changed. Mexico's percentage of debt at floating rates increased from 46.8 percent in the 1973–75 period to 82.4 percent in 1983. This increased dependence on commercial bank loans placed Mexico in a very precarious relationship with the U.S. government. As U.S. banks became more involved with Mexico's debt problem, Mexico's debt problem became more a concern for the U.S. government and financial community.

By March 1984, 9 of the leading U.S. banks had a total of $14.5 billion in loans to Mexico. By June 1984, the 209 major U.S. banks had $26 billion in loans to Mexico—almost 25 percent of their total loans to major Third World debtor countries.[3] Consequently they began to reduce their exposure. Looking at table 7–3, we can see that the banks reduced the amount of their primary capital as a percent of loans considerably over the 1982–85 period. Citicorp, for example, in 1982 had $3.4 billion in loans to Mexico, which represented 62 percent of its primary capital (shareholders equity plus allowance for loan losses). But by 1985, Citicorp had reduced its exposure in Mexico to $2.8 billion, which represented only 25 percent of primary capital. And all U.S. banks reduced their exposure in Mexico from 35 percent of primary capital in 1981 to 23 percent in 1985.

So although the situation has improved somewhat, it is still precarious. If the top ten U.S. lenders to Mexico had not received any interest payments from Mexico in 1985, they would have suffered a pretax earnings reduction of 19 percent. This might be *temporarily* tolerable, but very soon such losses would certainly trigger a sequence of events that would create a financial panic, which is what almost occurred in 1986 when the collapse of oil prices (from $25 to

Table 7–2
Mexico's Balance of Payments: 1960–1989

	Exports of Goods, fob	Imports of Goods, fob	Trade Balance	Net Service (Freight, Insurance, travel)	Net Factor Services (Interest, Profit)
1960	780	1131	− 352	150	− 112
1970	1348	2236	− 888	216	− 451
1975	3007	6278	− 3272	872	1783
1980	16067	18897	− 2830	601	− 6209
1981	19938	24038	− 4100	− 557	− 9531
1982	21230	14434	6796	− 493	− 12815
1983	22320	8553	13767	726	− 9373
1984	24185	11288	12897	1124	− 10251
1985	21667	13218	8450	809	− 9060
1986	16028	13218	2810	1127	− 7861
1987	20649	12199	8450	2083	− 7195
1988	20648	18945	1703	2426	− 7712
1989	22700	22900	− 200	2400	− 8380

Source: Economic Commission for Latin America and the Caribbean, *Statistical Yearbook for Latin America and the Caribbean* 1988. Data for 1987–89 from "Preliminary Overview of the Economy of Latin America and the Caribbean."

$12.5 per barrel) again put Mexico on the brink of collapse and potential default. This sent a shock wave throughout the international financial system. Once again Mexico needed a major rescue operation.

The 1986 Rescue Package

Mexican oil revenues decreased from $14.7 billion in 1985 to under $6 billion in 1986, and it was clear that Mexico could no longer meet its debt obligations. The 1986 crisis provoked widespread debate about the causes, consequences, and costs of the debt. A popular public point of view was that Mexico could not and should not have to face more years of harsh austerity just to satisfy the IMF and commercial bankers. More conservative elements in the Mexican government felt that it was critical that Mexico meet the demands of the IMF and obtain the loans necessary to avoid a default. Others argued that the loans were necessary but felt that real concessions should be made by the IMF and the international banking community. This faction argued the Mexico had attempted to restructure

Payments to Foreign Capital (Freight, Insurance, & Travel, plus Profits and Net Interest)	Current Account	Capital Account (Short- and Long-Term Unrequited Official Transfers, Errors, and Ommissions)	Net Payments to Foreign Capital, LA & cari	Mexico/LA (%)
38	− 320	310		
− 235	− 1098	1128	− 3954.8	5.94
− 911	− 4124	4327	− 8609.5	10.59
− 5608	− 8306	9262	− 27479.1	20.41
− 10088	− 14075	15151	− 39288.1	25.78
− 13308	− 6416	2847	− 50288.1	26.46
− 8647	5242	− 3207	− 39506.8	21.89
− 9128	3999	− 1866	− 40553.2	22.51
− 8251	510	− 3273	− 38729.1	21.30
− 6734	1897	1730	− 35798.2	18.81
− 5112	3722	1951	− 34618	14.77
− 5286	− 3130	− 3666	− 37915	13.94
− 5980	− 5500	6500	− 41775	14.31

its economy and had imposed austerity. The unfortunate collapse of oil prices in 1986, they argued, should be a responsibility shared by the commercial banks and the international financial institutions.

By October 1986 the outline of a comprehensive new loan package was visible. In essence, it provided for a loan package of over $12 billion over the period 1986–87. As is shown in table 7–4, the package involved all the major players: the IMF, the World Bank, the Inter-American Development Bank, the commercial banks, and the U.S. government.

Interestingly, this package appears to be consistent with U.S. Treasury Secretary Baker's Third World debt program. As the *Wall Street Journal* put it:

> The Baker plan . . . emphasized that the debt crisis could only be resolved through sustained growth by the debtor countries—that austerity alone would be self-defeating in the longer run. To achieve the requisite growth, the plan prescribed orthodox programs of economic reform and structural adjustment for the debtor countries, including greater reliance on the private sector, curtailment of state subsidies and price controls, measures to stim-

Table 7–3
Exposure of Major U.S. Banks to Mexican Debt, 1982, 1985
(billions of $)

	1982		1985	
	Loans	Loans as a Percentage of Capital	Loans	Loans as a Percentage of Capital
Citicorp	$3.4	62	$2.8	25
Bank of America	2.5	51	2.7	37
Manufacturers Hanover	1.7	52	1.8	37
Chase Manhattan	1.4	37	1.7	28
Chemical	1.5	62	1.5	36
Bankers Trust	0.8	48	1.3	39
Morgan Guaranty	1.1	33	1.1	21
First Chicago	0.8	47	0.9	32
First Interstate	0.7	33	0.7	24
Wells Fargo	0.6	45	0.6	27

Source: Keefe, Bruyette & Woods.

Table 7–4
Mexican Loan Package, 1986
(millions of $)

Source	1986	1987	Total
International Monetary Fund	$ 700	$ 900	$1,600
World Bank	900	1,000	1,900
Inter-American Development Bank	200	200	400
Commercial banks	2,500	3,500	6,000
International export credits	500	1,000	1,500
U.S. farm credits	200	600	800
Total	$5,000	$7000	$12,200

Source: U.S. Treasury, June 22, 1986.

ulate both foreign and domestic investment, and export promotion and trade liberalization. The plan also called on private banks and multinational institutions to step up sharply their lending to the indebted countries. The banks were urged to provide new commercial credits of $20 billion over a three-year period while the

World Bank and the Inter-American Development Bank would
contribute an additional $9 billion in loans.[4]

The proposed rescue package called for the commercial banks to
generate approximately $6 billion in new loans. The IMF and
World Bank loans were contingent on the commercial bank loans
being secured. This package also contained some concessions for
Mexico. The World Bank agreed to provide additional credit if real
economic growth was less than 3.5 percent in 1987. The IMF loan
of $1.6 billion guaranteed additional credit if oil prices fell below $9
per barrel. In exchange for this jumbo loan package, the IMF
required Mexico to continue to sell off and reduce the number of
state-owned enterprises, to liberalize trade, to attract more foreign
investment, and to reduce its domestic deficit by 3 percent of GDP.

A binding constraint of this package was the willingness of the
commercial banks to extend additional loans of this magnitude and
to make interest rate concessions. Most were not anxious to do so
and were put off by insistent monetary authorities eager for them to
commit new money for risky loans.

Furthermore, the package did not address the long-term needs
of the Mexican economy. Rather than reduce the amount of debt
Mexico had to service, the addition of another $12 billion merely
increased the nation's long-term debt service obligations. Most
important, this loan package did not reverse the negative transfer of
capital from Mexico to the industrial nations. Instead, the package
merely perpetuated negative flows. This hemorrhaging of capital
required that the Mexican people suffer through more years of austerity and a further decline in their already low standard of living.

Reductions in government spending left the Mexican economy
and people in a state of shock. *¿Qué nos pasa?* (What happened to
us?) became the slogan of the Mexican people. Political unrest contributed to the weakening of the PRI, the powerful government
party. Figures 7–6 through 7–8 present an overview of the costs of
austerity. Inflation accelerated to historic levels, reaching 160 percent in 1987 as confidence in the government was eroded. Real
wages continued their downward march as economic austerity,
combined with accelerating prices, eroded the purchasing power of
the Mexican people. Per capita GDP fell nearly 6 percent in 1986
and continued negative in 1987 and 1988 as the Mexican people

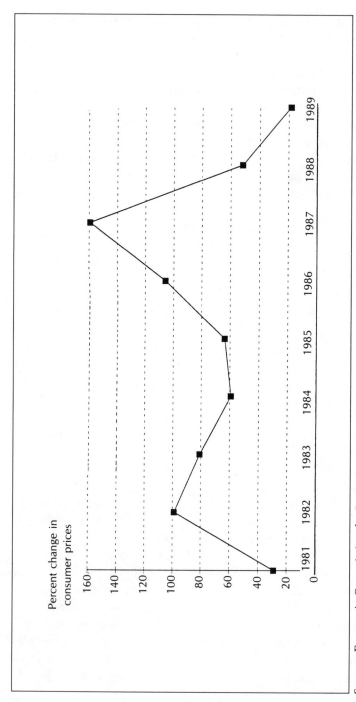

Figure 7–6. *Mexican Inflation, 1981–1989*

Source: Economic Commission for Latin America and the Caribbean, *Statistical Yearbook for Latin America and the Caribbean 1988*, table 38, p. 65, and *Preliminary Overview of the Economy 1989*.

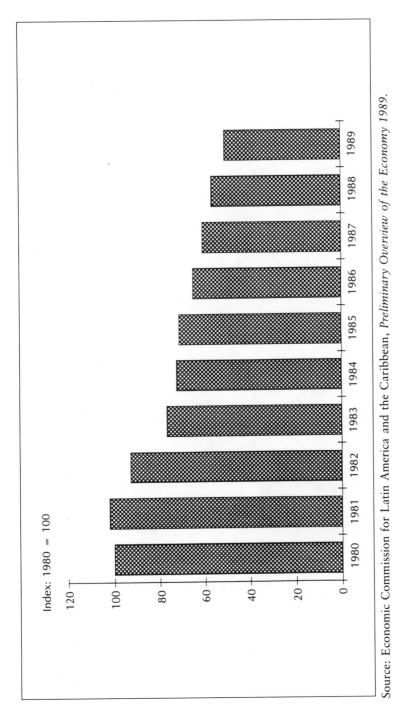

Index: 1980 = 100

Figure 7-7. *Urban Real Wages in Mexico, 1980–1989*

Source: Economic Commission for Latin America and the Caribbean, *Preliminary Overview of the Economy 1989.*

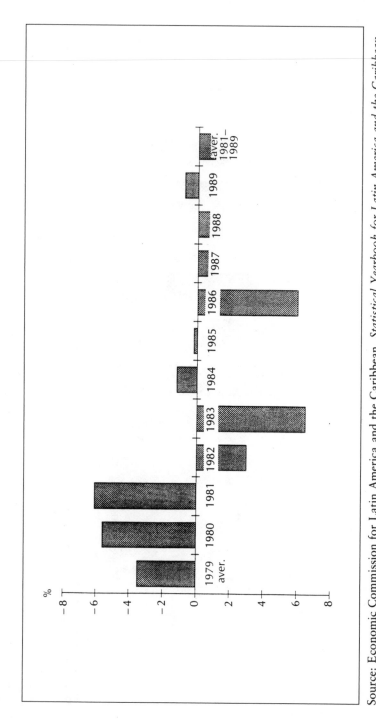

Figure 7–8. *Growth of Per Capita GDP at Constant Prices*

Source: Economic Commission for Latin America and the Caribbean, *Statistical Yearbook for Latin America and the Caribbean 1988*, and *Preliminary Overview of the Economy 1989.*

became progressively worse off. Those wealthy enough to leave fled to the United States, worsening the problem of capital flight. For those left behind, real per capita income, rather than growing over the decade, was stuck at the level of the late 1970s.

The Presidency of Carlos Salinas de Gortari
(1988–   )

In December of 1988, just as he took office, newly elected president Carlos Salinas de Gortari announced the continuation of the economic solidarity pact designed to decrease inflationary pressures and stabilize the economy which was implemented a year before. This agreement adjusted public sector prices better to reflect costs, increased minimum wages slightly, and began a program of daily depreciations of the peso to promote exports. The rate of growth of the money supply was also slowed. But, as *The Economist* reported, Mexican workers, having lost a minimum of two-fifths of their purchasing power since the debt crisis struck in 1982, booed and shouted obscenities as the finance minister tried to present his budget.[5]

In the external sector, Mexico had become a member of the General Agreement on Tariffs and Trade (GATT) in 1986 in an attempt to promote an outward orientation. Lowering its tariffs to an average of 11 percent and eliminating many quotas and nontariff barriers, Mexico received as its reward an influx of imports. As can be seen in figure 7–9, the difference between exports and imports began to narrow in 1986, and by 1989 Mexico was left with its first merchandise trade deficit since the beginning of the decade. In 1988, with weak oil prices, Mexico's export revenues were down, and the United States was forced to make an emergency loan of $3.5 billion to avert collapse.

The Brady Plan: Once Again,
Halfway Is Not Far Enough

It became increasingly clear that despite Mexico's good behavior in tightening its economic belt to comply with the austerity measures

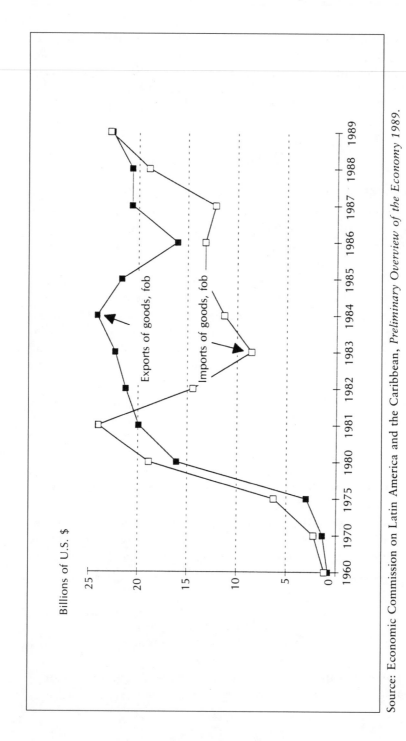

Billions of U.S. $

Exports of goods, fob

Imports of goods, fob

Source: Economic Commission on Latin America and the Caribbean, *Preliminary Overview of the Economy 1989.*

Figure 7–9. *Mexico's Imports versus Exports, 1960–1989*

imposed by the international financial community, and in reducing protectionist barriers, the 1986 Baker initiative package did little to stimulate growth. Faster growth was essential to absorb Mexico's growing population, but investment was stymied by the negative flow of resources back to industrialized countries. Indeed, long before the politicians, the international market recognized the impossibility of full repayment of debt. As is shown in figure 7–10, the secondary market value of Mexican debt was nearly half its face value by the end of 1987.

On February 4, 1990, a new agreement was reached between Mexico and its creditors on $48.5 billion of its international debt. Consistent with the objectives of the 1989 Brady Plan and the market's signals, this package, initially announced in July 1989, incorporated a critical new element: the *possibility* of debt reduction for Mexico. In return for reducing the face value, interest and principal payments on the remaining debt would be guaranteed by a fund of $7 billion put up by the IMF, the World Bank, the United States, Japan, and Mexico itself. The banks were allowed to choose from a menu of options including:

1. A 35 percent discount on the nominal value of the loans, with the remaining debt converted into thirty-year bonds with an interest rate of LIBOR plus 13/16 percent

2. A reduction of interest rates to a fixed, below-market rate of 6.25 percent on the full value of the debt, which would be converted into thirty-year bonds

3. New lending set at 25 percent of the bank's loans to the country repaid over fifteen years after a seven-year grace period at LIBOR plus 13/16 percent to finance the interest payments due to them on old loans, and to reduce, temporarily, the negative flow of resources

Essentially, this package was built on three principles: to reduce then outstanding value of the debt or the interest payment burden, to expand the repayment time period, and to provide fresh capital to promote growth. In concert with the traditional orthodox measures of fiscal and monetary restraint, the growth generated by the infusion of new money would be sufficient, it was hoped, to repay

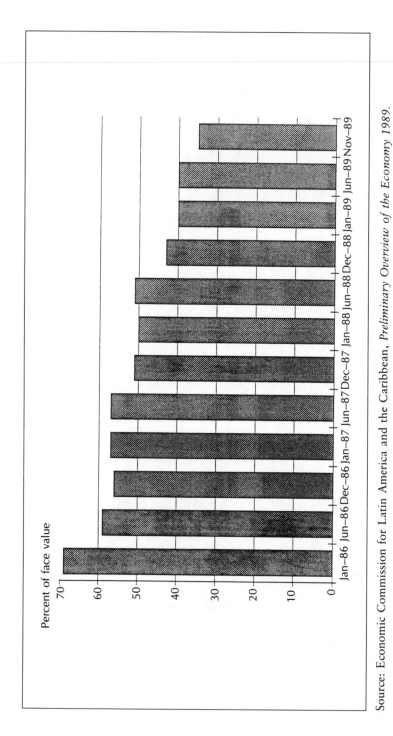

Figure 7–10. *Secondary Market Value of External Mexican Debt*

Source: Economic Commission for Latin America and the Caribbean, *Preliminary Overview of the Economy 1989.*

the outstanding loans. Under this scenario, then, with an enhanced probability of repayment, the loans became more valuable to the banks. The deal was further sweetened for the banks with a recapture clause that allowed a higher interest rate after July 1996 should the real price of oil surpass fourteen dollars a barrel. Thus, everyone was ostensibly made better off: Mexico should grow, and the banks' profitability should improve. There were also predicted indirect effects. As the debt and debt service burden are lessened, domestic investment should rise, particularly since it could be fueled by capital returning to Mexico because of renewed confidence in the economy. As President Salinas noted in his State of the Union address in 1989, the accord "opens up a breathing space in which we can renew growth."[6]

Nevertheless, the implementation of the plan has not matched initial expectations. When the Brady Plan was first announced in March 1989, it was estimated that Mexico might reduce $20 billion, or 20 percent, of its outstanding external debt. When the Mexican package was negotiated in concert with the Brady objectives, the projection was reduced to $8 billion. In practice, the returns are likely to be even more minimal. To finance the guarantees, Mexico assumed $5.7 billion in new loans from Japan, the World Bank, and the IMF and must make interest payments on a special U.S. Treasury bond. In fact, by January 1990 the *Wall Street Journal* was predicting that Mexico's foreign debt would be rising, not falling, over the coming years.[7] Furthermore, new loans (option 3, mentioned earlier) were not forthcoming. Although Mexico had anticipated receiving approximately $9 billion in fresh funding, only half that was received, with only 10 percent rather than 20 percent of the banks electing this route.

There have been a variety of criticisms of the Brady Plan. Many contend that the plan's primary beneficiary was not Mexico but the banks. The discount on the outstanding debt, for example, was not nearly so steep as the secondary market, making extraction from the country fairly attractive for banks. But as the *Wall Street Journal* points out, as commercial banks flee, industrial country governments—read taxpayers—are left holding the bag for bad loans made in the 1970s.[8] Furthermore, as Jorge Castaneda, a noted Mexican analyst, argues, Mexico has lost a prime bargaining chip in future negotiations: the suspension of payments. With the interest and principal guarantees built into the package, the next time Mexico needs money the banking community will be protected for at least eighteen months no matter the country's actions.[9] Additionally, since Mexico dealt with the international financial community unilaterally, its prospects for joint action with other Latin American debtors are further dampened.

On the other hand, there have been positive economic results in Mexico. As a result of raising public sector prices, engaging in a comprehensive tax reform, and aggressively selling state-owned enterprises, the government now registers a surplus of over 8 percent of GDP in its primary budget (not including interest payments), a reversal from the negative 7.4 percent in 1982. Domestic interest rates came down over 20 points, from 56 percent in July 1989 to 35 percent in September, reducing the interest burden on domestically held debt. By 1989 tax revenue had increased to 10.5 percent of GDP, despite a cut in the top personal and corporate taxes. This was accomplished by closing loopholes and beefing up enforcement and collection of taxes. The exchange rate has been subject to regular devaluations, promoting the competitiveness of Mexican products. By 1989 inflation has reached a manageable level of 20 percent annually. In October 1989 Mexico and the United States signed an agreement to expand trade between the two nations, and discussions of a free trade area among Mexico, the United States, and Canada have begun. It is argued that the net external transfers of 6 percent a year between 1983 and 1988 will be reduced to 2 percent a year during 1990–94.[10] But the debt overhang still retards investment, and the long-run ability of the Mexican economy to improve the well-being of its growing population is critically sensitive to the health of the international economy, and especially to its neighbor to the north. Most Mexicans still live in extreme poverty, and as the following story of one family shows, they have been the bearers of the country's debt burden.

A Mexican Family Copes with Hardship

High on a shanty-scarred hilltop just north of Acapulco's glittering strip of luxury hotels, Ofelia Romero sweeps the dirt floor of her shack almost obsessively, striving to impose order on a chaotic world.

The old order began to break down for the former middle-class housewife six years ago, when a bitter divorce coincided with the most jolting economic crisis in Mexican history. She lived off the generosity of friends for a few years, but soon found herself at the bottom: no money, no job, and seven children to feed.

But by pulling together, the Romero family is climbing back.

Like millions of Mexican families pounded in the crucible of *la crisis,* the Romeros are relying on the only real social security that still exists in Mexico: the family safety net.

In so doing, the Romeros are a testament to the durable and flexible Mexican family, whose ingenious strategies for survival have cushioned the blow of a crisis that might have sparked revolution in any other country.

The crisis, which erupted eight years ago when oil prices slumped and Mexico was left holding an enormous foreign debt, threw the country's development into reverse.

The once profligate government implemented a severe austerity program to meet its large debt-service payments. It cut the bloated government budget, trimmed real wages, and eventually sold off most of its inefficient state industries.

These were all sound macroeconomic decisions. But with real wages slashed to 1960 levels and state services and subsidies virtually eliminated, the average Mexican family has been forced to make sacrifices and pool its resources to survive.

"We would never be able to rebuild our lives if the whole family didn't contribute," says Mrs. Romero, whose determination is leavened by a buoyant demeanor. "Everyone has had to make a sacrifice, even the youngest."

She stops sweeping long enough to look down at her youngest child, Marco Antonio, playing with a ragged stuffed gorilla that would walk and clap its hands—if only it had batteries.

Toño turned six two days earlier, but Romero could not afford a party, a new toy, or even a pair of batteries. Her sole aim now is to raise the $150 needed to build a sturdy new house to replace the slap-dash mixture of plywood, tree branches, and burlap sacks that they currently call home.

Pulling Together to Survive

Each family member pulls his own weight.

Romero entered the job market last year for the first time. With the help of family friends, she landed a job as a cook in an

Acapulco hotel. She earns $5.50 a day and feels lucky to be able to bring home an occasional leftover sandwich for the children.

Her 19-year-old son, Oton, frustrated and unemployed, took off for the United States two months ago, vowing to earn enough money to help his family build a brick house. Romero carries his only letter from Florida neatly folded in her purse, pulling it out to peruse its hopeful words during her break.

Raul, a married son living in Hidalgo State, sends her the $25 a month he receives for renting out part of his house. He also takes care of his younger brother Mauricio, who works part-time in a glass shop.

Romero's three teenage daughters have also made sacrifices.

Carolina, a 13-year-old tomboy, had to give up her first and only love: basketball. The 13-year-old flunked out of school a few years ago due to a bout of "basketball fever."

She daydreamed about behind-the-back passes and fancy dribbling. She skipped classes to test her mettle with the older girls.

So her mother made her give up the game. "My mom told me that if I didn't try harder [in school] she wouldn't let me go back," says Carolina, toes wriggling in the dirt. "She said, 'All my efforts to feed this family can't be in vain.' Otherwise, she said I would have to become a nanny. Ugh!"

Julieta, a boy-crazy 16-year-old, reluctantly forgoes rock concerts and parties to stay home and run the family when her mother is working. She is also training to be a secretary so she can add more money to the family till—and buy the kind of stylish clothes worn by her teen idols.

All three of the girls, including 15-year-old Blanca, take care of Toño when their mother is absent. They also share responsibility for the family soda stand, hauling 24-bottle cases of Coke and huge cubes of ice up the steep incline every day.

Operated out of an old, unrefrigerated ice chest, the enterprise has become the settlement's hilltop watering hole—and the family's biggest breadwinner. The girls put about $7 a day into the family's between-the-mattresses "savings account."

Family as Cradle of Stability

Such family solidarity and sacrifice has been one of the keys to Mexico's remarkable political stability, social scientists say.

Many outside observers expected the worst for Mexico in 1988, when popular discontent over the economic crisis was exacerbated by widespread charges of fraud in the presidential elections. They predicted everything from massive protests to an outright insurrection.

But despite isolated incidents of conflict, calm has prevailed even in the poorest barrios.

"We've been surprised to find that, instead of increasing, people's participation in social protest movements has decreased during the crisis," says anthropologist Mercedes González de la Rocha. Social violence has dropped as well, she says.

The reason? "People are too concerned about feeding their families and going to work to think about participating" in protests, she says.

In a 1988 study of 95 urban working-class families, Ms. González de la Rocha showed how families band together to combat the crisis. Households grew by an average of about 10 percent as they incorporated more wage-earning cousins, uncles, and in-laws. And the number of young males and adult females pushed into the work force rose 25 percent.

Mexico has never been a welfare state. But what little social security existed here—especially in food subsidies, health care, and rural credits—either has been eliminated or greatly reduced.

With such a panorama, says political scientist Juan Molinar, "the family unit is the only way this country has been able to make it."

But the Mexican family is more than just a safety net. It has become the cradle of entrepreneurial creativity here.

With a knack for creativity born of necessity, families throughout Mexico have set up thousands of off-the-books businesses, ranging from soda stands to sidewalk flea markets, to in-the-home textile factories. This informal economy has grown so fast during the crisis that experts say it now accounts for more than one-third of Mexico's gross domestic product.

Finding a Place to Call Home

But having a successful enterprise—or even loads of money—does not guarantee a piece of property to call one's own. It takes connections too.

The battle for land on the outskirts of cities such as Acapulco and Mexico City has been exacerbated by urban population pressures and incoming peasants escaping the rural depression. Many people end up renting rooms in squalid downtown buildings with other families.

But Romero was fortunate.

She wanted to move back to her native Acapulco after 22 years away from her mother and sister. One day early last year, her sister told her about an illegal takeover of unused private property being organized by her political party, the Authentica Party of the Mexican Revolution.

Did she want a plot?

Wasting no time to take advantage of her family connections, Romero and four children packed up and moved to the shantytown, appropriately named the New Era settlement. Her mother, Ageda Tagle Hernandez, even helped clear out the hilltop plot, which has a million-dollar view of the Pacific Ocean.

In April 1989, a few days after the family had moved in, about 500 Army troops stormed the settlement, tore down the shacks, and threw the 258 families out. Dozens of families with nowhere to go camped out on the side of the coastal highway. Romero and her children squeezed into her mother's apartment in a more established settlement nearby.

One month later, party leaders negotiated an agreement that allowed the settlers to return to the hillside—for a price. Each family will eventually have to pay the equivalent of $900 to the landowner.

Now the struggle is for basic services. A few families have pirated electricity from the power lines that follow the coastal road below. But the Romeros and other families living up above cannot afford the hundreds of feet of cable they would need. Community leaders are petitioning the government for help.

There is no running water either. The Romero daughters lug six buckets of water a day from a makeshift faucet shared by some 70 families. At the same faucet, fully clothed shantytown dwellers splash soapy water on themselves and call it a shower.

Likewise, the Romeros have dug a hole in the ground, surrounded it with plywood and plastic, and called it a bathroom. On this particular day, Toño emerges from the outhouse announcing a minor discovery: "Mommy, there are worms in there." Romero sighs. "Despite the situation here, I feel much happier than I was before," she says, remembering without nostalgia the days when she seemed to have it all—a cement-block house, a refrigerator, and a color television. "I'm back home now, close to my family."

Carolina calls for her mother from outside. Romero hurries to put on a dab of perfume so the children can lead her and their grandmother down the slippery slope to the settlement's long-awaited Mother's Day party.

At the bottom of the hill, about 100 mothers and children

gather around a makeshift dirt stage to watch some nervous teen-agers dance the *lambada* and lip-sync Mexican rock songs to a scratchy sound system.

There is even a raffle, in which each mother wins a water jug or a plastic bucket.

Later, up at her home, Romero seems free to dream again.

"Come back in two years and this will all be changed," she says, standing on the postage-stamp–sized lot where she hopes to build the new house. Her eyes dance across the shantytown out to the crashing waves of the Pacific Ocean. "We'll even have a room for you."[11]

This story of economic hardship is not unique to Mexico. Throughout the developing world there are high human costs to ser-vicing the debt.

Notes

1. Miguel de la Madrid, "Mexico: The New Challenges," *Foreign Affairs* (Fall 1984): 62–76.
2. Morgan Guaranty Trust Company, "LDC Capital Flight," *World Financial Markets* (March 1986): 13–25; and Manuel Pastor, Jr., "Capital Flight from Latin America," *World Development* 18:1 (1990):1–18.
3. Anatole Kaletsky, *The Costs of Default* (New York: Priority Press, 1985), p. 113, table 6.4.
4. Peter Hakim, "The Baker Plan: Unfulfilled Promises," *Challenge* (Sept.–Oct. 1986): 55–59, James A. Baker III, Secretary of the Treasury, Statement before the Committee on Foreign Relations, U.S. Senate, Oct. 23, 1985.
5. "Mexico: A Softer Grip," *The Economist,* Dec. 24, 1988, pp. 52–53.
6. "President of Mexico Awaits Action on Debt," *New York Times,* Nov. 2, 1989, p. D1.
7. Peter Truell, "Brady Strategy: Rest in Peace," *Wall Street Journal,* Jan. 22, 1990, p. 1.
8. Ibid.
9. Jorge C. Castaneda, "Mexico's Dismal Debt Deal," *New York Times,* Feb. 25, 1990, p. F13.
10. José Angel Gurria (under secretary for international finance affairs, Mexican Ministry of Finance), "Mexico Is on the Move Again," *Wall Street Journal,* March 9, 1990, p. A13.
11. Brook Larmer, "A Mexican Family Copes with Hardship," *Christian Science Monitor,* May 29, 1990, pp. 10–11.

8

A New Bretton Woods?

The international financial system is in need of repair. The U.S. debt crisis and the debt crisis of the Third World are symptoms of fundamental disequilibrium in the international financial system. There is general agreement that any new restructuring of the international financial system must confront the problem of more equitable flows of trade and capital. This means, in essence, that the Third World debt problem must be addressed and resolved and that unsustainable economic spending in the United States must be corrected. Any system that does not resolve these problems will simply prolong and exacerbate the current crisis. There is less agreement, however, on how to go about resolving the problems, although there is no shortage of suggestions.

The Case Against

There are those who argue that there is no need for a new system because the current system already has in place mechanisms to correct imbalances. The IMF, some argue, could initiate the necessary discussions and implement appropriate policies. But the IMF already holds annual conferences, and little seems to be accomplished. Indeed, many argue, the conservative policies of the IMF, which attempt to correct exchange rate distortions through "conditional" loans, have been one of the primary causes of the problem.

Others argue that the current problems could easily be resolved if the United States would only put in place appropriate monetary and fiscal policies to end inflation and to lower interest rates, but that has already happened over the past several years and the overall situation has simply worsened.

A related argument is that a restructuring of the international financial system would almost certainly be opposed by any U.S. administration, and that, therefore, even thinking about it is a waste of everybody's time. But, like it or not, the crisis has reached such proportions and the trends are so troubling that soon there will be no choice. The question is whether the process will be planned and orderly or forced and chaotic.

As Morris Miller, former executive director of the World Bank, has put it in an insightful analysis of the problem:

> It matters whether the movement toward a new Bretton Woods is made by design or forced by events. The preferred method is to be guided by forethought and design, but even the second-best route to the destination may suffice—if we don't fall off the figurative cliff in the meantime. Once the current debt crisis is seen as an integral part of a deep-seated transformation of the global economic and financial system, the door is open to considering policy approaches that have the breadth and depth commensurate to the problem.[1]

There is a growing recognition that a turning point requiring a series of hard choices is imminent. There is, however, less recognition that the profound changes wrought over the past four decades are of a structural nature both in terms of (1) how trade and finance are handled and the size and direction of these flows, and (2) the ability of the United States to take on the type of leadership responsibilities that were assumed at Bretton Woods in 1944 and the necessity of the United States' sharing such leadership with Japan and other nations.

Under such conditions it is not surprising that, in light of the present instability of the international financial system, there should be increasing calls for a new system based on something more stable than the U.S. dollar, which is now out of control, literally and figuratively. Even such staid observers of the international scene as former secretary of state Henry Kissinger have taken up the cause:

> The biggest politico-economic challenge to statesmen is to integrate national policies into a global perspective, to resolve the discordance between the international economy and the political system

based on the nation state . . . . The spirit that produced Bretton Woods reflected the realization that in the long run the national welfare can only be safeguarded within the framework of the general welfare. . . . In [today's] circumstances the international economic system operates—if at all—as crisis management. The risk is, of course, that some day crisis management may be inadequate. The world will then face a disaster its lack of foresight has made inevitable. . . . My major point is that the world needs new arrangements.[2]

Put in this context, the rationale for international monetary reform seems overwhelming because, first, no system of policy coordination exists to replace the declining U.S. leadership role; second, there is no "early warning" system to signal impending crisis and no adequate response mechanism for coping with crises when they do occur; and third, there is no control mechanism over the mobility of capital. Furthermore, the problem just seems too big. Foreign exchange transactions now conducted instantaneously by computer links amount to more than *$200 billion a day.*[3]

But, as the stock market crash on October 19, 1987 ("Black Monday") dramatically demonstrated, the financial system cannot function efficiently in such a volatile climate. As such, the agenda for a new Bretton Woods is a long one, and the issues are pressing to the point of urgency.

Agenda for a New Bretton Woods

Those who favor a new Bretton Woods Conference argue that it should not be held in a climate of panic, should not be held without considerable prior preparation, and should not attempt to map out a plan for what might be done in the future. Rather, they suggest, it must address the fundamental structural imbalances that are disrupting the present outmoded system.

In *Toward World Prosperity,* a penetrating book on the topic, Irving Friedman has suggested that there are six basic issues that must be included in a new Bretton Woods Conference if it is to be successful.

First, a new financial system must be developed that will provide the framework for world prosperity, sustained growth, and structural change. Such a system, Friedman argues, must above all protect the developing countries from the continuing and worsening levels of high unemployment, low growth rates, and inadequate rates of saving.

Second, a system of exchange rates must be established that is realistic, equitable, and stable. Many of the present problems have come from the continual roller coaster movements of the dollar from strong to weak, weak to strong, a process that has disrupted the smooth functioning of the system, helped no one, and generated unnecessary instability and uncertainty.

Third, the whole process of international capital movements must be reexamined. Capital is supposed to move from the more industrialized world to the underdeveloped countries. Instead, as we discussed earlier, the opposite has occurred. If the system is ever to regain stability, this must be corrected. Is it feasible, Friedman asks, for a code of international behavior in this area to be established? If so, who would administer it?

Fourth, something has to be done to stop worldwide inflation, which has reached epidemic proportions in the underdeveloped countries and is a persistent problem in the industrialized world as well. No one knows how to stop inflation without at the same time slowing economic growth and increasing unemployment, a bitter pill that few nations are willing to swallow. Friedman asks, is it feasible that exchange rate adjustments could be tied to inflation rates in a more formal manner, perhaps administered by the International Monetary Fund?

Fifth, Friedman asks,

> Do the existing governmental rules and practices serve world business, which has become interdependent and integrated to a degree that represents a quantum change from the past? . . .
>
> Interdependence and global integration have created a world in which nations and their businesses have lost their freedom of action, however, reluctantly and angrily. The linkages of world markets . . . mean new definitions of what is national, what is meant by national interest, and what is meant by unfair national competitive practices.

Finally, he asks, "Is the international financial system suited to a world that has become very different because of the miracles of modern technology?"[4]

The Major Question: Policy Coordination

Any restructuring of the international financial system must be considered in the context of overall *policy coordination* among the major industrial powers, and between them and the less developed countries—which include *80 percent* of the world's population, some 4 billion people.

The present system gives only lip service to policy coordination, while each of the industrial powers continues "beggar-thy-neighbor" policies of studied self-interest that do not have long-run viability.

In a sense there *has* been an international economic policy in place since 1980, a policy of no policy. The theoretical rationale of the Reagan administration was that capitalism functions best when it is left alone—to the free market. When it became clear in 1985 that laissez-faire economics didn't always work to everyone's advantage, especially that of the United States, haphazard intervention in the exchange markets became the "policy" that pushed the dollar down by some 50 percent against the currencies of the major U.S. trading partners. That move produced virtually no results, as the U.S. trade deficit hovered at levels over $150 billion two years after the intervention. And *policy coordination,* which is simply another way of saying international economic planning, became the buzzword in Washington and in the financial press.

For international policy coordination to have any long-run effect, three key questions have to be addressed. First, trade imbalances must be resolved, or at least financed in an orderly manner. Second, exchange rates must be stabilized and anchored to *something* that provides stability as well as coordinated flexibility. Third, capital flows must be redirected so that they produce growth instead of leading to long-run stagnation. In addition, and directly related to the problem of capital flows, the Third World debt crisis must be resolved. Until that happens, talk of a new Bretton Woods Conference and policy coordination will ring as hollow as the rhetoric of laissez-faire.

Coordination and Trade

The issues that must be addressed at a new Bretton Woods Conference fall into three major interrelated categories: the trade imbalance, a workable system of exchange rate adjustment, and capital flows, including the still unresolved Third World debt question. The latter two are subsets of the overall trade question.

As long as the United States continues to run record-high trade deficits and, essentially, to exchange those deficits for recycled paper IOUs, the international financial system will continue to be dangerously fragile *and* the United States will pay the price, as will the Third World debtor countries. The problem could perhaps be resolved by some combination of increasing American manufacturing productivity—that is, restoring the United States' "competitive position"—and/or devising some way to induce a reluctant Japan and West Germany (and others) to stimulate their economies to the extent that they could absorb more exports, or by somehow convincing American consumers to reduce their level of consumption of imported products.

But although there are indications that U.S. productivity is improving, there is little evidence—as we have seen—that the trade imbalance, which is also *gradually* improving, will reverse itself to the extent that it would make any *real* difference in the foreseeable future. A new Bretton Woods Conference can't dictate to American consumers, it can't tell U.S. industry to be more productive, and certainly it can't tell Japanese, European, South Korean, and Taiwanese manufacturers to stop trying to sell their products abroad. Therefore the burden falls on some sort of agreement that will stabilize exchange rates at levels consistent with trade equilibrium, and on some sort of agreement to normalize capital flows, at least to the extent that funds begin flowing *from* the industrialized world to the developing world, instead of the reverse as is happening now. There are many proposals to modify the exchange rate system to rectify the Third World debt problem. Some are viable; some, in the current political climate, are not. Whether any kind of change in the exchange rate system would be sufficient to resolve the overall problem of imbalance and inequality in the international economy remains to be seen.

The Exchange Rate Problem

As we have already seen, the Reagan administration allowed the value of the dollar to decline in an effort to make U.S. exports more competitive and imports more expensive (see figure 8–1). This strat-

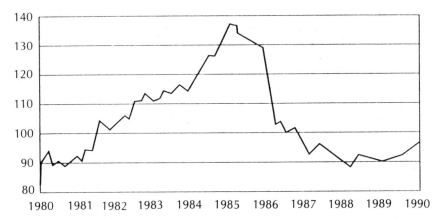

Source: *Economic Report of the President, 1989* (Washington, D.C.: Government Printing Office, 1989).
Index: 1980–1982 = 100.

Figure 8–1. *Index of the Dollar's Value against Fifteen Industrial Country Currencies*

egy has been somewhat less than successful. Even though the dollar declined as much as 40 percent against the yen and deutsche mark, the U.S. merchandise trade deficit for 1987 was a record $171.2 billion. The dollar decline did generate a significant 20 percent increase in manufacturing exports; yet, the American appetite for the even more expensive imports continued unabated.

Several prominent economists, including former chairman of the Council of Economic Advisers Martin Feldstein, proposed that the dollar be allowed to fall further.[5] This position suggested that the bottom had not yet been reached. But the Reagan administration was cautious about letting the dollar sink too low, too fast, given the need to finance the federal deficit and maintain interest rates at levels high enough to keep attracting foreign money. So one of two things has happened. Either there is something wrong with the economic theory guiding exchange rate policy or there are structural factors at work in the economy thwarting exchange rate policy. In any case, it is clear that, as Professor Paul Krugman, an international economist at the Massachusetts Institute of Technology, has pointed out, "the U.S. trade balance has shown less turnaround than anyone's model predicted." In theory the decline of the dollar since 1985 should have resulted in a reversal of export and import prices. But instead, much less of the yen and deutsche mark appreciation has been passed through to the American consumer in the form of higher import prices than was expected. This explains the high level of imports and the continued high trade deficit. The trade-weighted dollar has declined 28.8 percent since 1985, while import prices have increased only 18.8 percent.

Many economists have attempted to explain the lack of success of the U.S. exchange rate policy in terms of the J-curve. The J-curve theory argues that at first there will be a rise in the trade deficit after the dollar declines because consumers only slowly adjust to the higher-priced imports. The higher price multiplied by the same quantity results in a temporarily higher import bill. After consumers adjust to the new prices of imports, a reduction in imports will occur as exports are expanding and the trade deficit will begin to decline. But this has not been the case. Although there have been some improvements in the U.S. trade deficit, the failure of the J-curve theory to explain the situation continues to puzzle economists.

By the mid-1980s, foreign producers had successfully held down their export prices despite the enormous changes in currency values prompted by the U.S. devaluation of the dollar. So, the relative prices of imports and domestic products did not change significantly. This limited the predicted benefits of a cheaper dollar. What appears to have happened is that foreign companies, especially Japanese firms, were more adept at "pricing the market"—that is to say, at adjusting to competitive conditions—than anyone expected. American firms seem to be less successful at adjusting pricing policies to market conditions changed by currency value shifts.

How do foreign companies manage to hold down export prices in the face of a declining dollar? Or, put differently, why are U.S. firms unable to price to the market? Harvard economist Jeffrey Sachs has argued and demonstrated that the focus on the dollar itself is allowing for a misdirected policy. His argument is that the dollar strategy, which is largely based upon monetary policy—that is, the manipulation of interest rates—is wrong. It is, he argues, ill-conceived because it does not address the reality of the U.S. budget deficits and the relationship of these deficits to the trade deficit. Sachs maintains that the low interest rates required to encourage the decline of the dollar also encourage consumer spending and demand for imports. In addition, the existence of budget deficits (in the vicinity of $160 billion a year) stimulates consumer demand for imports because discretionary income is larger than it would be if taxes were increased or spending decreased in an attempt to reduce the budget deficits. So, both lower interest rates and budget deficits drive the seemingly insatiable demand for imports on the part of American consumers in spite of the falling dollar.

There are, in addition, other factors behind the lack of success of the dollar devaluation strategy which help explain why the prices of imported goods have not followed the appreciation of the yen and deutsche mark. Economist Robert Kuttner has identified five major explanations.

To begin with, he argues, most raw materials are priced in dollars. Therefore, a 70 percent decline in the dollar also means a 70 percent decline in the cost of oil, iron ore, chemical feedstocks, and other commodities. This, he suggests, substantially offsets the effect of the higher exchange rate on the price of finished products.

Second, all currencies have not appreciated against the dollar. Both American and Japanese producers have increasingly moved production to cheap currency, low-wage countries like Korea, Taiwan, Singapore, China, and Mexico.

Third, capital costs are far lower in Japan and Germany than in the United States. This means that a Japanese firm can cut profit margins to hold the line on prices, and still make acceptable returns.

Fourth, many foreign producers did not pass along the full savings to U.S. customers when the dollar was expensive, so they had a substantial cushion to absorb anticipated price increases as the dollar got cheaper.

Finally, Kuttner points out, a large share of imports today are marketed in the United States by American retailers or wholesalers, who often share the foreign producer's interest in holding down the price.[6]

These factors make it clear that the decline of the dollar will not *automatically* reduce the trade deficit. They mean, among other things, that the present one-dimensional policy approach will only result in a decline in the standard of living of American citizens as the cost of imports increases and inflation follows. The gradual resurgence in U.S. exports, though a positive factor, is tempered by the fact that continued export growth is held captive by the continued growth of other advanced industrial nations' export capacity, and by the decrease in the demand for U.S. exports on the part of developing nations because of their inability to maintain growth rates and export earnings sufficient to service their debt and at the same time buy more U.S. exports. In addition, an American recession would exacerbate all these issues.

To complicate this situation further, the global economy is suffering from excess capacity, especially for export-oriented goods like steel and automobiles. Also, many American firms that successfully adapted to the new competitive environment of the 1980s now find themselves so "lean" they are unable to increase output without higher costs or having to expand their capacity. So they are unlikely to be inclined to expand capacity rapidly in the short run to take advantage of what may be only a temporary increase in demand in the face of a potential global recession in the early 1990s. Moreover, many firms dismantled their marketing networks when the dollar was strong and are unable to respond swiftly to the new, more competitive conditions. Finally, there is the maze of regulations peculiar to every nation in this interdependent global economy. Such regulations make doing business more difficult and time-consuming, thus slowing down any rapid response to changing currency swings. Faced with this set of realities and uncertainties, firms find it virtually impossible to make decisions about whether to expand capacity at all or where to add it in the face of increasing global production.

To conclude, it seems clear that the weaker dollar in itself will not cure the trade deficit. Deborah Allen Oliver, president of Clarement Economics Institute, has argued that "the dollar's plunge against a few key currencies is not and cannot be a broad program of relief from foreign competition. Rather, it is a highly specific and narrow subsidy that will provide only limited help to a few producers." She asserts that the trade balance will be restored only when U.S. industries regain international competitiveness through increased productivity and greater efficiency.[7] Also, economist Michael Hudson has pointed out that the benefits of a cheap dollar are limited. He maintains that "the really important variables in the comparative trade advantages of countries are their labor costs, interest rates, and tax obligations." Hudson argues that as automation becomes more and more widespread, production will depend more on capital and financing and less on the cost of labor. The problem with policymakers, he says, is that they ignore these realities and choose to concentrate instead on relative currency values, which are of secondary importance and, we would add, only a temporary, short-run solution.[8]

The crucial question now becomes this: Given the seemingly inherent limitations of the declining dollar strategy (currency devaluation) of the United States and the other G-7 countries (Great Britain, France, Germany, Japan, Italy, and Canada), is there a workable strategy for the coordination of exchange rates among the G-7 countries that would resolve the problem of trade imbalance?

Exchange Rate Coordination

The one significant thing to come out of the Tokyo Summit of 1986 was a tacit agreement among the G-7 countries to construct an indicator system to help guide the international coordination of macroeconomic policies. This agreement was informal and voluntary, but it was a step toward a mechanism for setting target zones for exchange rates.

Although the Louvre Accord negotiated in February 1987 called for the further development of and a commitment to such an indicator system, it became readily apparent that what was really needed was a more formal mechanism for establishing agreed-upon parameters (target zones) between which exchange rates could fluctuate.

Since the Plaza Agreement in 1985, the G-7 nations have engaged in a form of international exchange rate coordination that has been largely based upon interventionist actions on the part of central banks, rather than on a systematic assessment of domestic macroeconomic policy coordination. For the United States, international monetary policy has essentially involved direct intervention in exchange markets by the Federal Reserve and the manipulation of interest rates to control the decline of the U.S. dollar.

Thus, as we have seen, the dollar debate has been reduced to a discussion of how low the dollar should be allowed to fall, how fast, and how far. But at the same time the dollar has been held hostage by the trade deficit and the budget deficit.

The lesson of all this is that it is vital to understand that any reconstruction of the international monetary system will of necessity require a formal method and system for setting and maintaining stability in foreign exchange markets. This means going beyond discretionary interventionism and monetary policy. This policy, for example, forced foreign central banks to buy $115 billion more dollars than they sold between November 1986 and November 1987. These were, in essence, unwanted dollars that in reality represented loans to the U.S. Treasury to finance the U.S. deficit. As Paul Farba, a columnist for *Le Monde,* has argued, this is a hidden danger of such currency cooperation because it indirectly fuels American consumers' purchasing power to buy imports and does not contribute to a systematic or structural solution to the continued stability of exchange rates.[9]

A newly conceived international monetary system will have to go beyond informal indicators and loose policy coordination. Several such systems have been proposed. Ronald I. McKinnon, an economist from Stanford, has for years been proposing versions of a basic model for currency cooperation. He argues that a trade deficit is not a monetary phenomenon. Instead, he says, it simply indicates that an economy is saving too little or investing too much. In the case of the United States, he identifies the problem (as have many others) as a federal deficit that is too large.

For McKinnon the central question is the ability to establish exchange rates without having to drive the dollar up and down with monetary policy. Therefore, he proposes that the Western world adopt a system of *purchasing power parity* (PPP) as a theoretical guide for central banks and financial markets. Such a "benchmark" would allow for the calculation of nominal exchange rates that would align national price levels of internationally tradable goods as measured by producer price indexes. These exchange rates—within narrow bands—would serve as the official exchange rate target range for governments.

Under such a scheme, international trade and mutual monetary adjustment would ensure convergence to the same rate of commodity price inflation. Eventually, McKinnon argues, tradable goods prices would then be aligned and relative growth in national money claims would reflect differentials in productivity growth.

How would such a system be coordinated? McKinnon suggests that the country with a weak currency would slow its domestic money growth, if necessary raising short-term interest rates relative to those abroad, while monetary policy in the strong currency market became more expansionary. Thus, the aggregate money stock would remain unchanged.

Though the mechanics of a system like that proposed by McKinnon are certainly more complicated than spelled out here, such a system clearly could be implemented without great difficulty *if* a general agreement could be reached.[10]

Another similar proposal has been developed by John Williamson, an economist with the Institute for International Economics, who calls for the establishment of international macroeconomic policy coordination in a manner that transcends anything the G-7 countries have done to date.

The primary goal of international policy coordination is, of course, to maintain as high a level of economic growth as possible while avoiding excessive inflation and disruptive, destabilizing financial disequilibrium—especially excessive trade and budget deficits.

The Williamson proposal calls for the determination of target zones for exchange rates for each of the major G-7 countries. Such target zones would be consistent with the internal domestic policies of each country. The basic policy objectives of increasing growth, lowering inflation, increasing employment, and balancing payments would necessarily reflect normal timing lags.

To implement such a program successfully, it would be necessary to set targets for exchange rates and the rate of growth of nominal domestic demand (demand not adjusted for inflation). The exchange rate, which is the central determinant of the division of demand between domestic and foreign sources, and of supply between domestic and foreign markets, is, Williamson argues, the central determinant of the current account. Thus, to have a target for the current account means having a target for the exchange rate. Such a target must also focus on the real effective exchange rate because it is this rate that is most relevant to competitiveness and the balance of payments. According to Williamson, such a target would be the fundamental equilibrium exchange rate (FEER), defined as the rate "which is expected to generate a current account surplus or deficit equal to the underlying capital flow over the cycle."

To implement such a scheme, it is necessary to convert a target for the real exchange rate into one for the inflation-adjusted exchange rate, which is a technical exercise. Following this, the need for intervention is eliminated, and the monetary policy can adequately adjust misalignment if the exchange rate moves out of the agreed-upon zone by a margin of 10 percent. For the purposes of making policy, this would require managing interest rates and over-all fiscal policy in each country to achieve the targets for a set of growth rates of nominal domestic demand and (mutually consistent) real effective exchange rates.

To accomplish these objectives, Williamson states that all participants would have to agree to modify their monetary and fiscal policies according to the following principles:

1. The average level of world (real) short-term interest rates should be revised up (down) if aggregate growth of nominal income is threatening to exceed (fall short of) the sum of the target growth of nominal demand for the participating countries

2. Differences in short-term interest rates among countries should be revised when necessary to supplement intervention in the exchange markets to prevent the deviation of currencies from their target ranges

3. National fiscal policies should be revised with a view to achieving national target rates of growth of domestic demand[11]

The proponents of such an approach to the coordination of exchange rates have used simulations of such policies for the G-7 countries to demonstrate that if such an indicator system had been adopted between 1980 and 1987, the instability experienced during those years would have been essentially eliminated.

One must bear in mind, however, that all efforts designed to expand and implement mechanisms for exchange rate coordination and overall international economic cooperation *assume* that the participants will be willing to sacrifice some measure of national sovereignty.

A World Version of the European Monetary System

Experts such as France's minister of finance, Edouard Balladur, have proposed that a world version of the European Monetary System (EMS) might provide a guide to the future.[12] Such a model would, as the EMS does, provide for automatic trigger mechanisms and appropriate sanctions. An EMS model would require a monetary reference unit that would be determined by a weighted average of international currencies, and this would serve as the standard for such a new system. Under such a system, each nation would be required to adhere to margins of fluctuations set around the target rate defined for each currency. Thus, each central bank would have to be prepared to intervene in exchange markets to ensure that its currency did not exceed the limits.

The obligation to intervene to maintain the value of its currency would force each country's central bank either to spend its reserves or to borrow from its trading partners when necessary. These required changes in reserves would be an indirect sanction. If it became necessary to redefine fundamentally the current currency standard (parity realignment), this could be done only with the consent of all.

The all-important difference between such a system and the old Bretton Woods arrangement is that the beleaguered U.S. dollar—now the world's key currency—would be replaced by a world currency. Thus, redefining the role of the U.S. dollar is one of the most important considerations in reconstructing the international monetary system. So this process should be among the top priorities at a new Bretton Woods Conference.

Eventually resolving the crisis of imbalance will require that, in addition to the basic areas of trade and exchange rates, the problem of Third World external debt be confronted. The central challenge here is to devise an approach that offers genuine debt relief to the overindebted nations, while allowing for the growth and stability of the world economy simultaneously. This is a tall order, but it is not impossible.

Third World Debt Relief

By 1987 the external liabilities of developing countries had reached over $1.3 trillion. As we have seen in previous chapters, by the early 1980s the problem (especially for the major debtors) had become a debt service burden that resulted in the net transfer of capital *from* the debtor countries *to* the creditor countries. This reverse capital flow has made it virtually impossible for nations to find the resources necessary to promote balanced domestic economic growth. The need to service debt has forced the debtor nations into transforming their economies into open export-oriented economies with increased emphasis on market solutions for their economic problems. This adjustment and restructuring, which seems necessary under current arrangements, has not been without serious consequences. Third World standards of living have steadily declined even though, on the surface, balance of trade conditions appear to have improved.

Although the Bush administration's commitment to the Brady Plan appears to be unwaivering, many experts consider the plan unsuccessful and insufficient. Critics maintain that the Third World debt problem is one of structural overindebtedness—that is, a long-run solvency problem rather than a short-run problem. Virtually all the private commercial banks seem to agree, since they have in recent years drastically reduced the level of new loans to debtor nations (see table 8–1). They have begun to recognize that they need to prepare for the time when they will have to accept large losses because the loans will never be paid back. In anticipation, many banks have increased their loan-loss reserves, which is money set aside to cover potential losses on the Third World loans. Higher loan-loss reserves will enable the banks to reduce their total debt

Table 8–1
Debt Relief and New Loans, 1980–1987
(billions of U.S. $)

Debt Relief	January 1980– September 1987	1983	1984	1985	1986	1987 (through September)
Debt restructuring bank	321.4	43.8	87.0	22.9	72.4	84.1
Official creditors	68.4	8.9	4.1	16.4	13.6	18.8
Total	389.8	52.7	91.1	39.3	86.0	102.9
New long-term money disbursed	42.2	13.0	10.4	5.3	2.7	9.5
Concerted short-term credit facilities	36.2	29.4	34.9	32.0	31.5	31.1

Source: World Bank, *World Debt Tables, I* (Washington, D.C.: World Bank, 1988), p. 22.

Table 8–2

Big Lenders to Developing Countries

(billions of U.S. $)

	Loans to LDCs	Added to Loss Reserves	1987 Earnings (Loss)	1986 Earnings (Loss)
Citibank	15.59	3.0	1.06	(1.00)
Bank America	10.00	1.1	(0.52)	(0.75)
Manufacturers Hanover	8.4	1.7	0.41	(1.05)
Chase Manhattan	8.7	1.6	0.59	(0.85)
Morgan Guaranty	6.0[a]	[b]	0.87[a]	0.92[a]
Chemical	5.9	1.1	0.40	(0.71)
Bankers Trust	4.0	0.7	0.43	(0.18)
First Chicago	2.8	0.8	0.28	(0.44)
Security Pacific	1.9	0.5	0.39	0.15
Wells Fargo	1.9	[b]	0.27	0.33[a]
First Interstate	1.6	0.75	0.34	(0.20)

Source: Morgan Guaranty Trust Company, 1987.

[a] Estimated.

[b] Nothing added so far in 1987.

exposure to levels that are more realistic in terms of potential repayment (see table 8–2). Such losses will inevitably reduce bank equity and capital base, and this will eventually be reflected in the bank stock prices and profits.

Viewing the developing country debt problem as a solvency problem means seriously considering ways in which a solution can be developed which produces concessionary debt relief. Debt relief requires that debt-servicing requirements be significantly reduced so that debtor countries can again begin to generate a positive capital inflow from the advanced creditor nations. Such flows are vital if the debtor nations are to have any chance of developing balanced, sustainable economic growth and improvements in their standards of living, which are now sliding backward.

There are numerous debt relief proposals. Most, however, involve at least one or some combination of the following five categories:

1. Canceling part of the debt or declaring a moratorium on payments for a stipulated period of time

2. Subsidizing interest rates or in some manner reducing real interest rates

3. Capping interest rates on variable rate loans or issuing variable maturity loans that become operative when the interest rate exceeds some predetermined limit set in relation to measurable indicators such as the debt service/export ratio

4. Capping the percentage of export earnings to be devoted to servicing foreign debt

5. Enabling developing nations to convert part of their short- and medium-term debts into longer-term obligations

One of the more imaginative plans has been described by Morris Miller in his book *Coping Is Not Enough.*[13] Miller argues for a comprehensive debt policy that would guarantee debt relief by the rescheduling of principal payments, coupled with reductions in real interest rates, so that the overall debt-servicing burden is significantly reduced.

Miller emphasizes, however, that although significantly reducing the debt-servicing burden is vital, it alone is not enough; it is also necessary for net capital to flow to the debtor nations. The unlikelihood that this will occur through an expansion of private commercial bank loans, he thinks, requires that the World Bank increase its capital resources available for debtor nations and, in addition, liberalize the conditions of the World Bank's structural adjustment loans. Miller also wants to see the International Monetary Fund support debtor nations' domestic economic policies that are growth-oriented, as opposed to austerity-driven. In *Debt and Disorder: External Financing for Development,* John Loxley has detailed how such an approach might work:

> [In summary, such a] . . . policy package would be tailored to the specific structural characteristics of the economy in question. It would rely more on selective policy instruments designed to influence behaviour in particular sectors or industries than on blunt instruments designed to have an economy-wide impact. It would be more sensitive to distributional implications and especially to the importance of preserving and/or extending the provision of basic needs, goods, and services. Above all it would seek to establish broad political support for adjustment efforts, thereby main-

taining, or even strengthening, democratic institutions. Such a package would undoubtedly imply less reliance on unfettered market forces and greater use of selective direct controls (including exchange controls, import controls, some price control, and a general incomes policy than would orthodox packages). It would put national economic integration and the meeting of basic needs to the forefront of economic strategy.[14]

Loxley's alternative stabilization approach assumes the debtor countries will undergo significant internal adjustment and economic restructuring but in a way that allows for diversity. This diversity, he argues, should reflect the unique character of each country and its situation.

Several noted advocates of debt relief proposals focus more specifically on the debt service problem and less on (somewhat unrealistic) overall comprehensive policies that involve the World Bank, the IMF, and debtor country responsibilities. For example, Stanley Fischer, an international economist from MIT, has made the case for debt relief on distributional (welfare) arguments. He proposes that the debt burden (interest and amortization) tied to commercial bank loans be reduced to 65 percent of the initial contracted value. This would result in a decline of approximately $10 billion a year in interest payments. In his proposal, commercial banks would gradually record these losses without serious financial consequences. Fischer believes, however, that such debt relief should be contingent upon each debtor country's agreeing to a comprehensive growth-oriented economic policy program approved by the IMF.[15]

A perhaps more realistic proposal by Jeffrey Sachs would have an international agency (the World Bank, for example) purchase commercial bank debt at the secondary market rate. The purchase, Sachs suggests, could be made with marketable bonds issued by the agency. This would reduce the debt burden to 60 percent of the current amount. Sachs argues that banks could afford this because their losses have already been reflected in their stock market valuations and loan-loss reserves. Like Fischer, Sachs also assumes that the debtor nations would agree to pursue adjustment programs approved by the IMF and/or the World Bank.[16]

In the past few years a number of other concessionary debt relief proposals have been presented. Each involves the creditor commercial banks' absorbing some losses, while facilitating an increase in capital flows to the debtor nations and/or increasing availability of foreign exchange. Sen. Bill Bradley (D–N.J.) has proposed a plan whereby commercial banks would forgive annually 3 percent of the interest and 3 percent of the principal for a period of three years, after which debtors would resume standard obligations on the remaining debt. His plan also gives each debtor nation control over economic policy during this period.

The commercial banking institutions of the creditor nations, not surprisingly, have refused to consider such a proposal. It is also unclear whether the U.S. Congress could constitutionally legislate such a program, and it is almost certain that the banks would not voluntarily participate. In addition, William R. Cline of the Institute for International Economics has estimated that the Bradley Plan, even if it were enacted, would really do very little to help debtor nations and might even be harmful in the long run. Cline's empirical research on Mexico tends to support these conclusions.[17] So, most analysts think the Bradley Plan does not go far enough to provide any long-term resolution of the problem.

Others, like Peter Kenen, a Princeton economist, Sen. Paul Sarbanes (D–Md.), and Congressman John J. LaFalce (D–N.Y.), have each proposed versions of a plan whereby some international entity would buy Third World debt from the banks at a discount. And in fact such a proposal has recently come from a member of the IMF's executive board, Arjun Sengupta. He has proposed that the IMF establish an International Debt Facility. This new entity would then buy portions of a debtor country's debt at an agreed-upon discount. In return, IMF bonds would be given to the banks. Then the debtor country's obligation would be to the IMF for that portion of the debt held by the IMF, but in addition, the debtor nation would have to agree to an IMF-specified economic policy program for domestic adjustment and stabilization.[18]

The inescapable conclusion is that as long as debt relief schemes, however imaginative, are voluntary and involve banks' accepting losses, they will be generally insignificant, as the Brady Plan has been. They will expand the growing menu of options available but will not themselves bring about long-term, concessionary debt relief.

Clearly, there is no shortage of ideas when it comes to solving the problem of developing countries' external indebtedness (see figure 8–2). The technical mechanisms and imaginative comprehensive

In his statement at the 1987 Annual Meetings of the IMF and World Bank, James A Baker, U.S. Secretary of the Treasury, listed instruments suitable for inclusion in an expanded range ("menu") of financing options for commercial banks participating in rescheduling agreements. The list included the following instruments:

- Trade and project loans, which enable banks to channel more funds directly to the private sector. Such loans, viewed by banks as providing more easily identifiable returns, encourage imports of investment goods.

- On-lending, which enables banks to channel funds to specific end-users (mostly in the private sector) under their general balance of payments loan agreements with governments, thus supporting their commercial relationships.

- New money bonds, which are viewed by many banks as more attractive than participation in a syndicated loan as the vehicle for new money, as bonds have some characteristics of a senior claim on the issuing country.

- Notes or bonds convertible into local equity, which can facilitate debt-equity swaps, thus helping reduce external debt service burdens and stimulate domestic activity.

- Exit bonds, which are also known as "alternative participation instruments," were used for the first time in the 1987 Argentine rescheduling. . . . Exit bonds enable banks with small exposure to avoid future new money obligations by accepting negotiable low-interest bonds.

- External debt conversions, which are now established in many countries as a means of reducing debt and debt-servicing burdens. They permit the conversion of external claims into domestic currency denominated bonds and equity, or, in some cases, into currency itself.

- Interst capitalization, which reduces interest service directly. Secretary Baker indicated that mutually agreed-upon interest capitalization may be appropriate in selected cases, particularly for small debtors.

- Balance of payments loans, which are the standard form new money loans have taken hitherto. Such loans to debtor country governments will continue to be an essential component of future new money packages.

Source: World Bank, *World Debt Tables 1988* (Washington, D.C.: World Bank, 1988).

Figure 8–2. *Debt Relief Financing Options*

proposals we've discussed demonstrate that debt relief is possible, but until there is general agreement that the crisis must be resolved or, more likely, a financial crisis of major proportions, the problem will linger and continue to stifle real economic progress.

Toward a Stable International Economy

In this chapter we have argued that there is great need for a realignment of international priorities and that to accomplish this a new Bretton Woods Conference is needed. The demand for a new set of rules is that much more urgent as the international system scrambles to incorporate the Soviet Union and Eastern Europe as trading partners. The agenda for such a conference has been outlined and described in detail. Clearly the leaders of the world need to come together to discuss the issues of trade, exchange rates, capital flows, and Third World debt as interrelated problems, solutions to which will require unprecedented international cooperation.

Conservative market-oriented prescriptions have not worked, and liberal structural-adjustment schemes are not realistic as long as the interests of the banking community do not coincide with the needs of the deteriorating Third World economies and the desires of the industrialized world.

To suggest that world leaders come together and try seriously to resolve the problem of international imbalance seems almost Pollyannaish. Capitalism is by definition a competitive system, not a cooperative one. Beyond that the contradictions of present world economic arrangements may be too great. This idea was summarized eloquently by Harry Magdoff and Paul Sweezy in 1987:

> The idea that far-reaching international cooperation is feasible under these conditions is about as remote from reality as one can get. Each step in an attempt to eliminate imbalance tends to produce a net set of problems. Thus, if the U.S. were to reduce imports sufficiently to eliminate its trade deficit, the economies of countries exporting to the U.S. would suffer. This would especially hurt Third-World countries who would then have even greater difficulty servicing their debts. To achieve stability in the foreign exchange markets a lid would have to be put on speculation and some means found to stabilize exchange rates. But how

can stability be achieved if an exchange rate that favors one country harms another? To reap balance out of imbalance some countries would have to accept a voluntary reduction in income, leading to growth in unemployment, reduction in welfare, and a possible financial collapse. The list of contradictions could go on and on: the main point to keep in mind is that capitalism and its market system are by their very nature anarchic. To advocate eliminating anarchy—whether in domestic or international affairs—while maintaining the system serves only to foster the worst kind of illusions.[19] [However, despite the utopian nature and the constant that someone has to lose, what other choices do we have if we want a stable, sustainable international system?]

Notes

1. Morris Miller, *Coping Is Not Enough: The International Debt Crisis and the Roles of the World Bank and the IMF* (Homewood, IL.: Irwin, 1987), p. 169–170.
2. Henry Kissinger, "The Future of the Global Economy," *The Washington Post,* November 22, 1984; and Miller, ibid., p. 143.
3. Miller, op. cit., p. 146.
4. Irving S. Friedman, *Toward World Prosperity* (Lexington, MA: Lexington Books, 1986), p. 291–293.
5. Martin Feldstein, "The End of Policy Coordination," *The New York Times,* November 9, 1987.
6. Robert Kuttner, "The Theory Gap," *The New York Times,* January 17, 1988.
7. Deborah Allen Oliver, "Few Industries Benefit from the Weaker Dollar," *The Wall Street Journal,* January 30, 1987.
8. Michael Hudson, "A Cheap Dollar Won't Cure the Deficit," *The New York Times,* January 24, 1988.
9. Paul Farba, "Hidden Dangers of Currency Cooperation," *The Wall Street Journal,* November 23, 1987.
10. Ronald I. McKinnon, "A Model for Currency Cooperation," *The Wall Street Journal,* September 21, 1987; McKinnon, "When Capital Flowed and Exchange Rates Held," *The Wall Street Journal,* March 28, 1988; McKinnon, "Monetary and Exchange Rate Policies for International Financial Stability: A Proposal," *Journal of Economic Perspectives,* Vol. 2, No. 1, Winter 1988, p. 83–103; McKinnon, *An International Standard for Monetary Stabilization,* Institute for International Economics, Washington, D.C., 1984. See also Rudiger Dornbusch, "Doubts About the McKinnon Standard," and John Williamson, "Comment on McKinnon's Monetary Rule," *Journal of Economic Perspectives,* Vol. 2, No. 1, Winter 1988, pp. 105–112 and pp. 113–119, respectively.

11. John Williamson and Marcus E. Miller, *Targets and Indicators: A Blueprint for the International Coordination of Economic Policy.* Institute for International Economics, Washington, D.C., No. 22, September 1987.

12. Edouard Balladur, "Rebuilding an International Monetary System," *The Wall Street Journal,* February 23, 1988.

13. Miller, op. cit., ch. 8. "Banks Step Up Third World Debt Disposal," *The Wall Street Journal,* July 26, 1988.

14. John Loxley, *Debt and Disorder: External Financing for Development* (Boulder, CO: Westview Press, 1986), p. 44–50.

15. Stanley Fischer, "Sharing the Burden of the International Debt Crisis," *American Economic Review,* Vol. 77, No. 2, May 1985, p. 165–170.

16. Jeffrey D. Sachs, "It's the Right Time to Offer Real Relief," *The New York Times,* August 9, 1987.

17. William R. Cline, *Mobilizing Bank Lending to Debtor Countries* (Washington, D.C.: Institute for International Economics, June 1987), p. 80–92.

18. Clyde Farnsworth, "IMF Studying Plan to Ease Debt Burden," *The New York Times,* March 8, 1988.

19. Harry Magdoff and Paul Sweezy, "International Cooperation: A Way Out?" *Monthly Review,* November 1987, p. 18–19.

Suggested Reading

Jahangir Amuzegar, "Dealing with Debt," *Foreign Policy,* no. 68, Fall 1987.

C. Fred Bergsten, *America in the World Economy: A Strategy for the 1990s* (Washington, D.C.: Institute for International Economics, 1988).

C. Fred Bergsten and William R. Cline, *The United States-Japan Economic Problem* (Washington, D.C.: Institute for International Economics, October 1985).

Fred Block, *The Origins of International Economic Disorder* (Berkeley: University of California Press, 1977).

Don Bonker, *America's Trade Crisis: The Making of the U.S. Trade Deficit* (Boston: Houghton Mifflin, 1988).

Samuel Bowles, David Gordon, and Thomas Weisskopf, *Beyond the Wasteland* (New York: Anchor/Doubleday, 1982).

Anthony Brewer, *Marxist Theories of Imperialism: A Critical Survey* (London: Routledge and Kegan Paul, 1980).

Ralph C. Bryant, Gerald Holtham, and Peter Hooper, eds., *External Deficits and the Dollar: The Pit and the Pendulum* (Washington: The Brookings Institution, 1988).

David P. Calleo, *The Imperious Economy* (Cambridge: Harvard University Press, 1982).

James A. Caporaso, ed., "Dependence and Dependency in the Global System," *International Organization,* No. 32, pp. 1–300, 1978.

Mark Casson, ed., *The Growth of International Business* (London: George Allen and Unwin, 1983).

Richard E. Caves, *Multinational Enterprise and Economic Analysis* (New York: Cambridge University Press, 1982).

William R. Cline, *United States External Adjustment and the World Economy* (Washington, D.C.: Institute for International Economics, 1989).

———, *American Trade Adjustment: The Global Impact* (Washington, D.C.: Institute for International Economics, 1989).

———, *International Debt and the Stability of the World Economy* (Washington, D.C.: Institute for International Economics, 1983).

———, *Mobilizing Bank Lending to Debtor Countries* (Washington, D.C.: Institute for International Economics, 1987).

Benjamin Cohen, *The Question of Imperialism: The Political Economy of Dominance and Dependence* (New York: Basic Books, 1973).

Michael L. Dertouzos, Richard K. Lester, Robert M. Solow, and the MIT Commission on Industrial Productivity, *Made in America: Regaining the Productive Edge* (Cambridge: MIT Press, 1989).

I.M. Destler, *American Trade Politics: System under Stress* (Washington, D.C.: Institute for International Economics, 1986).

Theotonio Dos Santos, "The Structure of Dependence," *American Economic Review,* No. 60, pp. 231–236, 1970.

Gerald Epstein, "The Triple Debt Crisis," *World Policy,* Vol. 2, No. 4, Fall 1985.

Peter Evans, *Dependent Development: The Alliance of Multinational, State, and Local Capital in Brazil* (Princeton: Princeton University Press, 1979).

Martin Feldstein, "American Economic Policy and the World Economy," *Foreign Affairs,* No. 63, pp. 995–1008, 1985.

Andre Gunder Frank, *Latin America: Underdevelopment or Revolution?* (New York: Monthly Review Press, 1970).

Jeffrey Frieden, "Third World Indebted Industrialization: International Finance and State Capitalism in Mexico, Brazil, Algeria, and South Korea," *International Organization,* No. 35, pp. 407–431, 1981.

Irving S. Friedman, *Toward World Prosperity* (Lexington, MA: Lexington Books, 1986).

Theodore Geiger, *The Future of the International System: The United States and the World Political Economy* (Boston: Allen and Unwin, 1988).

Robert Gilpin, *The Political Economy of International Relations* (Princeton: Princeton University Press, 1987).

H. Peter Gray, *International Economic Problems and Policies* (New York: St. Martin's Press, 1987).

Keith Griffin, *Alternative Strategies for Economic Development* (New York: St. Martin's Press, 1988).

David Gordon, "Do We Need To Be No. 1" *Atlantic Monthly,* April 1986.

Stephanie Griffith-Jones, ed., *Managing World Debt* (New York: St. Martin's, 1988).

Stephanie Griffith-Jones and Osvaldo Sunkel, *Debt and Development in Latin America: The End of an Illusion* (New York: Oxford University Press, 1986).

Joseph Grunwald and Kenneth Flamm, *The Global Factory: Foreign Assembly in International Trade* (Washington: The Brookings Institution, 1985).

Gary Clyde Hufbauer and Jeffrey J. Schott, *Economic Sanctions Reconsidered: History and Current Policy* (Washington: Institute for International Economics, 1985).

Stephen Hymer, *The International Operations of National Firms: A Study of Foreign Direct Investment,* Ph.D. dissertation, Dept. of Economics, MIT, 1960; published by MIT Press, 1976.

"Human Capital: The Decline of America's Work Force," *Business Week,* Sept. 19, 1988, Special Report.

Inter-American Development Bank, *Economic and Social Progress Report* (Washington, D.C.: IADB, 1987).

International Monetary Fund, *World Economic Outlook* (Washington, D.C.: IMF, April 1988).

Anatole Kaletsky, *The Costs of Default* (New York: Priority Press, 1985).

Paul Kennedy, *The Rise and Fall of the Great Powers* (New York: Random House, 1988).

Joyce Kolko, *Restructuring the World Economy* (New York: Pantheon, 1988).

Paul R. Krugman, ed., *Strategic Trade Policy and the New International Economics* (Cambridge, MA: MIT Press, 1987).

Pedro-Pablo Kuczynski, *Latin American Debt* (Baltimore: Johns Hopkins University Press, 1988).

Robert Z. Lawrence, *Can America Compete?* (Washington, D.C.: The Brookings Institution, 1984).

Donald R. Lessard and John Williamson, *Financial Intermediation Beyond the Debt Crisis* (Washington, D.C.: Institute for International Economics, 1985).

———, *Capital Flight and Third World Debt* (Washington, D.C.: Institute for International Economics, 1987).

Harold Lever and Christopher Huhne, *Debt and Danger: The World Financial Crisis* (New York: Atlantic Monthly Press, 1985).

John Loxley, *Debt and Disorder: External Financing for Development* (Boulder: Westview Press, 1986).

Ira Magaziner and Mark Patinkin, *The Silent War: Inside the Global Business Battles Shaping America's Future* (New York: Random House, 1989).

John H. Makin, *The Global Debt Crisis: America's Growing Involvement* (New York: Basic Books, 1984).

Alfred Malabre, *Beyond Our Means* (New York: Basic Books, 1987).

Stephen Marris, *Deficits and the Dollar: The World Economy at Risk*

(Washington, D.C.: Institute for International Economics, 1985). Updated in 1988.

Ronald I. McKinnon, *An International Standard for Monetary Stabilization* (Washington, D.C.: Institute for International Economics, 1984).

Morris Miller, *Coping Is Not Enough: The International Debt Crisis and the Roles of the World Bank and the International Monetary Fund* (Dow Jones-Irwin, 1986).

Peter Peterson, "The Morning After," *Atlantic Monthly,* October 1987.

Michael J. Piore and Charles F. Sabel, *The Second Industrial Divide* (New York: Basic Books, 1984).

Robert Pirog and Stephen C. Stamos, *Energy Economics: Theory and Policy* (Englewood Cliffs: Prentice-Hall, 1987).

John Charles Pool and Ross M. LaRoe, *Default* (New York: St. Martin's Press, 1987).

John Charles Pool and Stephen C. Stamos, *The ABC's of International Finance* (Lexington, MA: Lexington Books, 1987).

——— *International Economic Policy: Beyond the Trade and Debt Crisis* (Lexington, MA: Lexington Books, 1989).

———, *The Instant Economist* (Reading, MA: Addison-Wesley, 1985).

Robert B. Reich, *The Next American Frontier* (New York: Times Books, 1983).

———, *Tales of a New America* (New York: Times Books, 1987).

Resolving the Global Economic Crisis: After Wall Street. A Statement by Thirty-three Economists from Thirteen Countries (Washington, D.C.: Institute for International Economics, Special Report 6, December 1987).

Thomas Riddell, Jean Shackelford, and Stephen C. Stamos, *Economics: A Tool for Understanding Society* (Reading, MA: Addison-Wesley, 1987). Third Edition.

Martin K. Starr, ed., *Global Competitiveness: Getting the U.S. Bank on Track* (New York: Norton, 1988).

Howard Wachtel, *The Money Mandarins: The Making of a Supranational Economic Order* (New York: Pantheon, 1986).

Murray Weidenbaum, *Rendezvous with Reality: The American Economy after Reagan* (New York: Basic Books, 1988).

John Williamson, *The Exchange Rate System* (Washington, D.C.: Institute for International Economics, 1983).

John Williamson and Marcus H. Miller, *Targets and Indicators: A Blueprint for the International Coordination of Economic Policy* (Washington, D.C.: Institute for International Economics, 1987).

World Bank, *World Debt Tables: External Debt of Developing Countries,* Vol. I. Analysis and Summary Tables (Washington, D.C.: World Bank, 1988).

Index

Absolute advantage, theory of international trade, 13–17; and productivity, 14–17; and specialization, 15, 17

Agricultural industry (U.S.): government protection of, 94, 97; and imports, 96, 97; overproduction in, 93–97; and technology, 93, 96

Argentina: and currency, new, 134, 135; and exchange rates, devaluing of, 134–135; and GDP (1980s), 144; inflation rates in, 133–134, 135

Baker Plan: and adjustment with growth program, 136–137; lending institutions involved in, 136, 165–167

Balance of payment accounts: and balance of trade, 40; and capital account, 40–41, 61; and current account, 40, 41; and investment income, 40, 41, 58–59, 61–62; and reserve account, 41–42; and statistical discrepancies, 42

Balance of payment adjustments, theory of, with floating exchange rates, 43–51, 53, 57; and equilibrium, 51, 53, 55–56; and foreign exchange markets, 46, 48–51; and foreign exchange rates, 43, 46–48, 56–57

Banking system, U.S., 4, 6; and debt exposure, 110, 111, 112, 125, 133; and European banking,

differences in, 72; and government regulation, 112; and loan process, 127, 129; and OPEC investments, 75–76, 107, 130; and petrodollar recycling, 75–77, 130; and rescheduling of debts, 5, 6; and reserve requirement, 72–73; and transfers to Third World, 4–5, 76, 77, 108, 110–115. *See also* Banks, private commercial; Loans, to developing countries

Banks, private commercial: and Baker Plan, role in, 166–167; and Bradley Plan, role in, 202; and Brady Plan, role in, 175–176; and debt exposure, 110–111, 112, 163; and loan-loss reserves, 198–199; and Mexico, loans to, 130, 163, 175–176; and new loans (mid-1980s) to Third World, 82, 111, 198; and petrodollar recycling, 76–77, 107, 130. *See also* Loans, to developing countries

Black Monday (1987), 89–90

Bradley Plan, 202

Brady Plan, 138, 198; and Mexican debt crisis, 171, 173, 175–176

Brazil: and currency, new, 134, 135; and economic growth (1985–86), 135; and environmental problems in, 145–146; and exchange rates, devaluing of, 134–135; and foreign debt, payment of, 135; inflation rates in, 133–134, 135

Bretton Woods (dollar) system, 52, 53; and Bretton Woods conference, 67–68; collapse of, 75

Capital flight: definition of, 79; extent of (1976–85), 79–80

Capitalism, free-market: definitions of, 12; and free competition, 12–13; and free trade, 29, 30

Carter administration: and inflation, efforts to curb, 105–107, 130–131; and U.S. debt crisis, 105–107

Castaneda, Jorge, on Brady Plan, 175–176

Cline, William R., on Bradley Plan, 202

Comparative advantage, theory of international trade, 17; and gains from trade, 17, 19, 31–32, 36; and relative prices, 19, 31–32; and specialization, 19, 32

Consumer debt, U.S., 122, 124

Corporate debt, U.S.: and bonds, issuing of, 117, 122; and R&D, effects on, 122

Currency, and foreign exchange rates. *See* Exchange rates

Debtor nations, developing or industrialized: and adjustment with growth program, 136–137; and austerity measures, 83, 84, 136, 146–147; and capital flight, 79–80; and commercial bank loans, 82, 108, 110–112, 130, 131, 137, 198; and currency, devaluing of, 83; and debt indicators, 125–126; and debt relief, proposals for, 197–202, 204–205; and debt reduction, mechanisms for, 137–138; and default by, 125; and development, long-run, 133, 138, 145, 199; and environmental problems in, 145–147; and export capacity, 5; and export markets, recession in (1973–78), 129, 131; and foreign debt (1974–90), 125, 126; and GDP, growth of, 87; and gross domestic investment per capita, 145; and IMF agreements, 80, 82–84, 136; and inflation, 83, 111, 133–134; and interest payments, 125, 126; and interest rates, 5–6, 86, 112; and rescheduling, 5; and reverse capital flow, 127, 129, 138, 139, 197–198; and structural overindebtedness, 198, 199; transfers to, 4, 61. *See also* Loans, to developing countries; Mexican debt crisis

Debt reduction, mechanisms for: Brady Plan, 138; debt equity swaps, 137; debt for nature exchanges, 137

Debts, external, developing countries, 61; rescheduling of, 5, 6, 61–62. *See also* Developing countries; Loans, to developing countries; Mexican debt crisis

Deficits, balancing of. *See* Equilibrium, of balance of payment accounts

de la Madrid, Miguel, presidency of (Mexico): and economic program of, 155, 157; and IMF austerity measures (1983–86), 155, 157, 160–161

Developing countries: and balance of payments, deficits (mid-1970s), 78–79, 86, 87, 129–130; and balance of trade, adjustments to, 67; and capital flight, 129–130; and exports, increase in, 5, 33, 83–84; and foreign markets, dependence on, 33–34; and imports, decrease in, 83, 84, 145; international trade by, and comparative advantage, theory of, 31–36; and per capita GNP (1967–87), 144; and primary products, export of, 33–34; transfers to 4, 61, 76, 111–112. *See also* Debtor nations, developing or industrialized

Dollar: decline of, 105; and Eurodollar market, 72–73; as equivalent to gold, 73–74; floating of, 74, 75, 186; and gold, advantages over, 68; glut, origins of, 69–71; and Plaza Agreement, 88; stability of, 184, 186; strength of, 58, 88, 108, 117, 131; in U.S.-Japanese trade, 49–51; value of, 51, 55, 57, 58, 88, 90; as world currency, 4, 53, 65, 67–68, 73;

and yen/dollar exchange rates
(1973–90), 43, 45–48, 49–50
Dollar, devaluation strategy in
monetary policy, 187, 188–189,
190–191, 193; and imports, cost
of, 188, 189, 190, 191; and U.S.
exports, growth of, 188, 189,
191–192

Echeverria, Luis, presidency of
(Mexico): and economic reforms,
152–153; and shared development,
153
Economic Rights and Duties of States,
Charter of, 84–85
Environment: and debt crisis,
145–146; and sustainable
development, 146–147
Equilibrium, of balance of payment
accounts, 39, 40, 42–43; and
exchange rate systems, 51, 53,
55–56; and trade deficits,
correcting of, 65, 66
Eurodollars: as new money supply,
72–73; and rise of market, 72–73,
78
European Economic Community
(EEC), and free trade, 34–36
European Monetary System, world
version of, 196–197
Exchange rates, 43, 45, 46; and
balance of payment accounts,
56–57; calculating of, 45; and
derived demand, 48, 49–51;
devaluing of, 134; fluctuations in,
43, 45, 46–48; and foreign
exchange markets, 46, 49, 53, 55.
See also Exchange rate systems
Exchange rate systems: and balance of
payment equilibrium, 51, 53,
55–56, 57; coordination of,
193–196; dollar system (fixed), 53;
free-flexible exchange rate
(floating), 51, 53; gold standard
(fixed), 51, 52–53; and IMS,
reconstruction of, 193–196; and
Louvre Accord, 193; and managing
of, 53, 55–56, 188, 190; and Plaza
Agreement, 53, 88, 193; and
Tokyo Summit, 193
Export platforming, 104

Exports. *See* International trade;
World exports

Farba, Paul, 194
Federal deficit, U.S.: and consumer
debt, 122, 124; and corporate
debt, 117, 122; extent of
(1960–89), 115, 117; and
investment in U.S. economy,
62–63, 117
Federal Reserve Bank, and U.S.
money supply: control of, 72;
reduction of (1979–82), 130–131,
136
Fischer, Stanley, 201
Foreign exchange market, 46, 49, 53,
55; and derived demand, 48,
49–51
Free-flexible exchange rate system. *See*
International finance: floating
exchange rates
Free trade: and balance of payments
adjustment, 57; and EEC, 34–36;
and GATT, 29–30. *See also* International trade, theories of
Friedman, Irving, *Toward World
Prosperity,* 185–186

GATT (General Agreement on Tariffs
and Trade), 29–30; and Cairns
Group, 97
Germany. *See* West Germany
Gold standard: and balance of trade
deficits, 65; demise of, 4, 67,
73–75; as fixed rate system,
51–52, 73; and "Golden Rule," 67;
and New Economic Policy, 73–74;
and price of gold, post-WWII, 67
Group of Seven nations, economic
summit (1987), 90
Gwynne, S.C., 112, 115

Heckscher, Eli, 20, 21
High-technology industries, U.S.:
performance in, 97–98
Hudson, Michael, 192–193

Imports: in developing countries,
decrease in, 83, 84, 85; in U.S.
economy, increase in, 34, 102,

Imports *(continued)*
    104. *See also* International trade,
    theory of
Industrial nations: and advanced
    technology, control over, 22; and
    gross domestic product (GDP)
    (1978–83), 87; and NIEC, role in,
    85–86
Industries, U.S.: agriculture, 94, 97;
    and government protection, 29, 34;
    high-tech, performance in, 97–99;
    steel, 25; and trade with Canada,
    29. *See also* U.S. economy, and
    international trade
Inflation, rates of, and measures to
    decrease: in developing countries,
    133–135; and IMF requirements,
    83; in U.S., 105, 108, 130–131
International finance, 39; and balance
    of payment accounts, 40–43, 66;
    crisis in, 33, 60–64, 71; and dollar
    strength, 57–59; and exchange rate
    systems, 51–53, 55–57; and
    floating exchange rates, 43, 45–51,
    53; and foreign exchange market,
    46, 48–51; statistical sources to,
    6–7; and U.S. banking system, 4
International financial system,
    restructuring of, 183–185; and
    European Monetary System, world
    version of, 196–197; and foreign
    exchange markets, systems in,
    193–194; IMF, role in, 183; and
    participants in, 193, 196, 204–205;
    and policy coordination, 187,
    193–196; and U.S. dollar, role of,
    184, 197. *See also* New Bretton
    Woods, agenda for
International Monetary Fund, 42, 68;
    and Baker Plan, role in, 165, 167;
    and Brady Plan, 173, 175; and
    commercial banks, role of, 82; and
    conditionality requirement, 80,
    82–84, 136; and debt relief, role
    in, 202; and developing countries,
    transfers to, 4–5, 78, 80, 82–84;
    and international financial system,
    restructuring of, 183; as lender, 68,
    78, 82, 83; and loan capability,
    107; as monitor, of trade
    discipline, 68, 82; and NEP, 75.

See also de la Madrid, Miguel,
    presidency of (Mexico): and IMF
    austerity measures
International monetary system: and
    capital flight, 79–80; and dollar
    glut, 69–71; and Eurodollar
    market, 72–73, 78; and gold,
    demise of, 65, 73–75; and IMF,
    80–84; and international finance as
    disciplinary force, 65–66, 67, 68;
    and new international economic
    order, 84–86; and oil price shock
    (1973–74), 75, 77–79; and
    petrodollar recycling, 4–5, 75–77,
    78; and Plaza Agreement, 88, 193;
    and reconstruction of, 193–195;
    and Tokyo Summit, 88–89, 193;
    and U.S. as special case, 67–68;
    and U.S. dollar, as world currency,
    4, 65
International trade: and balance of,
    adjustments made, 22, 66–67; and
    barriers to, 12–13, 23, 29–30; and
    capital and labor factors, 20–21,
    32–33; and consumption, 11; and
    employment growth, 22; and excess
    capital, 192; and free market
    capital, 12–13; and loss, 23, 25;
    and production possibilities, 14,
    15, 16; and productivity, 11, 14;
    and specialization, 11, 12, 15, 32;
    and technology, role of, 21, 22–23;
    and world exports, 11–12, 22,
    34–36. *See also* U.S. economy, and
    international trade
International trade, theories of:
    absolute advantage, 13–17;
    comparative advantage, 17–19, 31;
    contemporary, 20–23; Heckscher-
    Ohlin model, 20–21; Leontief
    Paradox, 21; protectionism, 13,
    23–30
Investment income: definition, 40; in
    U.S. economy (1970–89), 58–59,
    61–62

Japan, and trade with U.S.: and
    competitive industries, 98; and
    investment in U.S., 117; and trade
    flows, 46, 47–48, 49–51; and
    value of yen, 43, 45, 46, 49

Japan, and world exports: pricing of, 190, 191; share in, 100–101

Keynes, John Maynard, at Bretton Woods conference, 67
Kissinger, Henry, on international monetary reform, 185
Krugman, Paul, 21, 189–190
Kuttner, Robert, 191

Leontief, Wassily, and "Leontief Paradox," 20–21
Lever, Harold, *Debt and Danger,* 139
Liquidity constraint, 53
Loans, to developing countries, 4–6, 107; and debt equity swaps, 137; and debt for nature exchanges, 137; and default, possibility of, 110–111, 125, 163–164; and foreign debt owed (1974–90), 125, 126; and interest payments, 125, 126; and interest rates, 5, 6, 57, 130, 131; and lending process, 127, 129; and loan-loss reserves, 198–199; and loan personnel, 112, 115; and rescheduling of debts, 5, 6; and reverse capital flow, 127, 129, 138, 139, 141–142, 143–144, 197–198; volume of, 112. *See also* Mexican debt crisis
Louvre Accord, 193
Loxley, John, *Debt and Disorder,* 200–201

McKinnon, Robert I., 194–195
Madoff, Henry, 204–205
Mexican debt crisis: and Brady Plan, 171, 173, 175–176; de la Madrid, Miguel, and IMF austerity measures (1983–86), 155, 157, 161, 163–164; Echeverria, Luis, and economic reforms (1968–76), 152–153; economic and political background of (1940–68), 152; and foreign debt, extent of (1970–89), 149, 151, 155; and inflation (1976–86), 151, 153, 155; and loans, from private commercial banks, 163, 164, 166–167, 175–176; Lopez Portillo, José, and petroleum-driven

development strategy (1976–82), 153–155, 160; and net payment to foreign capital, 161; and new borrowing, 157, 160; and oil development, loans for, 154, 161; and oil revenues, 6, 151, 155, 163–164, 171; and rescheduling, 5, 157, 165–167, 173, 175; and rescue package, 1986 crisis (Baker Plan), 164–167, 171; and resource transfer flow, 160, 167, 173; and Salinas de Gortari, Carlos, economic policies of (1988–), 171, 175, 176
Mexico, economy of: and austerity measures, 151, 157, 167; and balance of payment deficits (1970–82), 154–155, 160–161, 163; and capital flight, 79, 153, 155, 161, 171; collapse of (1982), 157, 160; currency (peso), devaluing of, 151, 155, 161; and debt service payments (1971–86), 151, 157, 160, 163, 164–165, 167, 173, 175; and dependency, on U.S. markets, 153; and development, long-term, 167; and exchange rates, 155, 157; expansion of (1940–68), 152; and export market, 153, 154, 161, 171; and foreign investment controls, 153; and GDP, growth of, 151, 153, 167, 176; and imports, 154, 161, 171; and inflation (1976–87), 151, 153, 155, 167; and living conditions in, case study of, 176–181; and manufacturing sector, 154; and oil, development of, 153–154, 161; and oil revenues, 151, 155, 164, 171; and real wages, 167, 177
Miller, Morris, 184, 200
Multinational corporations (MNCs): and Baker Plan, role in, 166; and debt, secondary markets for, 137; and Eurodollars, use of, 72; and international trade routes, 21; and production abroad, 102, 104

New Bretton Woods, agenda for, 185–204; and exchange rates,

New Bretton Woods (continued)
coordination of, 186, 188,
193–196; and international capital
flows, 186, 188, 197–198; and
new international financial system,
development of, 185–186, 187;
and stable international economy,
204–205; and trade, coordination
of, 187–188; and U.S. dollar,
replacement of, 186, 187
New Economic Policy (NEP),
provisions of, 73, 74; and Bretton
Woods system, 75; and dollar,
floating of, 74, 75; and gold,
pricing of, 73–74
Newly industrializing countries (NICs),
and high-tech industries, 98
New International Economic Order
(NIEO): and developing countries,
needs of, 84, 85; and industrial
nations, role of, 85–86
Nixon, Richard M., and NEP, 73, 74

Ohlin, Bertil, 20
Oil: and demand, decline of (1982),
86; exporters of, and petrodollars,
4; importers of, 4, 75; and non-
OPEC producers, 86; and OPEC,
4, 86, 105–106; and price, decline
in, 5–6, 86; price shocks, 4, 75,
77–79, 105–106, 129. See also
Mexico, economy of
Oliver, Deborah Allen, 192
Omnibus Trade and Competitiveness
Act (1988), 30
OPEC (Organization of Petroleum
Producing Countries): demise of, 5,
86; and oil embargo (1973–74),
75, 77–79; and oil price increases,
4, 75, 82, 105–106, 130; and
investments, 4, 75, 76
Outsourcing, 104

Petrodollars, 4; deposits of, 4, 107,
130; and Eurodollar market, 78;
and recycling, 4–5, 75–77, 78, 130
Plaza Agreement (1985), 53, 88, 193
Pollin, Robert, 122, 124
Porter, Michael, 21
Price elasticity, 96
Product market, 48–49; and pricing of

goods, 46, 47–48, 56–57; and
supply and demand, 49–51
Protectionism, 29, 30; and tariffs,
costs of, 25, 28, 29; theory of, 23,
25

Reagan administration (1981–1989),
U.S. economy during: budget and
trade deficits, 108, 117, 191; and
dollar, strength of, 59, 108, 117,
187, 189–190; and federal deficit,
115, 117; and interest rates, 59,
108, 117; and monetary policy,
108, 115, 193
Reaganomics, 108, 115
Regan, Donald, on developing
nations, loans to, 110–111
Research and development (nondefense), U.S. expenditures in
(1972–87), 98, 100
Resource transfer flow, in developing
countries: and current account
deficit, 139; and net flows, 140,
141–143; and net investment
income, 139, 140; and net
transfers, 141, 142, 197–198; and
reverse capital flow, 127, 129,
138, 139; and world debt crisis,
144–145, 197–198
Ricardo, David, 13; and absolute
advantage, theory of, 14–17

Sachs, Jeffrey, on dollar strategy,
190–191; on debt relief, 201
Salinas de Gortari, Carlos, presidency
of (Mexico), economic program of,
171, 175, 176
Sengupta, Arjun, 202
Smith, Adam, The Wealth of Nations,
12
Smithsonian Agreement, 74
Stagflation: definition of, 107; in U.S.
economy, 86, 87
Stock market crash (U.S.), 1987,
89–90; and dollar, value of, 90

Tariffs: cost of, 25, 28, 29; and
GATT, 29–30; theory of, 23, 25
Technology transfer, and developing
countries, 22–23
Tello, Carlos (finance minister,

Mexico), economic program of,
155
Third World countries. *See* Developing
countries
Tokyo Summit (1986), 88–89
Trade deficit, U.S. *See* U.S. debt
crisis; U.S. economy, and
international trade

U.S. debt crisis: and banking system,
4, 5, 110–114; and consumer debt,
122, 124; and corporate debt, 117,
122; and dollar glut, 69–71; and
inflation, efforts to curb, 105, 108,
130–131; and monetary policy
(1979–82), 130–131; and national
debt, 60–61, 63, 64, 115; and
Reagan era, legacy of, 115, 117,
122; and trade deficit, 7, 57–59,
100–102, 104, 108, 131, 188–190;
and U.S. as debtor nation, 9,
61–62, 63, 64; and U.S. industry,
93–99, 122. *See also* Banking
system, U.S.
U.S. economy, and international
trade: and agricultural industry,
93–97; and high-tech industries,
competition in, 98, 104, 122; and
exchange rate policy, 188–189,
190–193; and exports, 22, 29, 34,
101; and free trade, 30; and
imports, 22, 29, 34, 102, 104; and
job loss, 29, 102; and
multinationals, production abroad,
102, 104; and tariffs, 29. *See also*
Reagan administration, U.S.
economy during; U.S. debt crisis

U.S. economy, post WWII–1965: and
export surpluses, 69, 94; and gold
reserves, 73, 74; strength of,
67–68, 69. *See also* U.S. debt crisis

Volcker, Paul, 105

Wachtel, Howard, *The Money
Mandarins,* 112, 115
West Germany: and investments, GDP
percentage of, 117; and stock
market crash (U.S.), 90; and world
exports, share in, 101, 188
Williamson, John, 195–196
World Bank: and Baker Plan, role in,
165, 167; and Brady Plan, role in,
173, 175
World debt crisis, 125–126; and
adjustment with growth measures,
136–137; and austerity measures,
136; causes and origins of, 4, 33,
127, 129; chronology of, 86–87,
129–131, 133–135; and debt
reduction, 137–138; impact of,
110–111, 138–139; managing of,
international attempts at, 61, 88,
89–90, 135–138; and resource
transfer flow, 139, 141–142,
144–147, 197–198. *See also*
International financial system,
restructuring of
World exports: and international
trade, 11–12, 22, 34–36; and U.S.
share in (1960–89), 100–102;
volume of, 13, 34, 36. *See also*
Debtor nations, developing or
industrial; International trade,
theories of

About the Authors

John Charles Pool received his B.A. and M.B.A. from the University of Missouri, and his Ph.D. in economics from the University of Colorado. He is coauthor of *Economics: Enfoque America Latina, The Instant Economist, The ABCs of International Finance, First Edition* (Lexington Books 1987), *Default!, International Economic Policy* (Lexington Books 1988), *International Economics: Theory, Policy, and Practice* (Lexington Books 1990); and author of *Studying and Thinking about Economics and Society*. He has also published numerous articles on various economic topics and cowrites (with Ross M. LaRoe) a syndicated newspaper column entitled "The Instant Economist," which deals with current issues in economics. Dr. Pool is a professional economist–writer based in Rochester, New York. He has taught at Bucknell University and the Universities of Iowa and Missouri. For two years he was a Fulbright Professor in Mexico and is currently an adjunct professor of economics at St. John Fisher College.

Stephen C. Stamos, Jr., received a B.A. from San Diego State University, an M.S. in economics from Wright State University, and a Ph.D. in political economy from the Union Graduate School. He is coauthor of *Economics: A Tool for Understanding Society, Energy Economics: Theory and Policy, The ABCs of International Finance, First Edition* (Lexington Books 1987), *International Economic Policy* (Lexington Books 1988), and *International Economics: Theory, Policy, and Practice* (Lexington Books 1990); he has also published widely in professional journals on the topics of energy and international economics. Dr. Stamos is currently professor of economics and international relations at Bucknell University. He has been a visiting professor at Evergreen State College and at the University of Massachusetts at Amherst and was also a visiting fellow at the Center for U.S.–Mexican Studies, University of California at San Diego.

Patrice Franko Jones was educated at Bucknell University (B.A.) and later received her M.A. and Ph.D. at the University of Notre Dame. An assistant professor of economics and international studies at Colby College, Dr. Franko Jones has published on the Brazilian defense industry, including a forthcoming book with Westview Press on the subject. She has received an American Association for the Advancement of Science Arms Control and National Security Fellowship for a one-year appointment to the Department of Defense, International Security Affairs, Inter-American region.